STUDIES IN THE ODYSSEY

BY

J. A. K. THOMSON, M.A.

LATE SCHOLAR OF PEMBROKE COLLEGE, OXFORD
EXAMINER IN CLASSICS TO THE UNIVERSITY OF ABERDEEN

HASKELL HOUSE
Publishers of Scholarly Books
NEW YORK
1966

published by

HASKELL HOUSE

Publishers of Scholarly Books

30 East 10th Street • New York, N. Y. 10003

PRINTED IN UNITED STATES OF AMERICA

PREFACE

THE different lines of argument followed in these *Studies* lead to a fairly definite conclusion. But the Homeric Question is usually stated in a form so irrelevant to my intention, that some words of explanation appear to be necessary. So far as there exists a controversy between those who maintain and those who deny the artistic unity of the Homeric Poems, I am altogether with those who maintain it. I find in the Odyssey an almost perfect harmony of tone and colour, a structural symmetry almost complete. I have asked myself how this harmony and symmetry have been attained; and I have tried to find the answer in what we know or may reasonably infer concerning the conditions under which the Poems came into being. That the Iliad and Odyssey must be the work of a single age and a single poet because they are on the whole so consistent in detail, is a mere assumption, until we know whether this consistency cannot arise in some other way. The whole point at issue is here. Does homogeneity of style involve unity of authorship? Homer, it has been said, cannot be traditional poetry, because that cannot rise above a certain level, far beneath the art of Homer. This might be true; but I did not know it. What I did seem to myself to know was, that to determine on *a priori* grounds what excellence of art is in the nature of things attainable by one kind of poetry, and for ever unattainable by another, is unscientific, indeed a blasphemy against Art itself.

The question thus resolved itself into one of origins. If it could be shown that, as a matter of fact, the Homeric Poems are traditional, the aesthetic issue would so far settle itself. In this investigation I have had to make use of many instruments. If I deal chiefly with questions of mythology and religion, that is merely because they are for our problem the most fundamental of all. In my treatment of them I make no claim to originality either of method or of principle; what originality there may be lies in the conclusions to which I have been led. Miss Harrison's *Themis* has, I think, helped me most; but in this field I also owe much to Dr. Frazer, Professor Gilbert Murray, and others. It will be clear from this acknowledgement what view I accept of primitive religion, and in particular of the religion in Homer. Yet I feel more and more that a clear statement of the religious problem would lead to concessions on both sides. I do not suppose that any scholar who believes that Odysseus was an historical baron or chief would deny that he acquired some of the characteristics and mythology of a god or Hero. It is these characteristics and this mythology with which alone I concern myself, because of them I think that we can say something. I do not deny the existence of the Achaean chief, being quite unaware of any evidence either for or against it. I only say that the story of the Odyssey is the history, not of a man, but of a divinity. It is no part of my case to argue that a man may not become thus divine.

For the convenience of the reader in a matter of so much complexity, I will give here a brief analysis of the arguments elaborated in the book; and I will do this chapter by chapter, to avoid the appearance of confusion.

The first chapter is intended to reveal the depth of the background against which the shining figures of the Homeric poetry move; how much of latent and unexpurgated magic and savagery lurks in that unexplored region. Bearing this in mind, the reader will be prepared for what follows.

The second chapter discusses the origin of Odysseus. He is found to be in certain aspects a double of Autolykos, who again is a double of Hermes, in these aspects of the god's nature. Autolykos dwelt upon Parnassos; and in the shadow of the mountain is the Boeotian town of

Lebadeia, where was a buried hero called Arkesilaos. Arkeisios, the name of Odysseus's grandfather, the progenitor of the race, is a form of Arkesilaos; and a son of Odysseus and Penelope was in fact called Arkesilaos after his great-grandfather. This younger Arkesilaos was a reputed ancestor of the Battiad princes of Kyrene, who also claimed to be Minyans from Central Greece, descended from Euphemos the son of Europa of Lebadeia. This suggests that Arkeisios is identical with Arkesilaos of Lebadeia. Further evidence for the Boeotian origin of Odysseus is drawn from the eleventh book of the Odyssey, in which he consults the soul of 'Theban' Teiresias, and beholds the beautiful dead women, all or nearly all of whom have Minyan-Boeotian connexions. But is the Visit to the Dead an original part of the Odysseus-saga? The answer is, yes; there is no part older than that. For Odysseus is one of those divine or supernatural beings, made familiar to us by the *Golden Bough*, who are thought to die and come to life again, or to be obscured for a season only to reappear in renewed splendour. Unable to invent a better term, I have followed Miss Harrison in calling such a being an Eniautos-Daimon. The word Eniautos means, not so much a measured space of time, as the completed cycle of the seasons, at the moment of its completion; and it is just this cycle of birth, death, regeneration of everything that lives, which the Eniautos-Daimon represents in his own Life-story. So vague and yet stereotyped is his nature, that we cannot accurately call him a god, scarcely even a divinity. But the development of the religious sense in his worshippers may turn him into an actual god or 'Hero' with what we may call a personality of his own. This has happened to Odysseus. He is an Eniautos-Daimon, who has become a Hero.

The third chapter discusses the relation of Odysseus to Poseidon *Hippios*. A study of the cults of this god leads to the conclusion that his worship in all probability originated with the so-called Minyans in Central Greece, whence it spread into the Peloponnese. Local tradition maintained that it was introduced into Arcadia by Odysseus. The chief centre of its diffusion there was Mantineia; and at Old Mantineia was the grave-mound of Penelope. Analysis proves the authenticity of the Mantinean legends, and also makes it reasonably certain that Penelope was originally a Water-fowl divinity connected with the spring Arne near Mantineia. The marriage of Odysseus and Penelope is a mythological way of expressing an historical fact, the meeting and fusion of Odysseus-worshippers from Boeotia with the Arcadian people who worshipped Penelope.

The fourth chapter seeks to prove the reality of a migration on the part of a people of Minyan affinities and traditions from Central Greece by way of the Corinthian Isthmus through Arcadia to Triphylia in Elis and the Ionian Islands; further, that this people formed an important body of the settlers in Ionia, and carried with them the Poem of Odysseus.

Chapter V returns to Boeotia. A comparison of the Odyssey with the *Argonautica* helps us to disengage certain other Minyan-Boeotian elements in the Odysseus-saga, and leads to a tentative reconstruction of an original 'Boeotian Odyssey'. A somewhat similar method, using our knowledge of the lost *Telegoneia* epic for a criterion, leads in Chapter VI to an outline of the 'Arcadian Odyssey', with its addition of new matter. The next stage, the Ithacan Odyssey, was reached, when Odysseus had come to be represented as king of Ithaca, and the saga had travelled with him there, changing the scene of many adventures from Boeotia and Arcadia to Ithaca.

The seventh chapter attempts to answer the difficult question, Who were the Achaeans? arriving at the conclusion that they were a people of 'North-Western' affinities, and distinct from the Aeolians. The epos was not their creation nor their property, but belonged to the Ionians; the prominence in it of the Achaean name being due to the Achaean prestige at a formative stage in the growth of the heroic poetry. The subject is pursued in the next chapter, which shows that there has been a very consistent, but superficial, 'Achaeanization' of Homer, and that the Iliad and Odyssey are in substance pre-Achaean poems. The epic heroes are shown to be almost without exception non-Achaean, and the same is true of the Homeric gods. Traces of the ancient custom of inhumation are discernible side by side with the frequent and obvious burning of the dead, which was perhaps an Achean practice. The emphatic patriarchal tone of Homer has not quite expelled the evidences of another sentiment natural to a society in which women held an important position. Thus Odysseus is very closely associated with a goddess, Athene, by whose temple at Boeotian Alalkomenai he was born. Finally, the confusion of older and newer types of weapons and armature indicates the same process of superposition, Achaean (and perhaps post-Achaean) upon pre-Achaean.

The last two chapters (IX and X) treat of the conditions under which the Story of Odysseus took the form of our Odyssey. Homer, we know, was recited by rhapsodes. In Chapter IX the rhapsode is shown to be the successor of the Aoidos. He professes to deliver the words of 'Homer', but in practice he may alter or add to these up to a certain limit, defined for him by the approval of his audience. The Iliad and Odyssey attained their present form through the co-operation of two factors, the genius of successive poets working within the epic convention, and the controlling taste of successive audiences. Who, then, is 'Homer'? This question is answered in the last chapter. Homer was the traditional author of the hymn sung to Apollo at the festival held every four years at Delos. The hymn was sung by a chorus of maidens exactly corresponding to the chorus of the Muses. The expression applied to such a choir, φωνῇ ὁμηρεῦσαι, explains the name Ὅμηρος given to their leader. It is, therefore, not a personal but a functional name, although actual poets personated 'Homer'; for instance, the poet of the existing *Hymn to Apollo*. An investigation of the problem raised by the relation of the minstrel to the god leads to the conclusion that Homer is a double of, or a parallel to, Apollo himself in his capacity of Aoidos. The hymn sung at Delos had for its subject the Birth-story, as in that place the most significant part of the whole Life-story, of the god; and the Homeric epos is an expansion of the hymn. The conclusion is, that the Odyssey was from the first an Ionian poem, and that it gathered shape through the recitations at the Delian Festival, until that fell into decay, and Homer came to Athens.

I wish to express my thanks to Professor Gilbert Murray and Miss Jane Ellen Harrison, who read my manuscript and made a great many invaluable suggestions; to Mr. A. J. Toynbee for the privilege of reading an unpublished paper by him on the Foundations of Greek Nationality; to Dr. Walter Leaf for some interesting criticisms. I am obliged for a reference to Mr. H. B. Walters, of the British Museum. My debt is especially great to Professor Murray and Miss Harrison, to whom, and above all to Professor Murray, I owe more than I can acknowledge in detail, more, indeed, than could be expressed in a mere reckoning of obligations. No one, however, whom I have mentioned, is in any degree responsible for the main theory embodied in the book, in which I am conscious that there is much that challenges received opinion, and may appear presumptuous in so untried a writer. But I had this suggestion to make, and it seemed best to make it at once. The value of any suggestion depends so much upon the promptness with which it is offered, that, if I had waited until I had made myself a better scholar, half the virtue would have gone out of mine.

J. A. K. THOMSON.

CONTENTS

CHAPTER I

ANTELUCANA

ἦμος δ' οὔτ' ἄρ πω ἠώς, ἔτι δ' ἀμφιλύκη νύξ.

To write the history of the Odyssey, to trace the story to its origins and disentangle the intricate processes of its growth, is a perilous adventure to be justified perhaps only by some novelty or suggestiveness in the argument. On the other hand, when the argument cannot in the nature of things be final, no more than these qualities should be required of it. However much further research and discussion may come to settle regarding the source and development of the Homeric Poems, all this fresh knowledge will aid us only in so far as we can use it to correct and define the picture our imaginations form of a time so remote, and, as we say, prehistoric. It is the business of the student to make this use of all the information available to him; and for that purpose any hypothesis which allows him to correlate the facts is better than none at all. Generally a new theory has the quality, excellent for the intellect, of provocativeness. It invites examination and concentrates criticism. Better still, where Homer is the subject, it may redirect attention to certain, perhaps half-forgotten, characteristics of his poetry. If the argument developed here does that, it will do so much that no other merit need be claimed for it. To stimulate thought is hard at all times, but doubly so on a matter so obscure as the origin of the Greek Epic, where one has to contend not only with so much ignorance in one's own mind, but also with a more insidious danger from the imagination, which is very subtle to introduce its own colours and its own logic into what is merely vague and disconnected in the actual evidence. It is a danger against which the scholar cannot be too vigilantly on guard, and it is likely to be great in proportion to his capacity for original research. What is needed is an imagination as sensitive as possible, yet never playing fast and loose with the facts—a conscientious imagination. It is the rarest of gifts, yet scholarship has never progressed very far without it.

Now it is becoming plain to us that Greek mythology, like most other mythologies, came into existence among a people holding beliefs about the natural and spiritual world which, to all except a few mystical and exceptional minds in modern times, are hardly even intelligible. The men of the early world, even when they were Greeks, were so bound in illusion and fantasy that solid objects seemed to melt before their eyes and pass into other forms, common things acquired a divine significance, and the very air was crowded with supernatural presences. The limits of human and superhuman, material and immaterial, were but dimly realized. There was something in common between gods and men and the beasts of the field and all growing things, and a pathway between the living and the dead. The strange beggar who came to your gate might be a god disguised ; for do not the Immortals wander here and there over the earth in the likeness of strangers out of foreign lands, ξείνοισιν ἐοικότες ἀλλοδαποῖσιν? Night and mist and the blowing wind took bodily shape and became a most ancient goddess, and a spirit rising from the sea, and a swift youth outrunning the Thracian horses. They could believe that a god, whose shape was the shape of a goat, pursued a maiden and clasped a reed. Dreams would come and in faint voices speak to them in words false or true. Every tree might be like the elm Aeneas saw in the entrance to the world of the dead, haunted by the phantoms that abuse the mind of the sleeper, so many of them that they clustered under every leaf, *foliis sub omnibus haerent.*[1] Every stream and oak and mountain was the habitation of a spiritual being whose nature was on the borderland between the human and the divine and partook of both. And

[1] *Aeneid* vi. 284.

so weak was the sense of identity, that with a touch of magic it was felt the barrier might be passed, and a man become a wolf or a serpent or a hoopoe or a purple lily. He might renew his youth; he might be raised from the dead. With waving of a branch and sprinkled waterdrops the wizard might bring a rain-shower down the side of Lykaios. Like Melampous he might understand the language of all living creatures, even the woodworms in the decaying rafters, and say with Alkman 'I know the songs of all the birds';[1] while the poets by the power of their music built cities and uprooted forests. Ancient popular literature, and not least the Greek, is full of gods in human forms, and divine beasts, and animate and powerful material objects. It is in such imaginings, which have their origin in religious rather than aesthetic emotions, that a mythology takes root and grows; when these disappear, the mythology which grew out of them dies likewise, or hardens into typical forms, which also is a kind of death. We can never understand the mythology of a people unless by an effort of sympathetic imagination we learn to see with their eyes and think with their simplicity. With the Greeks this is the more necessary because they began so early to cultivate poetry for its own sake; which means dissociating it from religion. In Homer the dissociation is already quite deliberate and complete. There is nothing, for instance, more characteristic of him than his entirely adequate perception of the difference between gods and men. You cannot bridge that gulf, he understands: but this is rather because of the weakness of human nature, the disabling handicap of old age and death, than because the gods are physically or morally unlike us. Zeus is the father of gods and men. The anthropomorphizing tendency of the Greek spirit is nowhere more active than in Homer, not only fashioning its divinities in the image of man, but filling them with human emotions, and engaging them actively in human affairs. But let us disregard it for the moment as less illuminating here than the effect upon the Homeric Poems of the Tradition itself. The Tradition, which

[1] *Fr.* 67.

still speaks of the War about Troy as a contest of gods and godlike men, arose among a people for whose eyes the earth was a theatre of magic and the gods only a mightier race of magicians than men or animals. So in the Iliad and Odyssey we find the old way of belief asserting itself in the constant transformations of the Immortals into shapes other than their ideal or typical shapes, into the semblance of a particular hero, or an old woman, or a young girl carrying a pitcher, or a vulture or a swallow. *Transformations* we should perhaps not call them, because they are so often not quite complete, but in some mysterious way a certain unmistakably Olympian dignity or beauty in the aspect or gestures of the god makes itself felt through the fleshly veil. But if we accept it as the most expressive word, how are we to think of these transformations? Not as part of the epic machinery, although in Homer they serve that purpose too. They are not in origin an artistic device but an article of primitive religion, as indeed we all now recognize—the dreams of men who believed that the Olympian gods in battle with the Giants assumed the forms of the mean animals, and who discovered a dreadful sanctity in an oak-grove or a blackened stone.

Thus in the Iliad Apollo becomes like Asios,[1] like Mentes,[2] like Periphas,[3] like Phainops the son of Asios;[4] at another time like Lykaon Priam's son[5] and Agenor.[6] Athene has the semblance of a herald,[7] Laodokos,[8] Phoinix,[9] a man,[10] Deiphobos,[11] Mentes king of the Taphians,[12] Mentor in the Odyssey frequently, Telemachos,[13] a young girl,[14] the herald of Alkinoos,[15] a young shepherd,[16] a woman tall and beautiful —her ideal form.[17] In the same way other gods, Iris and Hera and Hermes, Poseidon and Ares and Aphrodite, appear in human guise. The River Skamandros when he threatens Achilles has the appearance of a man.[18] And the *eidola* and dreams in Homer take human shapes and seem to speak

[1] Π 716. [2] Ρ 73. [3] Ρ 323. [4] Ρ 583. [5] Υ 81.
[6] Φ 600. [7] Β 280. [8] Δ 87. [9] Ρ 555. [10] Φ 285.
[11] Χ 227. [12] α 105. [13] β 383. [14] η 20. [15] θ 8.
[16] ν 222. [17] ν 288, π 157. [18] Φ 213.

with human voices. Nor is it only in the forms of men that the gods reveal themselves. Athene and Apollo become vultures and perch upon a lofty oak;[1] Athene is changed to a 'sea-eagle',[2] and a swallow,[3] and some other bird.[4] When Sleep alights upon the branches of a fir-tree on Mount Ida, the poet thinks of a certain hill bird with a shrill note—'the gods call it the *chalkis*, men, the *kymindis*'.[5]

When one remembers how full Greek mythology (like the old Irish and Finnish mythology) is of these shape-shiftings—so that Ovid writes the fifteen books of his *Metamorphoses* upon nothing else—one finds it easy to believe that in the earliest tellings of the stories of Troy and Odysseus they were even more numerous than in our Iliad and Odyssey. Something has happened—the intervention of a great poet, one critic will say, a long process of expurgation according to another—partly to expel, partly to disguise where that is possible, the supernatural element, still large enough in the Poems as we have them. If then there has been an unconscious, or only half-conscious, or quite deliberate attempt to eliminate the supernatural, one may expect to find indications of this. I think they may be found. 'So spake she and departed, the grey-eyed Athene, and like a sea-eagle she flew away . . . and he marked the thing and was amazed, for he deemed that it was a god.'[6] That is a clear case of transformation. But read in connexion with it the curious passage in the thirteenth book of the Iliad where Poseidon manifests his divinity.[7] He had appeared to the Aiantes in the semblance of Kalchas, urging them to battle; and then, as he took his departure, *ὥς τ' ἴρηξ ὠκύπτερος ὦρτο πέτεσθαι . . . τοῖιν δ' ἔγνω πρόσθεν 'Οιλῆος ταχὺς Αἴας*, 'the son of Oileus was the first to recognize him', and said to the son of Telamon: 'Aias, this is not Kalchas, but an Olympian god in the likeness of a prophet'—*ἴχνια γὰρ μετόπισθε ποδῶν ἠδὲ κνημάων ῥεῖ' ἔγνων ἀπιόντος*, 'I made out the traces of his feet and legs as he went away'. For, when he went away, 'like

[1] H 59. [2] γ 372. [3] χ 240. [4] α 320. [5] Ξ 291. [6] α 319 f. [7] 62 f.

a hawk he rose into flight', as Athene in the Odyssey vanishes in the shape of an eagle. Is not this a transformation rather than a simile, a transformation on the way to become a simile? Or take a passage where the poet is again speaking of Athene:[1] ἠΰτε πορφυρέην ἶριν θνητοῖσι τανύσσῃ Ζεὺς ἐξ οὐρανόθεν ... ὣς ἡ πορφυρέῃ νεφέλῃ πυκάσασα ἓ αὐτὴν δύσετ' Ἀχαιῶν ἔθνος, 'as Zeus bends his shining rainbow in men's sight, so she clothed herself in a shining cloud'. The poet is not thinking of Athene as like the rainbow so much as actually in the rainbow, as the rainbow itself. Is not this another disguised transformation, a transformation on the way to becoming a simile? When Poseidon smote the Phiakian bark, changing it into a rock νηὶ θοῇ ἴκελον,[2] it became more than a curiously formed reef, it became an enchanted ship. Similarities of that kind have something prodigious about them to simple people, who are always ready to confuse similarity with identity. To take a well-known example outside of Homer, instead of comparing a girl to a flower they say she is made out of flowers, like Blodeuwedd in the *Mabinogion* whom Math, the son of Mathonwy, and Gwydion made out of the blossoms of the oak and the broom and the meadowsweet. It is all part of that magic which they find so natural, which enabled Proteus and Thetis to pass at will into fire or water or a high-foliaged tree, and inspires so many of the Ballads, as *Tam Lane* and *Earl Mar's Daughter*. When Thetis arose from the waters, they saw her ἠΰτ' ὀμίχλη, 'like a mist'.[3] Modern readers call this a simile because they are educated. But the audience who listened when that image of the sea-fog was first used imagined, or half imagined, the goddess as physically bodied forth in it. And if we ourselves read our Homer with some sympathy with the frame of mind which makes such a conception possible, we shall be surprised to find how much of the beauty of the image depends upon a half conscious identification of the divine and weeping mother with the grey mist lifting from the sea at dawn. When Athene is sent by Zeus from Olympos, she darts to

[1] P 547 f. [2] ν 157. [3] A 359.

earth like a shooting star: τῷ εἰκυῖ' ἧιξεν ἐπὶ χθόνα Παλλὰς Ἀθήνη, κὰδ δ' ἔθορ' ἐς μέσσον· θάμβος δ' ἔχεν εἰσορόωντας, the beholders wondered, and said one to another, 'Surely evil war and dread strife will come again, or Zeus maketh friendship between the hosts'.[1] That is what one would expect them to say if a star fell. It was a star and not a woman tall and beautiful that flashed down between the armies. Immediately afterwards Athene put on the likeness of a man, namely Laodokos Antenor's son, and so persuaded Pandaros to shoot the fatal arrow that broke the truce.[2] Therefore, since the goddess passed unrecognized and seemed only a meteor, it is not a simile we have to do with here, although we may call it a simile in the making. The process must have been aided by the words expressive of likeness, ἐοικώς, εἰδόμενος, and the rest, with their ambiguous connotation of 'similar' and 'in the form of'. Indeed the history of these words would illustrate the change, which I find going on in Homer, from the primitive simplicity or confusion of thought which identifies things merely similar to more philosophical notions. It is of course a *tendency* of which I am speaking. No one would deny that (since men must always be comparing things) true similes have been in constant use from the beginnings of human speech. The Iliad in particular is full of them. But, besides these, there are others which, as we have seen, are formally similes, but in reality are disguised identifications or transformations. How far, one may ask, is the tendency actually traceable in the Homeric Poems? There is, for instance, the curious simile applied to Hera and Athene marching to battle: αἱ δὲ βάτην τρήρωσι πελειάσιν ἴθμαθ' ὁμοῖαι, 'they went on their way like timid doves in their going'—an almost humorously inappropriate description of two warlike goddesses stepping so daintily.[3] Is it a merely fanciful suggestion of Mr. Cook, that the explanation may lie in the relation of these divinities to Zeus, who, as the Odyssey itself implies,[4] was attended by sacred doves? Once doves in bodily form perhaps, they have become now only 'like unto

[1] Δ 75 f. [2] Δ 86 f. [3] Ε 778. [4] μ 62 f.

doves in their going'.[1] The very epithets they have in the Epic tradition, *βοῶπις*, *γλαυκῶπις*, concentrate in a word that way of thinking about the gods which even in Periclean Athens accepted the Snake Kekrops and the Bull that was Dionysos. Again, there is a superstition, current in places so far apart as France,[2] Australia, and the Ivory Coast of West Africa,[3] that the ghosts of the dead turn into bats—strange, crepuscular creatures with horrible wings and, it is whispered, a sinister taste for human blood, haunters of caverns and old tombs. The superstition is natural enough. That it existed in ancient Greece seems to me probable in itself, and a fair inference from certain references in Aristophanes to Chairephon, the friend of Socrates. The Chorus of the *Birds* in a comical little song, which is a parody of the *Nekyia*, tell how Socrates, like Odysseus, called up the dead, and Chairephon obeyed the summons—'Chairephon the Bat'.[4] Every one must feel how much this gains in point, if we suppose the audience familiar with the conception of the ghost as bat. And the other references to Chairephon,[5] which speak of his cadaverous complexion, give the explanation of the nickname. He was called the Bat because he was so like a ghost. If then the superstition was a familiar one in Greece, imagine how the opening lines of the last book of the Odyssey must have sounded in the ears of a popular audience, just such an audience as Aristophanes was addressing. The poet is telling how Hermes conducted the souls of the dead Suitors to the House of Hades; 'as when bats in the depths of an eerie cave squeak and flutter when one of them drops loose from the chain in which they cling to one another along the rock, so they went with him squeaking'.[6] How much of this is mere

[1] A. B. Cook, *Class. Review*, 1903, vol. xvii, *Zeus Jupiter and the Oak*, p. 186.

[2] A. Maury, *Croyances et légendes du Moyen Âge* (1891), p. 272.

[3] *Golden Bough*, vol. ii, ch. iii, § 12, p. 131, quoting J. C. Reichenbach, *Étude sur le royaume d'Assinie*. N. W. Thomas, art. *Animals* in Hastings's *Encycl. of Rel. and Ethics*, vol. i, p. 502.

[4] *Birds* 1553 f.

[5] *πύξινος* in the *Cities* of Eupolis, Νυκτὸς παῖς in the *Horae* of Aristophanes, *ἡμιθνής* in the *Clouds* 504. The explanation in the scholia *διὰ τὸ μέλας εἶναι καὶ λεπτόφωνος* is, of course, absurd.

[6] *ω* 6 f.

comparison, how much is identification? It might be difficult to say, and for my own part I feel that the doubt does in some subtle way enhance for me the charm of the quaint simile, just as one who has read *The Golden Bough* must feel a fresh significance in the simile of the mistletoe in the *Aeneid.* The likeness goes deeper than we had thought. Once more, when the sword of Poseidon was compared to the lightning-flash,[1] did it not pass through the mind of the hearer that the characteristic weapon of the god, the triple-pointed trident, was indeed in origin nothing else? Or was the poet who composed the simile ignorant of this?

Indeed, when one remembers out of what material the Iliad and Odyssey have been wrought, these lingering traces of a more ancient and naïve habit of thought can hardly appear other than inevitable. The Tale of Troy, the Story of Odysseus, are not the inventions of any single poet, however much they may be thought to owe to a single poet in form and spirit. That we all now admit. But the consequences of the admission are not always accepted, perhaps not always quite realized. For it follows that the great body of tradition which came down to Homer—'the author of the Iliad and Odyssey' here for the sake of the argument—which he shaped to the ends and in the spirit of his art, can never wholly have forgotten its origins. There was something for him to do in the way of selection and omission; how much one may guess from the most cursory glance at Hesiod. Homer, as Mr. Lang insisted, is silent about many cruel and grotesque and shameful things of whose existence in the tradition he could not be ignorant. He is indeed familiar with all the ancient histories, with the legend of Argo, for example, with all the horrors it contains, the black magic in it, and the echo it keeps of the savage ritual of the Laphystian Zeus. So those who praise, as we all do, the purifying breath of the Homeric Spirit in the two great Epics,

[1] Ξ 386. On this point see Dr. Chr. Blinkenberg, *The Thunder Weapon in Religion and Folk-lore* (Camb. Arch. and Ethnol. Series), 1911, ch. vii, pp. 51 ff.

should be prepared to find its effects here and there in the form of actual expurgation. There is, it may be confessed, something vaguely distasteful about the word 'expurgation' when used to describe a process dictated as much by an aesthetic as by an ethical motive. But it is the word in use, and the Greeks themselves would not have disliked it because it had a moral connotation. They were not so sensitive as we are to the distinction between the ideals of the artist and the moralist; they were even apt to deny it. They might do that because they had so strong an instinct to keep them right.

To take one instance out of many, there has been expurgation apparently in the story of Dolon as it is told in the tenth book of the Iliad. We read: 'He drew about him the hide of a grey wolf, and set upon his head a cap of marten's skin, and took a sharp javelin, and set out from the camp on his way to the ships'.[1] But in the *Rhesos*, which dramatizes the story, we find that the wolf skin is regarded not as a garment but as a disguise. Dolon is explaining to the Trojan sentinels who form the Chorus what he proposes to do. 'Will you change your raiment?' they ask. 'Yes . . . I will fasten about my back the skin of a wolf, and draw over my head the grinning mask of the beast, and fit to my arms the forelegs of the hide, and its limbs to my limbs, and walk wolf-fashion on four feet, deluding the enemy when I draw near their trenches and beaked ships; but when I come to a clear space, I shall walk on two feet like a man'.[2] Representations in art of the Slaying of Dolon also show him disguised. To pretend you are a wolf to deceive your enemies is a stratagem of primitive warfare—a genuinely archaic touch, one is bound to suppose, and therefore an original part of the tradition. Homer omits it, clearly 'expurgates' it, for a grotesqueness very alien, one feels at once, to the general tone of the Iliad.[3] Or

[1] K 334 f. [2] 208–15.

[3] *Class. Review*, 1911, vol. xxv, *Dolon the Wolf*, p. 238 f. The illustration given there—a fragmentary kylix by Euphronios—is perhaps unfortunately chosen, since the fragment has been in great measure restored. Cf. H. Usener, *Kleine Schriften*, 1913, vol. iv, *Heilige Handlung*, p. 453 f.

take another point, too large to be fully discussed here, the absence in Homer of all apparent traces of that belief in the 'jealousy of the gods' (φθόνος τῶν θεῶν) which is something like a dogma for the rest of Greek literature. The thought that God is jealous or envious of the eminent or fortunate man is, of course, however much it may be moralized, at heart entirely non-moral, and springs from a much lower and more primitive stage of religion than Homer's. Yet Homer's religion logically involves it, and, if it no longer appears in him, the reason must be that he has outgrown this particular part of the Olympian creed.[1] And no wonder; for in the last resort this jealousy is nothing better than the resentment of a divine being at the breach of some taboo, some non-moral obligation, whose sanction is supposed to lie with him, or at the usurpation of some privilege or special possession of his, which seems to put the usurper on the level of the god himself. To be very famous, to be very powerful, to be very happy are not for mortal man; for then he becomes too like the Immortals. Homer will have nothing to say to so crude a doctrine; but then he does not believe either that a man may be or become a god. Yet allow that possibility, and the jealousy of the gods becomes, if not a more amiable, at any rate a more intelligible thing. This gives us its historical explanation. The Divine or Medicine King was much worshipped in early Greece, and it must have been largely on the destruction of this worship, and by a very comprehensive and active jealousy of all other divinities, that Zeus and his favoured associates acquired the special position they have in Homer. Yet there the only clear traces of all that are on Olympos itself. The sovereignty of Zeus, for all his placability, is avowedly based on terrorism: it is plain enough by what methods he has made himself king of the gods; he has but followed the methods of his conquering worshippers. But what of his relation, say, to Agamemnon? In Homer Agamemnon is a mortal king; but at Sparta he was worshipped as a god and actually identified there with Zeus. That identification im-

[1] Cf. *Themis*, p. 168 f.

plies a fusion of cults, a conflict followed by a reconciliation.[1] Which is the original version of his death—Homer's, who makes it the result of a family feud, or the account of Aeschylus, who, in the significant scene in which he represents Agamemnon treading on purple as he enters the palace, plainly intends to show the conqueror guilty of *hybris*, the great offence of 'seeking to become a god'?[2] Again, what is the cause of the 'innumerable woes' of the Iliad? Is it the quarrel about the woman of Bresa? Not in the opinion of Agamemnon, who attributes it all to Ate, 'the eldest daughter of Zeus', sent by him, or coming of her own accord, from the mere pleasure of hurting, it seems.[3] And why is Achilles made to suffer? Is it not because he insists upon so monstrous a revenge for the insult done him, such revenge being the prerogative of the gods, since 'Vengeance is mine'? And why does Poseidon so persecute Odysseus? The blinding of Polyphemos cannot be the primary motive; it can only be what one may call the fictional motive. The story of Polyphemos has arisen to account for the wrath of the god, and *that* must have an historical explanation in the quarrel or jealousy of the two divinities, Poseidon and Odysseus. Thus penetrating beneath the surface of the Homeric Poems we seem to find the Jealousy of the Gods as a real agency in the movement of the plot. Why then is it so carefully disguised? For two reasons, I imagine; an aesthetic, or mainly aesthetic, and a moral one. The aesthetic reason is this: that when once a myth breaks loose from the ritual, to which it is related as theory is related to practice, it tends in the hands of poets and story tellers to lose its sacred or theological character; the actors in it from divine tend to become human, as we may see not only in Homer but also in the old Irish epic-romances, which are said to be full of such faded,

[1] If Agamemnon was simply a local representative of Zeus, a 'Zeus' from the beginning, our explanation will have to be put somewhat differently, but it will be essentially the same explanation. Agamemnon, like Salmoneus, was at first a quite legitimate 'Zeus', but came to be looked upon afterwards as a usurper. So he incurs *phthonos*.

[2] μὴ ματεύσῃ θεὸς γενέσθαι, Pind. *Ol.* v. 58. [3] T 86 f.

humanized divinities. This may explain why Agamemnon and Achilles and Odysseus are no more than mortal heroes for Homer; and we cannot dissever his insistence upon the difference between god and man from his repugnance to the doctrine of Phthonos, which, as we saw, is rooted in the belief that the difference may be overcome. Yet Herodotus and the Attic tragedians are not less conscious than Homer of the limitations of humanity, and they believe in the divine jealousy. So he must have had a moral reason as well. That is to say, there has been conscious or unconscious expurgation of this primitive doctrine inherent, we are bound to assume from all the evidence, in the earlier forms of the traditions.[1]

If this does not convince, there are the other examples of expurgation gathered by Professor Murray in his *Rise of the Greek Epic* (ch. v), and discussed there, surely very persuasively. It may be denied that there has been any substantial alteration in the text since it left the hands or lips of a supreme poet. But then the supreme poet must himself have made many expurgations in the traditions which went to the making of the Iliad and Odyssey; for we cannot assume the existence of a Homer before Homer, and so must believe that the legends he found did not differ in spirit from all other Greek legends, the spirit of which is on the whole singularly unhomeric. The expurgations are there in any case, and should be studied.

The Odyssey even more than the Iliad is full of these imaginations of an earlier world, imaginations permeated by a spirit not at all like the normal tone of the Iliad or the rest of the Odyssey. But these, we are told, are stories of adventures in strange lands and seas where marvellous things may be expected to happen; and scholars talk of the 'outer geography' of the Odyssey. But this does not explain everything; for many episodes in the poem are not only marvellous in a way not elsewhere evident in Homer, but are also of a

[1] The first non-Homeric passage which explicitly dissociates *φθόνος* from the divine nature seems to be Pl. *Phaedr.* 247 A *φθόνος γὰρ ἔξω θείου χοροῦ ἵσταται.* But the dissociation is implied in Aesch. *Ag.* 750 ff.

vast antiquity, as students of mythology can prove. There can hardly be perfect appreciation even of the poetical significance of the Odyssey until one realizes that it is fashioned out of materials of the most different ages, and can think oneself back, with however pitiful success, into a time when as yet our Odyssey did not exist at all. The *Alkinou Apologos* is built up out of the dreams of numberless generations of men, and one cannot even guess when first it was put into the mouth of Odysseus. But, it may be objected, we are helpless. To bid us try to conceive an Odyssey before the Homeric is a counsel of perfection, or rather of despair; it is bidding us stare into the darkness. Not altogether; for a great traditional poem, an epic really national, like the Odyssey, casts a light backwards as well as before it, and we need never pass out of that light. Moreover, even among dreams there are some that pass the Gate of Horn.

CHAPTER II

ODYSSEUS IN BOEOTIA

AUTOLYKOS dwelt on Mount Parnassos with his sons and his wife Amphithea. The young Odysseus, his daughter's son, came to him there from Ithaca, and took part in a boar-hunt, and, as it happened, was wounded in the thigh by the boar, a monstrous beast, which they found at dawn in a glade of the mountain forest. Autolykos excelled all men in thievishness and the use of the oath. The god Hermes gave him this gift, for he used to sacrifice the young of sheep and goats to Hermes; and the god was with him and showed him favour.[1] The legend was, or came to be, that Hermes was his father;[2] and Ulixes in Ovid says

> Est quoque per matrem Cyllenius addita nobis
> Altera nobilitas. Deus est in utroque parente.[3]

This relation of Hermes to Autolykos reveals an aspect of the god about which Homer is reticent, so reticent that we should hardly have observed it in him at all, if we had not the *Hymn to Hermes*. In the *Hymn* we find a very different picture from that idealized one presented with almost perfect consistency in the Iliad and Odyssey. He is no longer 'the herald Mercury' or the grave Conductor of Souls with golden rod, but a thief, a liar, a master of stratagem; the counterpart, in fine, of the knavish Autolykos. No one now asks whether the Homeric figure or that described with so much vivacity in the *Hymn* comes nearer to the traditional conception of the

[1] τ 392 f.

[2] Apollod. *Bibl.* i. 9, xvi. 8. See Roscher's Lexicon under *Autolykos.* His mother was Philonis daughter of Deion or Daidalos, or Chione daughter of Daidalion, or Telauge daughter of Heosphoros or Hermes.

[3] *Metam.* xiii. 146, 147.

god, even though one may admit that in the popular conception he had a graver and more menacing aspect, upon which the poet of the *Hymn* has not cared, or has had no occasion, to dwell. The Hermes of the *Hymn*, despite a certain obvious sophistication, is older, incomparably older, than the Hermes of the Epics, who indeed is not a god of primitive religion at all. In many respects the other is. He is the Hermes *Dolios* whom Pausanias found at Pellene 'ready to grant men's prayers', an idol of the old, rude, 'four-cornered' fashion.[1] He is the Hermes *Χαριδότης* whose singular ritual permitted the Samians to thieve and to steal, as Plutarch tells us in his *Greek Questions*.[2] And even in Homer he is sent by the gods to 'steal' the body of Hector.[3] Of this Hermes then Autolykos is the reflection or double, the embodiment in a typical figure of folk-lore of a certain ambiguous side of the god's nature which is evidently primitive just because it is so ambiguous. So that curious helmet worn by Odysseus when he set out with Diomedes to spy upon the Trojan camp had once been stolen by Autolykos from Amyntor Ormenides in Eleon.[4] The stories speak of him as above all a thief of cattle, like Hermes in the *Hymn*.[5] It is only when we remember all this that the passage in the Odyssey which speaks of Autolykos as the protégé of the god acquires its full significance. We see him now as a form of the Cunning Hermes; originally no doubt an independent figure, but very early identified with a divinity he so much resembled. He dwelt upon Parnassos, and he is named *Αὐτόλυκος*, 'Very Wolf'. Now at Delphi among the great precipices of Parnassos a Wolf-god was worshipped, for the inscription which records the ritual of the Delphian Labyadai in the fifth century before Christ assigns to him the skins of the sacrifice,[6] and Pausanias saw the image of a great wolf there, and tells a strange anecdote to account for it.[7] The

[1] vii. 27. 1. [2] 55. [3] Ω 24. [4] Κ 266, 267.

[5] Hesiod, *Fr.* 112 (Rzach); Pherekyd. 63.

[6] τὰ τῷ Λυκείῳ δάρματα . . . *Bull. Corr. Hell.*, 1895, p. 12, l. 37. Cf. Dittenb. 438. But see there note 82.

[7] x. 6. 2.

story connects the wolf with Apollo *Lykoreus*, and there was a town Lykoreia upon Parnassos. But although it was Apollo and not Hermes who was associated in historical times with this Parnassian cult, the cult itself was almost certainly in existence before it was taken over by Apollo. Thus there is no need for surprise that the associations of the Wolf Autolykos, who cannot be unconnected with the Wolf-god worshipped on his native mountain, are altogether with Hermes, although Parnassos was to become so much the holy hill of the lyric god that it has filled the verses of poets ever since with the echo of his fame.

Autolykos was the father of Antikleia the mother of Odysseus, and, according to the story in Homer, gave him his name Ὀδυσσεύς, the Son of Wrath, as the poet understands it to mean.[1] But in popular speech he was called not Ὀδυσσεύς but Ὀλυσσεύς; Ὀδυσσεύς is a literary, perhaps an Ionic, variant.[2] Which is the significant form, Odysseus or Olysseus? Unless philological reasons are decisive against it, one would say the form which persisted in living use in spite of the epic: other things being equal, for the philologist the spoken is better evidence than the written word. Great weight must be given to any arguments which seem to establish the historical connexion of Odysseus with a particular locality; if I can show, as I hope to do, that Odysseus came originally from Central Greece and was worshipped in Boeotia long before he became a hero of the Ionian Epos, then the Boeotian form of his name ought to have much influence with us. Now Boeotian pottery gives us the forms Ὀλυσ(σ)εύς, Ὀλυσσείδας. Attic and Corinthian vases also show the spelling with λ. Ibykos of Rhegion has Ὀλίξης,[3] the Sicilians perhaps said Οὐλίξης,[4] the Romans certainly Ulixes. A usage so general as this can hardly be treated as a mere local or dialectic variant and dismissed with λάφνη

[1] τ 403 f.

[2] P. Kretschmer, *Die griech. Vaseninschr.*, p. 146 f. He finds upon the vases ολυτευς, ολυττευς, ολυσευς, ολισευς, ωλυσσευς. Cf. *Einleitung*, p. 280 f.

[3] *Fr.* 11 b.

[4] Plut. *Marcell.* xx.

and λίσκος as an example of 'dissimilation'.[1] The stem of Ὀλυσσεύς is apparently *luk*, which is the stem of λύκος, a wolf, and so Autolykos gives his grandson his own name.[2] Olysseus and Autolykos are therefore apparently only two slightly varying names for the same god or hero named of the wolf. The cunning robber of Parnassos and the wise king of Ithaca are in origin identical. And although this conclusion is at first a little startling, and philological arguments are notoriously deceptive, there are others besides these which seem to bear it out.

We know how the Attic dramatists and Pindar habitually speak of Odysseus as the absolute knave, the typical rogue and dissembler. In this they are not creating a literary convention, they are listening to the voice of tradition, the original tradition which even the idealizing intention of the Iliad and Odyssey has not quite obscured, and which revealed itself, we may be sure, much more vividly in other epics of the Trojan Cycle where Odysseus was prominent, in the *Kypria*, for instance, and the *Little Iliad*. The epithets constantly applied to him, πολύμητις, πολυμήχανος, bewray his original character, just because, one might say, they are used so formally. In the *Epipolesis* in the fourth book of the Iliad, Agamemnon addresses him as 'master of mischievous wiles'.[3] It is true that Agamemnon is angry. But it is only with a smiling admiration that Athene uses a long series of epithets to the same effect, 'many-coloured mind ever framing some new craftiness.'[4] Then there is the whole episode of the Cyclops. In essentials that is a story admittedly of dateless antiquity, with many undoubted parallels in the folk-lore of other nations than the Greek. In Northern mythology the hero is called the Shifty Lad; while the Shifty Lad, as Mr. Lang observed, is only a human representative of the

[1] F. Solmsen, Kuhn's *Zeitschr.* 42, *Odysseus u. Penelope*, p. 207 f.

[2] Wilamowitz, *Hom. Unters.*, p. 18, n. 6. Bolling, in the *American Journal of Philology*, 1906, 65 f., takes Ὀλυσσεύς as actually an abbreviated form of Αὐτόλυσσος, a 'dedicatory' name from Αὐτόλυκος.

[3] Δ 339.

[4] ν 291 f.

Shifty Beast.[1] So Odysseus, the Shifty Lad of Greek mythology, is also the Wolf. It is in this character of the typically crafty hero that he is represented as the descendant of Autolykos, his other self; and, according to another tradition, as the son of Sisyphos, most cunning of men,[2] who outwitted Death in Ephyra; and, according to yet another, as the kinsman of Sinon, who beguiled the Trojans.

But if Odysseus is connected so closely with Autolykos, we must expect to find him standing in a not very different relation to Hermes from that of Autolykos. With this in one's mind it is interesting to observe the part played by Hermes in the Odyssey. There are two occasions on which he intervenes; the first, when he visits Kalypso in her island to announce the will of the gods that Odysseus return home; the second, when in that other island of Kirke he appears to Odysseus in the likeness of a young man in the most gracious season of youth.[3] The second occasion is the more illuminating, precisely because in the Odyssey it is left unmotived. We are not told that Hermes was sent by Zeus to give counsel to Odysseus in the Aiaian Isle, as he was sent to bear the message to Kalypso. But if we think of the relation between Autolykos and Odysseus, and recall the phrase describing the relation between Autolykos and Hermes 'He went with him and showed him favour', *ὁ δέ οἱ πρόφρων ἅμ' ὀπήδει*,[4] the motive will seem evident enough perhaps; while the whole position of Hermes in the Odyssey, so difficult to account for in view of the Iliad, looks very like a relic of his prominence as just such a patron and companion of the hero in some earlier form of the Odysseus legend. However that may be, the connexion remains to elucidate several things. It allows us to believe in the appearance of Hermes in Kirke's isle as an original part of the tradition, and not as merely copied from the incident in which he visits Kalypso. Then there is the adventure of the Thrinakian Isle, where the companions of Odysseus stole and slew the sacred kine of the Sun.[5] That is at the centre a most

[1] *Anthropology and the Classics*, p. 60.
[2] Ζ 153.
[3] ε 28 f., κ 277 f.
[4] τ 398.
[5] μ 352 f.

ancient tale, how the divine herds of the Light-god came to be stolen and slaughtered. It appears in the Vedas, where Ahi steals the cattle of Indra.[1] In varying forms it reappears in Greek mythology. The kine of Helios, which Apollonios describes as milk-white with golden horns,[2] are identical with the swan-white cows of Augeias the son of Helios,[3] and doubtless also with the red cattle of Geryoneus, which Herakles drove.[4] Above all, they are the kine of Apollo—belonging to him, as these parallels prove, in his capacity as a Light-god, perhaps definitely the Sun-god—of which the *Hymn to Hermes* speaks at such length, and mention was made in Hesiod[5] and Alcaeus,[6] from whom we learn that they too were snow-white and golden horned. What Hermes does in the *Hymn* the companions of Odysseus do in the Odyssey; the companions being, as one can scarcely doubt, 'secondary' and taking the place held in the original form of the myth by Odysseus himself, or at least borrowing their whole significance for students of mythology from their relation to him.

The shadow of Parnassos falls across the Boeotian Plain, and it is in Boeotia that one seems to find the earliest traces of Odysseus. The least expected of these is perhaps the most suggestive. It is the name of Arkeisios his father's father and the progenitor of the race. The importance of Arkeisios consists in this, that he is the significant ancestor; the whole issue at stake throughout the Odyssey being whether 'the blood of Arkeisios shall perish out of Ithaca'.[7] Who then was he? Homer does not tell us. The prevailing tradition speaks of him as a son of Zeus and Euryodeia,[8] but then un-

[1] Preller-Robert, i, p. 394. [2] *Argon.* iv. 976.
[3] Theocr. xxiv. 130. [4] Apollod. *Bibl.* ii. 5. 10 f.
[5] Anton. Liberal. 23. [6] Paus. vii. 20. 4. [7] ξ 182, &c.

[8] Schol. π 118; Eustath. p. 1796, 83. The alternative version represented him as the son of Kephalos of the Attic Thorikos, or the son of Keleos or Killeos son of Kephalos. Kephalos being childless had recourse to the god at Delphi, who bade him wed the first female he should meet upon his homeward journey. This, as it happened, was a she-bear, which was afterwards changed into a woman, and bore a son, Arkeisios. *Et. Mag.*, p. 144, 22; Heracl. Pont. 38; Eustath. p. 1961, 19. The myth is an etymological one, based on a fancied connexion between Ἀρκείσιος and ἄρκτος

fortunately falls silent. We should be left in entire perplexity if philology did not come to our aid with an analysis of the name Arkeisios which reveals a world of new possibilities. Ἀρκείσιος (Ἀρκέσσιος) is a *Kosename*, a 'hypocoristic' form of Ἀρκεσίλαος.[1] Now there was a hero of that name buried at Lebadeia in Boeotia,[2] who appears in the *Catalogue of the Ships* as a Boeotian chieftain.[3] His bones were carried home from Troy by his brother-in-arms, Leitos, and buried in Lebadeia; so ran the story, accounting for the tomb. He was killed by Hector,[4] who in his turn was buried at Thebes. Diodoros calls him the son of Ἀρχίλυκος,[5] the scholiast on *B* 494 the son of Ἀρηίλυκος, Hyginos the son of Λύκος, simply.[6] Arkesilaos son of the Wolf! Can that be accidental? We remember also that Lebadeia was the seat of the famous oracle of Trophonios, who, whatever his exact character may have been, was certainly a 'chthonian' divinity, one of many such in Boeotia, where the worship of Hades and the dead was widespread. It has been conjectured[7] that Ἀρκεσίλαος is one of the numerous titles acquired by the god of the underworld, and this is likely enough in the case of a hero with his grave at Lebadeia.

Something more may be gained from another source. Odysseus and Penelope, it was said, had a son called Arkesilaos.[8] The authority for this quoted by Eustathios was the 'Cyclic' poet Eugammon of Kyrene, who composed the *Telegoneia* telling of the death of Odysseus at the hands of his son Telegonos. A poet of Kyrene! The significance of that shines out when it is remembered that in the royal house of the Battiadai Arkesilaos was a hereditary name. If the Eusebian *Chronicle*

(ἄρκος) a bear. Kephalos is the eponym of Kephallenia. The story was in Aristotle's *Constitution of the Ithacans*.

[1] Bechtel and Fick, *Die griech. Personennamen*, p. 382.

[2] Paus. ix. 39. 3.

[3] B 495.

[4] O 329. Cf. E. Bethe, *Homer u. d. Heldensage*, p. 15.

[5] iv. 67.

[6] *Fab.* 97, p. 85.

[7] By Gruppe, who connects the Ἀρκέσιον ἄντρον in Crete with a possible Cretan or Phoenician god of death Arkesios = Arkesilaos, *Griech. Myth.* i. 253.

[8] Paus viii. 12; Eustath. p. 1796.

is right in assigning the *floruit* of Eugammon to the 53rd Olympiad, he may have been poet at the court of Arkesilaos I. Plainly, the kings of Kyrene were willing to have it believed that the blood of Odysseus ran in their veins, derived through a son of his, a certain Arkesilaos, not mentioned to be sure in Homer. The name of Odysseus' grandfather, Arkeisios, it is thought, may have suggested to the Battiadai or some courtly bard, Eugammon himself perhaps, so flattering a genealogy.[1] But the claim seems to find confirmation in a very curious series of facts which at least entitle us to believe that those who made it had more solid ground to proceed upon than an accidental resemblance of names. We may begin with the evidence of Herodotus, our capital authority for the early history of Kyrene. In the well-known chapters at the end of the fourth book of his History he has included a genealogy of the Battiad princes. The progenitor of the race was the Minyan Euphemos, one of the Argonauts.[2] That this was the received tradition is made certain by other proofs, above all by the great *Fourth Pythian* ode written for Arkesilas of Kyrene, in which Pindar relates how Euphemos obtained the clod of earth that was to serve him for a pledge that in days to come his descendants should occupy the Libyan shore.[3] Euphemos, we always hear, was a Minyan, son of the Earth-shaker according to Hesiod,[4] with whom Pindar agrees: 'Euphemos, the princely son of Poseidon Lord of Horses'—the Minyan god Poseidon *Hippios*—'Euphemos, whom in former days Tityos' daughter Europa bare by the banks of Kephisos'.[5] The genealogy thus expresses the claim of the House of Battos to Minyan descent. The claim may not have been historically justified. They may have based their pretensions solely on the associations of Euphemos with the promontory of Tainaron in South Laconia, from which the island of Thera, the birthplace of Battos, was anciently colonized.[6] My own belief is that they had more than this to

[1] Wilam., *Hom. Unters.* p. 184.
[2] iv. 150 Βάττος ὁ Πολυμνήστου, ἐὼν γένος Εὐφημίδης τῶν Μινυέων.
[3] 80 f. [4] *Fr.* 152 (Rzach). [5] *Pyth.* iv. 80 f. [6] *Pyth.* iv. 78.

go upon; but it is enough for my present purpose that the claim was made and in some way defended. Now on what grounds was it defended?

The kings of Kyrene said: 'We are by descent Minyans of the race of Euphemos and Arkesilaos son of Odysseus'. Our impulse is to dismiss this double claim as self-contradictory. But if the Battiadai themselves did not so regard it? We are at least bound to examine the evidence.—Euphemos, as we have seen, was a Boeotian, and the name of his mother, Europa, daughter of Tityos, enables us to say to what part of Boeotia he belonged. For, since the giant Tityos dwelt in Panopeus,[1] his daughter can be no other than that Europa who was worshipped at Lebadeia and was there regarded as the 'nurse' of Trophonios and a form of Demeter.[2] Now it was at Lebadeia that the hero Arkesilaos was buried.

Again, the mother of Euphemos was this Demeter-Europa; and the mother of Arkesilaos was *Εὐρυόδεια*, an epithet of Gaia the Earth, and an actual cult-title of Demeter at Skarphia on the Malian Gulf.[3] Again, there is some reason to think that *Εὔφημος* and *Ἀρκεσίλαος* are both titles of the god of the dead,[4] and Lebadeia was certainly a great centre of chthonian religion. Here, then, we seem to find the solution of the apparent inconsistency. The Battiadai claimed descent from Arkesilaos the son of Odysseus because this Arkesilaos was the great-grandson of Arkeisios, whom they identified with Arkesilaos of Lebadeia. One need not go on to argue that Euphemos and the Lebadean hero may be only different forms of a single divine being, although they have clearly something in common besides the place of their origin. For that merely local bond, taken along with the constant claim of the princes of Kyrene to a Boeotian origin—Theras, the

[1] λ 581.

[2] Paus. ix. 39. 4 ἔστι δὲ καὶ Δήμητρος ἱερὸν ἐπίκλησιν Εὐρώπης at Lebadeia. Cf. § 5. For the Europa legend, which spread from Lebadeia, see Ed. Meyer, *Gesch. d. Alt.* ii. 93.

[3] Hesych. s. v.

[4] Εὔφημος· ὁ Ζεὺς ἐν Λέσβῳ, Hesych. At Tainaron a cleft in the ground led to the underworld, Pind. *Pyth.* iv. 78.

founder of Thera, was a Kadmeian [1]—and with the persistence of the name Arkesilaos in their family, gives us what we desired, some historical justification of their pretensions. It is only when we assume that they regarded the son of Odysseus as directly descended from Arkesilaos of Lebadeia that the claim implied in the *Telegoneia* becomes intelligible. But on this assumption it is both intelligible and, as I hope will afterwards appear, in essence true.[2]

This speculation has withdrawn us a little from our main quest, the Boeotian affinities of Odysseus.[3] In the Odyssey itself the existence of certain apparently Boeotian elements has long been recognized. In especial it has been thought that the eleventh book, the *Nekyia*, must have been in its original character pure Boeotian saga. For the central part of it, the *Nekyomanteia* proper, is the visit of Odysseus to the realm of Persephone to consult the soul of the Theban Teiresias. This legend, or rather this form of a world-old and world-wide legend, would most naturally arise in the land where the prophet of Thebes was most in reputation. The scene of the *Nekyia* indeed is not in Boeotia but in the remotest West, at the limit of the River Okeanos. But could this have been the original form of the story? Whenever Homer speaks of the dead and of their world we are involved in a strange perplexity; for he speaks of them in one way, and historical Greek religion, at least for the most part and in its most genuine utterances, in quite another. For him, as Pater says, though not of Homer, the ghost is only 'a dream that lingers a moment, retreating in the dawn, incomplete, aimless, helpless: a thing with faint hearing, faint memory, faint power of touch; a breath, a flame in the doorway, a feather in the

[1] Her. iv. 147.

[2] Gruppe, *Griech. Myth.* i. 256, thinks that the Battiadai were only concerned to claim descent from Ikarios through Penelope, Ikarios being a Spartan and reputed the father of Tainaros. But it is enough to say in answer to this, that Arkesilaos is named after his paternal great-grandfather and not after any of his mother's race. The second Arkesilaos derives his whole significance from the first. But doubtless the Battiad kings were glad to be thought the descendants of Ikarios also.

[3] 'Boeotian' of course as belonging to Boeotia, not the Βοιωτοί, who were late comers.

wind'. For it the ghost is full of power, a being of gracious or maleficent activities, with bodily passions and desires that cry for appeasement. This difference in the philosophy of death accompanies, probably arises out of, a difference in the disposal of the dead, who are burned in Homer, whereas the older and always prevalent custom in Greece was to bury them.[1] Now if the legend of Odysseus' visit to the shades be very old—as it embodies one of the earliest imaginations of humanity—it will date from an age when inhumation prevailed and the ideas about the dead which go with inhumation. Then sooner or later the Homeric spirit entered into it and subdued the tradition to the mould of its own characteristic beliefs.[2] Yet, it would seem, not entirely. When Odysseus came to the verge of Okeanos, he drew his sword and dug a trench with it, and poured a libation, and vowed to sacrifice a black ram to Teiresias, and cut the throats of the sheep he had brought with him letting the blood flow into the trench, 'and the souls of the perished dead gathered up out of Erebos' and would have drunk of the blood, but Odysseus would not suffer them, until Teiresias had drunk and made his prophecy.[3] This feeding of the dead with blood poured into a *bothros* belongs to the service of the buried, not of the burned.[4] And it is significant that in the Odyssey itself Teiresias is distinguished from the other dead, who are mere 'shadows', by some superior vitality or vigour of intelligence surviving in him from his former life on earth;[5] this retention of faculties in death being again a privilege of the buried only, as one sees from so many examples of 'heroes'

[1] The evidence is collected by Zehetmaier, *Leichenverbrennung u. Leichenbestattung im alten Hellas* (1907). Inhumation was the rule in all periods, cremation the exception. But cremation was always practised.

[2] Need I say that by the 'Homeric spirit' I do not mean the private feeling of any individual poet regarding the dead, but the feeling of a certain Greek society at a certain stage in its development?

[3] λ 23 f., 90 f.

[4] All this is familiar to readers of Rohde's *Psyche*, esp. i, p. 49 f. Cf. the chapter on Inhumation, Cremation, and the Soul, in Ridgeway's *Early Age of Greece*, vol. i.

[5] κ 492 f.

regarded as lying in their graves, bodily entombed. Teiresias himself had his grave by the spring of Tilphossa, and an oracle at Orchomenos of the Minyans. He is already a famous seer in Homer; long before men must have sought counsel of the prophetic dead in his native Boeotia. And there was at least one well-known entrance to the lower world there, namely the cavern of Trophonios at Lebadeia, where the visitor sacrificed a ram to Agamedes the 'brother of Trophonios', before descending into that fearsome hollow.[1] Remembering this, one finds it easy to believe that the core of the Odyssean *Nekyia* is an actual, very ancient Boeotian tradition of a visit to consult Teiresias made by Odysseus, not at the edge of the world, but at the prophet's Boeotian home, where alone, according to normal Greek belief, he could drink the blood of sacrifice soaking down to his lips and make answer to his consultant; and if on other grounds we conclude that Odysseus was himself, to begin with, Boeotian, we shall find it all the easier.

Then there is the *Catalogue of Women*.[2] The wonderful beauty of the lines that conjure up for us one after another the ghosts of these famous queens of ancient song 'star-sweet on a gloom profound' need not blind us to the character of the art. Such 'Catalogues' were preserved and composed with especial piety in the Lokrian-Boeotian school of epic poetry, whose chief representative was Hesiod of Askra. To him is attributed the curiously named *Eoiai*, a list of Aeolian (Lokrian-Boeotian) heroines, who had been the brides of gods. The *Theogony* contains the genealogies of 'heroes', defined by the poet as the sons of divine mothers and mortal fathers. However difficult it may be to reconstruct the contents of the lost 'Hesiodic' poetry, there is no doubt of the predominance in it of this feature, as ancient scholars, who were in a better position than we to judge, themselves recognized. There is thus a *prima facie* case for assuming a Boeotian origin for this passage of the *Nekyia*. And when one proceeds to examine in the light of this suggestion the names and histories of the

[1] Paus. ix. 39. 6. [2] λ 225–330.

women mentioned there, one finds that they are in fact the names and the histories of Boeotian legend.[1] Odysseus saw Tyro daughter of Salmoneus, Antiope daughter of Asopos, Alkmene and Megara the mother and the wife of Herakles, 'the mother of Oidipodes fair Epikaste', Chloris and Leda and Iphimedeia, Phaidra and Prokris and Ariadne, Maira and Klymene and hateful Eriphyle. Of these, Tyro is a Minyan princess, mother of Pelias king in Iolkos and of Neleus king of Triphylian Pylos; a parallel tradition tells how her father Salmoneus came from Thessaly to Elis. Antiope is the mother of Amphion and Zethos, who built a wall of towers for Thebes. It was in Thebes also that Alkmene bare Herakles and Epikaste died, who was the mother and queen of Oedipus. Chloris was the youngest daughter of Amphion, who reigned in Minyan Orchomenos, and bare to the Minyan Neleus in Pylos Nestor and Chromios and Periklymenos and a daughter Pero, whose beauty was a thing to wonder at.[2] Iphimedeia was the mother of Otos and Ephialtes, who strove to put Ossa upon Olympos and Pelion upon Ossa—a Thessalian legend—and founded the worship of the Muses at Askra.[3] These, with the exception of Leda, whose fame as the mother of Helen may have won for her a place in the list, are all of whom the poet speaks at any length: that is to say, these are the heroines in whom the audience for which this passage was originally composed were chiefly interested. And they all belong, or all but Iphimedeia, to the same cycle of Minyan-Boeotian legend. How far the Odyssean Catalogue may be drawn from or dependent on similar Catalogues in other poems, the *Eoiai* in particular, is hardly determinable now.[4] Those who think of the Odyssey and the *Eoiai* as poems

[1] I use the word 'Boeotian' not in any strict geographical sense, but to designate a certain well-defined cycle of mythological tradition which clearly had for its centre the very ancient civilization of the Boeotian Plain. In fact, geographical terms could not be used with any precision, the land being so long unsettled and boundaries continually shifting in these remote days, with fragments of the same people finding their way into widely distant regions. What one discerns is only groups of more or less homogeneous tribes settled in more or less fixed habitations.

[2] λ 281 f. [3] Paus. ix. 29. 2. [4] Wilam., *Hom. Unters.* p. 147 f.

composed *d'un seul jet* by individual authors, familiar of course with much earlier poetry treating of their subjects, cannot entertain the theory that one epic may have borrowed from the other. But in either case, whether the Catalogue in the *Nekyia* be original or borrowed, it must have made a special appeal to a Boeotian audience and was therefore presumably composed or inserted for one, although time and the art of Homer have concealed any more obvious indications of this. The conclusion thus arrived at fits in with the prominence of the Theban hero-prophet Teiresias in the central episode. Properly understood, that episode is an essential part of the Odysseus legend, whereas the *Catalogue of Women* has a less organic connexion with the rest of the Odyssey; it is, as we say, a *mere* episode. What has preserved it is the fact that it also was, in its less vital way, part of the tradition, one of the Boeotian legends about Odysseus; that and, one would like to believe, the great and strange quality of its own inherent loveliness, 'beauty making beautiful old rhyme in praise of ladies dead.' With Homer, of course, the first impulse is to preserve the tradition; he does that even when it troubles and perplexes him. But, as we see in his handling of the myths, he is also perpetually striving to mould it into the most beautiful form of which it is capable, even if he is forced to do it a little violence. Here, however, he could keep the tradition entire. The *Catalogue of Women* made a great impression upon the imagination of antiquity, but the feeling it creates has been shared by imaginative minds in every age. One finds it in Dante's account of the Second Circle of Hell, where Francesca and her companions are, and in Faustus' vision of the face that launched a thousand ships against Ilium; it is the feeling of Propertius' *sunt apud infernos tot millia formosarum*.

How did the ancient fable of the Descent to Hades come to attach itself to Odysseus? The question is a little out of the way of our inquiry, and perhaps does not permit of a final answer. Yet I think one can see the direction in which the answer should be sought. Odysseus, it has been argued, was originally a mere double of Autolykos, who again was a double of Hermes. Now we know enough of Hermes to let us understand Odysseus a little better by aid of this analogy. Hermes, whose primary function it is to secure the fertility of the crops and trees and herds of his worshippers, has as a necessary means to the performance of this function control over the dead, from whom, according to primitive Greek belief, comes the fruitfulness of the earth. So perhaps we may explain the curious double aspect of the god. Homer indeed, except in the *Second Nekyia* (in the last book of the Odyssey), which is generally regarded as a 'spurious' or 'post-Homeric' addition, never directly refers to the chthonian functions of Hermes, although he knows of the golden charming-rod with which he puts to sleep and awakens again whomsoever he will. But, as we are continually finding, the silence of Homer is no argument against the existence in his age of any custom or belief in Greek religion, whatever we mean by the age of Homer. Hermes, a very ancient and apparently indigenous divinity in Greece, was certainly from the very first a god of death as well as of life; he was *Chthonios, Psychagogos, Psychopompos,*[1] the Conductor of the newly released soul to its future dwelling-place beneath the earth. It is interesting to find that the boy-ministers of Trophonios at Lebadeia were called *Hermai,*[2] Hermes here standing in the relation of *πρόπολος* to a confessedly chthonian Daimon. Well, Arkeisios-Arkesilaos was buried at Lebadeia. The fable of his visit to the Shades might come in this way to attach itself to Odysseus. But the true explanation goes deeper than this. One cannot understand the whole significance of Odysseus' adventure without comparing it with the Visits to the Dead of Herakles and Theseus and Orpheus and Dionysos. When we do that, we shall probably find that one explanation will cover them all;

[1] Conductor also of the ghost to upper air again. Indeed the normal meaning of *ψυχαγωγός* is 'necromancer'. See the Jena lekythos figured in *Themis*, p. 295. Cf. the curious passage E 385 f. where Hermes *ἐξέκλεψεν Ἄρηα ἤδη τειρόμενον*, when Ares had been shut up in a pithos for thirteen moon-months.

[2] Paus. ix. 39. 7.

they are part of the normal life-history of what Miss Harrison calls the Eniautos-Daimon. I am not so much concerned to prove that Odysseus is such an Eniautos-Daimon; one can never express the whole truth about any god or hero who has acquired a complicated mythology in a single formula. But one formula penetrates deeper than another, and the conception of the Year-Spirit guides us farther than any other into the original nature of the Hero Odysseus. Hermes, in so many ways his counterpart, is such a Spirit,[1] and Odysseus may be so too. Grant this, and we have a reasonable explanation of much that hitherto may have seemed mere accretion from originally alien sources gathering about the genuine story of Odysseus. The Visit to the Dead may now take its place as an authentic part of the story, an essential scene in the drama of the Eniautos-Daimon. The sojourn with Kalypso, the 'Concealer', may represent the periodic disappearance or obscuration of the god. And the relation of Odysseus to Helios, which affects his fortunes so deeply, may be understood from the similar relation of other Year-Spirits to the Sun-god. We have already discussed the analogy with Hermes, who stole and slaughtered the kine of Apollo. That the Eniautos-Daimon should come into contact with the Sun is seen to be inevitable when one reflects that the Eniautos is the Sun-Year. Thus the sojourn with Kalypso would seem to represent the winter feebleness of the Sun. And there is this also to observe: the sun which shines for us by day must shine somewhere else by night. Where, unless among the dead? Do we not see it every evening sink beneath the earth? Helios himself threatens that, if the gods deny him satisfaction for the killing of his sacred cattle in Thrinakie, he will descend into the house of Hades and shine among the dead—he means, shine permanently there.[2] Such a conception of Helios and his functions brings him very near to Hades himself.[3] It also brings him very near to Odysseus with his voyage to the sun-

[1] The Agathos Daimon. See J. E. Harrison, *Themis*, p. 294 f.

[2] μ 383.

[3] J. E. Harrison, *Class. Review*, 1908, vol. xxii, *Helios-Hades*, p. 15.

set and the land of ghosts. A comparison between Odysseus and Herakles, the Daimon of the Sun-Year,[1] would help us to establish still more clearly the substantial identity of these, and of many other Daimons and Heroes, all embodying the same fundamental conception. But this would take us beyond the limits of our argument.[2]

Every one remembers the tenderly imagined episode in which the White Goddess of the sea, Ino-Leukothea, saves the shipwrecked Odysseus by the gift of her magical veil.[3] Her intervention comes at a critical moment, and is so integral a part of the plot, that it ought not to be regarded as an interpolation. Who then was Leukothea? Homer knows her as 'the daughter of Kadmos',[4] the founder of Thebes. The Boeotian goddess succours the Boeotian hero. Again, (though we are now dealing with a mere interlude, from which we cannot argue with the same force as from an organic, necessarily original part of the story) the tale of the loves of Ares and Aphrodite recited by Demodokos[5] is clearly a romance woven about the joint worship of the god and goddess in some of the communities where we know that this common cult existed. What exactly their association implies, whether

[1] *Themis*, p. 369 f.

[2] Odysseus has important relations to Apollo also Apollo in his capacity of Sun-god. These were first indicated by Wilamowitz in *Homerische Untersuchungen*, and afterwards more fully elaborated by Seeck in his *Quellen der Odyssee*. If I may say so, I think Seeck makes the mistake of treating one part of Odysseus' nature as if it were the whole. It is quite true that in certain situations of the Odyssey Odysseus plays the part of Apollo. But it is equally certain that in others he seems the counterpart of Hermes and Poseidon, and at times a male embodiment of Athena. The explanation is that in his origin Odysseus was quite independent of these Olympians, and goes back to an age before their functions were differentiated as they were in Classical Greece. He and they were developed out of the same primitive type of divinity, and so we find him resembling now one of them, now another. It is the same with Herakles and Theseus and Achilles. They are as old and as divine as the Olympians, only they have not been so fortunate. In the moral order they are for the most part older. The Apollo of the Iliad is a later conception than the Odysseus of the *Doloneia*.

[3] ε 333 f. Mr. Lawson compares the magical qualities attributed to a nymph's scarf in Modern Greece. *Mod. Gk. Folk-lore*, &c., p. 37 f.

[4] ε 333.

[5] θ 266 f.

we have to think of Ares as originally a Thracian god and Aphrodite a Thracian goddess his wife, is still a disputed point.[1] But it is scarcely disputable that Thebes, which kept so persistent a tradition of Thracian occupation, first brought their association into prominence in Greece; indeed the Theban cult was always the most famous of its kind.[2] It looks then as if the Lay of Demodokos was a peculiarly Homeric handling of Boeotian matter.[3]

It is unnecessary to suggest other possibilities of this, not quite satisfactory, character. But by giving a new direction to the argument we reach a fresh conclusion singularly consonant with the hypothesis of a Boeotian origin for the Odysseus legend. This new line of reasoning derives from the religion of Poseidon. The part played in the Odyssey by the god of the sea is present to all our minds, the wrath of Poseidon being in fact the central motif of at least the first half of the poem. Homer tells us the cause of his wrath—the poetical cause, so to say, the Aition—namely the blinding by Odysseus of the god's uncouth son Polyphemos. But the Aition here, as in the myths generally, is really secondary. Poseidon is not angry because Odysseus blinds Polyphemos; Odysseus is made to blind him that Poseidon may have a reason for his anger. This is none the less true because the tale of the blinded giant is not Homer's invention, but an immensely ancient story retold in a new context. The Greek imagination, so logical in its inventiveness, would not easily tolerate an apparent irrationality—the motiveless wrath of

[1] More probably, Aphrodite came from the south to Thebes, where she was identified with the Theban Harmonia, whose association with Ares is clearly very ancient. See Gruppe, *Griech. Myth.* i. 86[4]; ii. 1330[7] ff.; 1356[6]; 1362[2]; Farnell, *Cults*, ii, p. 620 f.

[2] It reappears in the neighbourhood of *Mantineia*, Paus. ii. 25. 1 *κατὰ μὲν δὴ τοῦτο Ἀφροδίτης κεῖται ξόανον, πρὸς δὲ ἡλίου δυσμὰς Ἄρεως.* See pp. 41 ff.

[3] The Lay has somewhat the air of a *prooimion* to the joint gods Ares-Aphrodite. The humorous tone of it is not unlike that of the *Hymn to Hermes.* It is not suggested that the Lay is a Hymn which has strayed into the Odyssey, but only that the Homeric Hymns help us to understand how a poem like the Lay might come to be made in connexion with a particular ritual or festival.

Poseidon—at the basis of a fabric otherwise so consistently designed. For us, however, the wrath is the thing 'given', and we must begin from that. We have to discover the historical Aition instead of the mythical.

Why then is Poseidon the enemy of Odysseus? At first the question may seem to answer itself. What could be more natural than that the man who had wandered over so many seas and so often suffered shipwreck should be thought an object of the Sea-god's wrath?[1] But the mythopoeic spirit does not work in that way; it does not reason so deliberately; it does not reason at all. It merely trusts its instinct, not knowing how or whither that instinct will guide it. This is why the discussion of what is logical or reasonable in mythology—and the remark applies to the whole field of primitive religion—is for the most part really impertinent. Mythology indeed has its own logic and its own reasons, but they are not ours; and it is only when we adopt theirs and abandon our own that we can understand the whole significance of the myths. In the present case we are not helped by a mere assertion of the naturalness of Poseidon's anger in the story. How dangerous it would be to accept this explanation as adequate may be seen from the analogy of the *Argonautica* and the *Aeneid*. Jason and Aeneas like Odysseus were driven over remote and dangerous seas, yet it is not Poseidon or Neptune who persecutes them; in the case of Aeneas, Neptune is even favourable. If we are to find the true explanation, we must seek it on some surer ground.

[1] *Hom. Unters.*, p. 138.

CHAPTER III

ODYSSEUS AND PENELOPE

Such a rural queen
All Arcadia hath not seen.

POSEIDON as he appears in Homer striding from island to island or driving his divine horses over the waves in his golden chariot hardly answers to the picture one forms of him from the historical study of his worship in Greece. Yet this is rather because Homer consistently presents one aspect of his divinity and confines himself to that than from any positive discrepancy, such as one may suspect in the case of Hermes, between the character of the god in the epos and his character in the cults. Something is due no doubt to the very different feeling one has in reading Homer, who is always at his best when he speaks of Poseidon, and in reading the sober and fragmentary accounts of the ritual of the god. But Homer does give us a somewhat one-sided representation. For with him Poseidon is always the god of the sea; whereas in the cults, although his office as the great marine deity seems to be recognized everywhere, he has other provinces and functions ignored, or at most only dimly perceptible, in the epos. It is in fact now generally admitted that at first he had no part in the lordship of the sea at all. Following Mr. A. B. Cook,[1] who has explained the second part of the name *Ποσει-δῶν* as a parallel form of *Ζεύς*, I take him to be originally the Sky- and Thunder-god, who in descending to earth has not forgotten his weapon of the three-forked lightning, the trident. Hence perhaps a certain dreadfulness and splendour investing all his appearances in Homer. But there is nothing to prevent our thinking that Poseidon was also from the first a god of

[1] *Class. Review*, 1903, vol. xvii, *Zeus Jupiter and the Oak*, p. 175 f. Mr. Cook follows Ahrens.

the fertilizing waters, as a Thunder-god may well be; of the 'sweet waters' however, the fountain and the stream, not of the 'unvintaged' sea; and with his trident, as Moses with his rod, he can strike the waters from the rock, because he is also the Earth-shaker, the god of earthquakes. Besides this the records point to other, more unexpected, qualities of his, of which the most important for our purpose, as it is perhaps the strangest of them all, is his connexion with horses. For he was to the Greeks not more the ruler of the seas than the god of horses, *Poseidon Hippios*, creator of the first horse and the divine patron of chariotry. 'The gods have divided thine honour in twain', says the Homeric *Hymn to Poseidon*, 'that thou shouldst be at once tamer of horses and saviour of ships.'[1] And Aristophanes speaks of him as taking peculiar pleasure in the neighing of steeds and the ringing of the bronze-shod hooves as they strike like cymbals upon the ground.[2] Some faint recognition of this aspect of the god appears even in Homer, where the aged Nestor in counselling Antilochos speaks of his son as the pupil in horsemanship of Zeus and Poseidon.[3] At Onchestos, at Corinth, at Mantineia, three of the most ancient and important centres of his worship, and often elsewhere, we find Poseidon revered as above all *Hippios*, with the quaintest legends sometimes attaching to a local cult and unconsciously testifying to its original character. Of the horse Areion, for example, we have two substantially identical accounts, one connected with the spring Tilphousa in Boeotia, the other told by the people of Thelpousa in Arcadia, both stories agreeing in this, that Areion was the offspring of the god, who in the Boeotian legend is explicitly said himself to have assumed the form of a horse.[4] Was that the form then in which Poseidon of Tilphousa was originally worshipped?[5]

[1] 4, 5.

[2] *Knights* 551 f.

[3] Ψ 306 f. Why Zeus? Is it because he has a special regard for Antilochos as a future βασιλεύς?

[4] For the Tilphousian story see schol. Ψ 346, for the Thelpousian Paus. viii. 25. 4; cf. 42. 1.

[5] The horse Areion looks like an embodiment of the god himself. The regular title of both is κυανοχαίτης, an epithet at least as appropriate to

That the god of horses should have been figured in the imaginations of his early worshippers as himself a horse, if it can be proved, will not seem strange to the student of Greek religion. The proof of this, however, is not required to convince us that such stories as this of the divine horse Areion answer to something actual in the beliefs of men concerning their god, beliefs which in their turn answered to something actual in the ritual with which they served him. About the ritual we know a good deal. We hear of horses dedicated or sacrificed to the god. At Onchestos, where was 'the bright Poseidonian grove',[1] we learn from the Homeric *Hymn to Apollo*[2] that the charioteers prayed to Poseidon for skill and fortune in their driving. At the Isthmos the god was honoured as himself a charioteer.[3] Much more evidence might be accumulated, if it were necessary to prove the existence of Poseidon *Hippios*. Since that is not denied, it is more urgent to consider the bearing of such evidence as has been quoted upon the special problem which now confronts us—the relation of Odysseus to Poseidon, and the meaning of that relation.

What we find is that the worship of Poseidon *Hippios*, whatever its origin, was specially and characteristically Minyan; and I think it can be made very probable that its diffusion throughout Greece was from a Minyan centre. The earliest home of the Minyans when first they become discernible to the historian is in Boeotia, in the lands about the Kopaic Lake. That they dwelt for some time in Thessaly also, with Iolkos, the seaport at the head of the Pagasaean Gulf, for their capital there, seems to be a fair inference from the Minyan legends and the character of the discoveries made at Volos (the ancient Iolkos), which at least prove the existence in prehistoric times of a civilization here like that of the excavated Orchomenos. Where the Minyans originally came from hardly concerns us here.[4] The Kopaic district was, from the earliest times of which we need take cognizance, the

a horse—'with dark-blue mane'—as to a god. Is it a survival like γλαυκῶπις, βοῶπις?

[1] B 506. [2] 238. [3] Himerius 3. 10.

[4] See Additional Note, p. 236.

motherland of the Minyans: yet, since their myths have so many strands of Thessalian tradition woven into them, we may stop to consider the evidence they contain for the worship of the Horse-god in Thessaly. There are to begin with certain *a priori* probabilities. If the name *Poseidon* is rightly connected with *Zeus*, and the gods ultimately identical, we are almost bound to assume that Poseidon as well as Zeus entered Greece from the north. I am myself inclined to think of two great main divisions of the Greek race—an Aeolian-Ionian division (to use historical names by anticipation) which invaded by the way of Thrace and Olympos, and an Achaean-Dorian division which came from the north-west. The North Eastern section worshipped Poseidon, the North Western the same god under the name of Zeus. Some justification of this view will emerge, or be readily inferred, from the evidence I shall adduce for regarding the Achaeans as a people of 'North Western' affinities. But if for the present we disregard this hypothesis, it is certainly far more probable that the worship of the Horse-god arose in the famous horse-breeding plains of Thessaly and Boeotia than in the Corinthian Isthmus or in Arcadia. The Thessalian legends of the Centaurs show the dominance of the horse in the popular imagination of these lands. That Poseidon was the chief god of the Minyans appears certain. The genealogies of the Minyan heroes, with which the *Nekyia* deals so largely, would alone go far to prove this. The whole race seems to trace itself back to him as the ancestor, and through the female line; good evidence for the antiquity of the tradition. In the *Fourth Pythian* ode of Pindar, Jason addresses Pelias as 'Son of Poseidon of the Rock' (*Πετραῖος*).[1] The scholiast commenting on the passage says, 'The story is in Pherekydes: Pelias, he says, was sacrificing to Poseidon, and had summoned all men to be present.' That is, it was a tribal sacrifice; the god who was father of the king was the father, the *Theos Patrôos*, of the tribe as well. The scholiast proceeds to explain the epithet: 'Poseidon of the Rock is honoured among the Thessalians because he

[1] 138.

cleft the Thessalian mountains—I am speaking of Tempe—and has caused the River Peneios to run on between them.'[1]

Poseidon then is a Minyan god, but not, so far as we have seen, Poseidon in his special function as *Hippios*. It is merely as Earth-shaker that he creates the Pass of Tempe with a blow of his trident. We hear also of a Thessalian cult of Ἴμψιος.[2] But the great centre of the Horse-god's worship north of the Isthmos was Onchestos near Haliartos. This Onchestian cult was very ancient and influential. In it Poseidon was worshipped as *Hippios*. In the *alsos*, which Homer praised, the god was honoured with chariot-races. In the form of a horse he begat the dark-maned Areion 'by the spring Tilphousa' and gave him to Kopreus king of Haliartos. An Amphiktionic Assembly used to meet in the Haliartian territory—at Onchestos in fact.[3] We may be sure that it was of great antiquity; and its mere existence is proof enough of the position held by the sacred place where it met in the religious life of Boeotia; so that it was perhaps of this Assembly that Aristarchos was mainly thinking when he spoke of Boeotia as altogether sacred to Poseidon.[4] The chariot-racing in fact implies a meeting of neighbours. We know of another and more famous Amphiktiony in Greece which met for the common worship of Poseidon; its centre the little island of Kalaureia in the Saronic Gulf not far from Methana. One of its members was the Minyan Orchomenos.[5] That is interesting for us because it shows how important the worship of Poseidon was for Orchomenos. That being admitted, we cannot doubt that the god of Onchestos was honoured in at least an equal degree by the Orchomenians. That Poseidon was a Sea-god at Kalaureia, but a Horse-god at Onchestos, is not a matter of great moment here; they could worship him under either aspect. A legend, generally regarded as reflecting to some extent the actual balance of power in early Boeotia, says that Klymenos king of the Minyans was wounded to the death by Perieres, the charioteer of Menoikeus of Thebes, 'in

[1] See Additional Note, p. 236.

[2] Hesych. Ἴμψιος· Ποσειδῶν ὁ ζύγιος.

[3] Strabo, p. 412.

[4] *Et. Magn.* 547.

[5] Strabo, p. 374.

Onchestos, the *temenos* of Poseidon'; and that the son of Klymenos, Erginos of Orchomenos, avenged the murder by making war upon the Thebans and imposing upon them a fine or tribute of a hundred oxen yearly for twenty years.[1] Here we find the Minyan king in the *temenos* at Onchestos, certainly for a religious purpose. Evidently the Onchestian god was his god; and it may be that the ἑκατὸν βόες exacted from the Thebans were really a hecatomb offered to Poseidon to expiate the pollution brought upon his sacred grove. The story further implies the predominance of Orchomenos in all this region about the Kopaic marsh. We are taken back to a time when Orchomenos was the political, Onchestos the religious, capital of the district. Whether the Minyans superimposed their god Poseidon, the ancestor of their kings, upon some ancient Horse-god worshipped at Onchestos before their coming, we cannot tell; but that they worshipped Poseidon *Hippios* there is surely a fair inference from the evidence. This conclusion is very greatly strengthened by the circumstance that, wherever one finds a well-authenticated record of a Minyan settlement, there we find also the cult of Poseidon the Horse-god. Without saying then that the worship of *Hippios* originated with the Minyans in Central Greece we may assume with some confidence that they adopted it there.

The worship of Poseidon is notable for having served in important ways as a bond of political union, as for example in the case of the states of Ionia with their Pan-Ionic cult of Poseidon *Helikonios*. That epithet in itself is full of suggestion. It is certainly ancient, for it is known to Homer, who professedly does not know Ionia. Philologically it can mean one thing only, Poseidon of Helikon; and this was the opinion of Aristarchos, who would not admit the derivation from Helike.[2] Helike was a town in the Peloponnesian Achaia. It was from this Achaia that, according to the Ionian tradition, the main body of the settlers in Ionia came; so that the desire to connect *Helikonios* with Helike would be natural enough, and would seem all the more plausible because there was in fact an

[1] Apollod. *Bibl.* ii. 4. 11.

[2] *Et. Magn.* 547.

important cult of the god there. Helikon, of course, is the Boeotian mountain; and since we do find so many Ionian traditions and genealogies leading directly or ultimately back to Boeotia, and such evident proof of the prevalence there of Poseidon-worship, it seems unreasonable to reject the meaning 'god of Helikon' simply because there is no trace, or no positive trace, of any actual cult of Poseidon on the mountain in any historical record.[1] But in fact all the historical records, and the mythological evidence as well, pretty clearly indicate, as I hope to show in a later chapter, that the worship of Poseidon, or at least of Poseidon *Hippios*, passed down into Southern Greece from Boeotia. For instance, at Kolonos, as Sophocles tells us, the Horse-god was had in reverence;[2] and Kolonos was full of Boeotian memories, memories of Oedipus and Adrastos. Corinth was a great centre of his worship; and the Corinthians told how he strove with Helios,[3] the old god of the land, and won the Isthmos, where he was worshipped along with Ino-Leukothea and Melikertes-Palaimon, obviously 'conflated' divinities, Ino and Melikertes being Minyans, and bringing with them perhaps the Minyan legend of Argo, which received such important developments in Corinth. He was worshipped also in Elis, in the *altis* at Olympia;[4] and Herodotus is ready with a tale of Minyan settlers there,[5] while the excavations of Doerpfeld at Olympia have brought to light traces of an ancient culture of 'Northern' characteristics and allied to that discovered on a site identified by him with the Homeric Pylos, the town of the Minyan Nestor. At Sparta Poseidon was worshipped under the name of *Hippokourios*;[6] and Sparta also had its Boeotian traditions, the Theban clan of the Aigeidai reappearing, it seems, in Lacedaemon and by its name evidently connected with the god; while Minyan traditions were rife in Southern Laconia

[1] Cf. Gruppe, *Grioch. Myth.* i, p. 74. Wilamowitz says definitely, 'The lord of the *ἵππου κρήνη* must have had horse-form, is therefore Poseidon Helikonios', *Griech. Dichter-Fragm.* 1–2; *Episch. Fragm.* Korinna 1; *Helikon und Kithairon* ii, p. 26 f.

[2] See esp. *O. C.* 712 f.

[3] Paus. ii. 1. 6.

[4] Paus. v. 15. 5.

[5] iv. 145–8.

[6] Paus. iii. 14. 2.

generally, and always in association with the worship of Poseidon.[1] The cult of *Hippios* at Patrai in Peloponnesian Achaia goes with the cult of *Helikonios*.[2] The cult of *Hippegetes* in Delos[3] is Ionian; and the intimate connexion of Ionian and Minyan is a thing that can be proved.

One great cult of the Horse-god has been left unmentioned until now, because it leads directly to the relation between Odysseus and Poseidon. This is the cult at Mantineia in Arcadia. The Mantineans bore the trident for a device upon their shields,[4] and stamped the figure of the god upon their coins, and had among their tribes one named *Ποσοιδαία*;[5] and indeed the whole city was in a manner dedicated to his service. But although it was the chief, Mantineia was not the only site of his worship in Arcadia. Methydrion had its shrine.[6] At Thelpousa they worshipped Demeter under the strange title of *Erinys*, and Pausanias says, 'They assert that Demeter bore a daughter to Poseidon (but her name they are not wont to pronounce to the uninitiated), and the horse Areion. Therefore they were the first of the Arcadians with whom Poseidon came to be called of horses (*Ἵππιος*)'.[7] With the Thelpousians agreed the people of Phigaleia; only they held that 'it was not a horse that was born of Demeter but She that is given the title *Despoina*, Our Lady, by the Arcadians . . . and their image of her is made after this fashion — She is seated upon a stone and is woman all but her head; but she had the head and the mane of a horse'.[8] *Θέλπουσα* is *Τιλφοῦσσα*, a certain philological equation; and at Tilphousa, which is in Boeotia, the story ran that Poseidon loved Erinys, and their offspring was the horse Areion. Here then is a Boeotian temple-legend that Poseidon brought with him

[1] Sam Wide, *Lakon. Kulte*, pp. 40-3.

[2] Paus. vii. 21. 7.

[3] Schol. Lycophr. *Alex.* 766 (Kinkel, p. 140).

[4] Bacchyl. *Fr.* 6, p. 413; Jebb (*Fr.* 2 Kenyon), *Ποσει]δάνιον ὤ[ς Μαντ]ινέες τριό[δοντα χαλκοδαιδάλοισιν ἐν ἀσπίσι]ν φορεῦν[τες . . . ἀφ' ἱπποτρ]όφου πό[λιος* . . . Blass thought the passage came in a catalogue of the Greek forces who went to Troy. The schol. on Pind. *Ol.* xi. 83 quotes Didymos as saying *τὴν Μαντινέαν . . . ἱερὰν τοῦ Ποσειδῶνος.*

[5] Collitz 1203.

[6] Paus. viii. 36. 2.

[7] viii. 25. 4.

[8] viii. 42. 1; 3.

a memory of his earlier seat when he came to Arcadia.[1] At Mantineia the old temple of the Horse-god was called the work of Trophonios and Agamedes,[2] Lebadean heroes, the sons of Erginos king of the Minyan Orchomenos; and near it were the tombs of 'the daughters of Pelias', king of the Minyans,[3] and a spring called Ἄρνη, a North Greek name, by whose margin Rhea bare Poseidon. So that, even if there were no other evidence than this from the study of religion and the diffusion of cults, one is disposed to accept the conclusion arrived at by good authorities that Poseidon did indeed come from Boeotia to Arcadia bringing Boeotian legends and legendary persons with him.[4]

The Arcadians themselves believed that the worship of Poseidon was introduced into their land by Odysseus. The people of Pheneos had a story that Odysseus once lost some horses and, wandering through Greece to find them, had found them at last at this town of Pheneos in North Arcadia; so he built a shrine there to Artemis Εὑρίππα, Artemis the *Finder of Horses*, and dedicated a statue to Poseidon of Horses near the temple of Athena *Tritonia*.[5] And on Mount Boreion by Asea, at the sources of the Alpheios and Eurotas, were the ruins of a chapel said to have been erected by Odysseus after his return from Troy to Athena the Saviour and Poseidon.[6] These stories were not made out of the Odyssey, which could never have suggested them, although it may have suggested some of the details which have gathered round the historical elements at their centre. What these elements are may be partly discovered by an examination of the cults with which Odysseus is associated. Artemis the Horse Finder is a very ancient and quite authentic divinity, for the connexion of the

[1] So K. O. Müller, *Eumen.*, pp. 191, 195, Eng. tr.; Immerwahr, *Kulte u. Myth. Arkad.*, pp. 114, 115; Farnell, *Cults*, iii, pp. 53–5.

[2] Paus. viii. 10. 2.

[3] Ibid. 11. 2.

[4] A careful statement of the case for the Boeotian (Minyan-Ionian) origin of Poseidon Hippios in Farnell, *Cults*, iv (Poseidon). A very complete record of the evidence is also given by Gruppe, *Griech. Myth.* ii (Poseidon), p. 1137 f., who holds that the religion of Poseidon arose in the old Boeotian sphere of culture. Cf. i, p. 195 f.

[5] Paus. viii. 14. 5.

[6] Ibid. 14. 4.

goddess with horses is certain, and is perhaps one of her original characteristics, although in times nearer the 'historical' it had almost faded away,—living on, however, to blossom into one famous flower of poetry and romance, the legend of Hippolytus, and persisting in a more concrete form in an actual cult at Pheraia in Thessaly;[1] while we may perhaps infer from the appearance of *Ποτνια* leading a horse on Boeotian seventh-century pottery that the Horse-goddess was worshipped in Boeotia also.[2] The bronze image dedicated to Poseidon was near the temple of Athena *Tritonia*, She of Triton, a little torrent stream near Alalkomenai in Boeotia.[3] And then the connexion of Odysseus with the Horse-god both at Pheneos and Mount Boreion—— is that in itself likely to have been invented? The connexion of Odysseus with Poseidon you may indeed deduce from the Odyssey; his connexion with horses you could not by any ingenuity deduce.[4] And the way in which all the circumstances of these Arcadian legends trace themselves so innocently back to a common source in Northern Greece, in Boeotia evidently, helps to make it still more probable that Odysseus came with Poseidon *Hippios* from Boeotia to Arcadia.[5]

[1] Paus. viii. 14. 4. [2] Ibid. 44. 4. See Additional Note, p. 236.

[3] Paus. ix. 33. 7. If this is the meaning of Tritonia, it must evidently be distinguished from that other epithet of Athena, Τριτογένεια, which has quite a different explanation. See Miss Harrison, *Themis*, p. 499 f. (following Lippold). The Greeks themselves apparently confused the two epithets, for the local Boeotian legend was that Athena was born by the Triton stream. At a later date the settlers of Kyrene took this with their other Boeotian and Arcadian legends and cults, and said that Athena was born at Lake Tritonis in Libya.

[4] Sir William Geddes thought an actual repugnance to the horse characteristic of Odysseus, *The Problem of the Homeric Poems*, ch. xv (1878).

[5] Whether Odysseus came to be identified with the Horse-god is a question I do not feel competent to decide. One cannot build very much upon the legend in Sextus Empiricus (*Adv. Math.* A, § 264, Bekker 659) that Odysseus after his death was transformed into a horse—interesting as the legend is in its bearing upon his relation to Poseidon Hippios. Eduard Meyer in his *Gesch. d. Alterthums*, ii, p. 67, and more fully in an article in *Hermes* (1895), lxxx, p. 241 f., entitled *Der Ursprung des Odysseusmythus*, maintains that Odysseus has grown from a Mantinean cult of an 'Angry' Poseidon (ὀδύσσομαι). This view is supported on

At least the association with Poseidon in Arcadia remains to help us; and following this clue we discover at Mantineia . . . Penelope, established there as native goddess of the place! At Old Mantineia, the *Ptolis* as it was called—the town of classical times was of course a comparatively late foundation, at some distance from the original site—her grave-mound was shown.[1] Her Arcadian origin and her divinity are both implied in the statement of Herodotus that, according to the belief of the Greeks (not, it is rather important to observe, of the Arcadians or Mantineans alone), she was the mother of Pan.[2] The Mantineans in Pausanias' time had a profane story, which is almost too silly to quote, to account for her presence in their land so far from Ithaca. 'The story of the Mantineans about her says that Penelope was accused by Odysseus of bringing followers (ἐπισπαστούς) into the house, and, being sent away by him, went first of all to Lacedaemon, but afterwards left Sparta to reside in Mantineia, where she died.'[3] So difficult was it to find in Homer any overt recognition of the Mantinean cult. Yet the very ineffectiveness of the attempt to reconcile the account of her in the Odyssey with the existence of her tomb at Mantineia indicates the independence of the Arcadian traditions of Penelope, which were found so incapable of adjustment to the canonical epic tradition. Well, since at Mantineia we find a famous cult of Poseidon *Hippios*, and at Mantineia also memories of Penelope as an ancient goddess of the land, was it not here that Odysseus first met her? The Mantineans themselves believed that he was the founder of their worship of the Horse-god, if a somewhat cryptic device upon their coinage of the fourth century B.C.[4] is rightly interpreted as Odysseus in the act of

philological grounds by Solmsen in *Kuhn's Zeitschrift* (see above). There is no evidence for any such cult in Mantineia beyond this inference from the supposed etymology of Ὀδυσσεύς.

[1] Paus. viii. 12. 5.

[2] ii. 145 ἐκ ταύτης (i. e. Πηνελόπης) γὰρ καὶ Ἑρμέω λέγεται γενέσθαι ὑπὸ Ἑλλήνων ὁ Πάν. Cf. 146.

[3] Paus. viii. 12. 6.

[4] The Mantinean coinage is discussed by Svoronos in *Gaz. Archéol.* xiii. 257 f.

planting in the earth the oar he was carrying upon his shoulder, so fulfilling the injunction laid upon him by Teiresias the prophet, that after the slaying of the Wooers he should take an oar and go upon his way until he came among men ignorant of the sea, and there fix his oar in the earth and offer sacrifice to the Lord Poseidon.[1] There is no doubt that the darkness of this oracle conceals some historical fact. The oracle was remembered because it was fulfilled or, if one must take a more rational view, it was composed after the event. The real problem is to discover what was the event, the historical fact disengaged from its mythological surroundings. Now it is in a general way quite clear what the prophecy implies. It is the foundation of a cult of Poseidon in some inland place remote from the sea. This was observed by the ancients themselves.[2] Only they thought of Epirus, naming Bounima and Kelkea—'unintelligible noises of local place-names', as Eustathios says, *τινῶν τοπικῶν ὀνομάτων βαρβαροφώνους δούπους*—as the scene of Odysseus' sacrifice,[3] but sometimes substituting the town of Trampyia or Trampya;[4] while of these Bounima, it seems, passed for a foundation of his. We can only answer that these are legends we have really no means of controlling, from mere ignorance of ancient Epirus; while the fact that Epirus supplied the obvious solution of the riddle, if we suppose that the true solution had been lost, ought to make us suspicious. For where in historical times would one go from Ithaca to find a people ignorant of the sea unless to the tribes beyond Dodona, the last outpost of the Hellenic civilization? The Odyssey indeed knows of Dodona, so our scepticism must be qualified by that. But although a legend may travel with a people, and it is not to my mind an incredible thing that the people of Odysseus may at some time have penetrated as far as Trampyia, yet the original scene of the fulfilment of Teiresias' injunction was clearly Mantineia—the home of Penelope, the adopted home of

[1] λ 119 f.
[2] Eustath., ad loc., p. 1675.
[3] Eust., l. c., schol. λ 122; Steph. Byz., s. v., Βούνειμα.
[4] Tzetzes on Lykophron, 800. Cf. schol. vet. 800.

Odysseus, the seat of the great cult of Poseidon founded by him there in the heart of the Peloponnese.[1] We are led to remember that the poet of the *Boiotia* with its Boeotian outlook, not to be forgotten in connexion with Odysseus, and its 'un-Homeric' geography, says that Agamemnon furnished the Arcadians with ships because they had no skill in seamanship, ἐπεὶ οὔ σφι θαλάσσια ἔργα μεμήλει.[2] Mantineia answers all the requirements of the prophecy.

Every reader of Herodotus must experience a shock of surprise when he comes upon the statement, twice repeated, that Pan was the son of Penelope. Some indeed have found it quite incredible. Does Herodotus really mean this? May not Pan's mother have been not our Penelope but an Arcadian nymph bearing the same name?[3] These are idle questions. It is of course Homer's Penelope that Herodotus means, and all the authorities who really count agree with him. Indeed few things in Greek mythology are better attested. There is

[1] The actual Wrath of Poseidon may be a Boeotian story arising out of a clash of cults. But conceivably it may have arisen, after Poseidon became god of the sea, in answer to the question, How did Odysseus come to found a cult of the god so far from the sea? But because it was this question which produced the answer 'To appease the wrath of Poseidon', it does not follow that the wrath did not exist already.

[2] B 614. The view that Mantineia is referred to by Teiresias was propounded by Svoronos in the *Gaz. Archéolog.*, 1888, xiii. 257, *Ulysse chez les Arcadiens et la Télégonie d'Eugammon*, and maintained by Ed. Meyer in his *Geschichte* and in *Hermes*, 1895. It is interesting to find Teiresias himself connected in legend with Mount Kyllene, the hill of Hermes, near Pheneos, where we found traces of Odysseus (Hyg. *Fab.* 75).

[3] This is the view held by Roscher and before him by Welcker and Preller. Roscher can only quote Nonnos, who speaks of two Pans sons of Hermes, one by the Oread Soso, the other by the 'nymph Penelope' (*Dion.* xiv. 87 f.), and a comment of Tzetzes on Lykophron 772 'Pan is the son of Hermes and Penelope—not *Homer's* Penelope', ὁ Πάν . . . Ἑρμοῦ καὶ Πηνελόπης ἄλλης υἱὸς γέγονε. The evidence is not good enough! We must believe Pindar and Herodotus. Besides, is it not obvious that Tzetzes (or his authorities) is merely trying to solve the problem as Roscher is trying to solve it, by what seems to him the likeliest hypothesis? As for the passage in Nonnos, even if Roscher's interpretation of it is right it is not really decisive. He calls Penelope the mother of Pan an Arcadian nymph. That is not a contradiction of Herodotus.

some doubt about the father of Pan, for, while Herodotus calls him the son of Penelope and Hermes, which is the usual account, Pindar, followed by the learned Euphorion, called him the son of Apollo:[1] but always, except in one text, his mother is Penelope. The exception is illuminating. It is the Homeric *Hymn to Pan*. There the god is apparently represented as the son of Hermes and Dryope, the account accepted by Keats in that other Hymn to Pan in *Endymion*. Well, the *Hymn*, being the work of 'Homer', had to be consistent with Homer, must not represent the mother of Telemachos as the mother of an Arcadian god! Its evidence is not independent. In fine there is no just ground upon which we can reject a tradition so strongly supported. Neither is there any reason why we should even wish to reject it. Scholars are beginning more and more to recognize that not merely did local traditions in the strangest contradiction of Homer persist for long in Greece, but that these are more primitive and genuine than the idealized and delocalized versions of them in the Epics. If Helen was buried in Therapnai, why should not the tomb of Penelope be at Mantineia, as Pausanias says explicitly? If it be objected that Therapnai was near Old Sparta, where, according to Homer himself, Helen spent her last years upon earth, yet it is Homer himself who tells us that she did not die there, but was carried with Menelaos to the Elysian Plain.[1] Nor is it in any way a stranger thing that Penelope should be buried at Mantineia than that Agamemnon should be buried in Amyklai or Hector in Thebes or Protesilaos in Elaius. And since her grave-mound was there, the tradition that she was also the mother of the Arcadian Pan becomes entirely credible. Neither, when one remembers how many of Homer's heroes and heroines were worshipped as 'heroes' and 'heroines' of a quite different order, in some cases definitely as gods, and all this after the epos had denied their divinity, will it appear at all anomalous that Penelope, too, is

[1] Pind. *ap.* Servius *in Georg.* i. 16; Euphorion *ap.* schol. *Rhes.* 36.
[2] δ 563 f.

now discovered to be divine. For divine of course the Mother of Pan must be.[1]

Eustathios in his commentary on the Odyssey has a quotation from the great Homeric scholar Didymos: 'that Penelope is properly called *Ameirake* or *Arnakia*', τὴν δὲ Πηνελόπην Δίδυμος φησὶν Ἀμειράκην ἢ Ἀρνακίαν κυρίως καλεῖσθαι.[2] Tzetzes calls her *Arnaia*;[3] another form is found, *Arnea*.[4] What then of this other 'proper' name of Penelope? It comes from an unexceptionable source, and has besides an air of authenticity. I cannot explain Ameirake, but the other titles, Arnakia, Arnea, Arnaia, are I think capable of an obvious explanation. They mean *She of Arne*, the famous spring by Mantineia at whose edge Rhea gave birth to Poseidon.[5] But if this interpretation is correct, we get two results: confirmation of the tradition which made Penelope a Mantinean, and, in the second place, a definite connexion of her divinity with a spring of water; a circumstance which we shall come to see has its significance. For Eustathios proceeds to quote from Didymos a quaint myth telling how Penelope had once been saved from drowning by certain *penelopes*, a kind of waterfowl evidently indigenous to Greece. The story may be really the explanation, the Aition, of some ritual of the *Plynteria* type, such as formed a normal part in the service of every Kore; or it may be simply one of those naively invented fictions of ancient mythologists which carry upon their faces the evidences of their origin. But in either case it proves that the Greeks connected Πηνελόπη with πηνέλοψ; and so she is sometimes represented in art with a penelops beside her. Now in fact Penelope is derived from penelops, as certainly as Παρθενόπη from παρθένοψ or

[1] The evidence for the parentage of Pan was collected by Roscher in *Philologus*, lxiii. 1894; *Die Sagen v. d. Geburt d. Pan.* The stories clearly show that Homer's Penelope is meant, e.g. the statement of a scholiast on Theocritus that Pan was the son of Odysseus and Penelope. Others made him the son of Antinoos. Our chief source of information is a long *scholion* on the *Rhesos*, l. 36.

[2] On α 344. Cf. schol. δ 797.

[3] Lykophr. *Alex.* 792.

[4] Schol. Pind. *Ol.* ix. 85.

[5] Paus. viii. 8.

Μερόπη from *μέροψ*.[1] The penelops is a water or marsh bird, 'like a duck, but the size of a pigeon,'[2] familiar enough in the Greek λίμναι as early as Alcaeus and Ibykos. A scholiast on the *Birds* of Aristophanes has preserved for us the picturesque description of Alcaeus: '*What birds are these?* Penelopes come from Ocean and the ends of the earth with their long wings and necks of changeful hue.'[3] Was Penelope then herself at first a penelops, the Penelops-Kore of Arne? . . . One of the epithets of Artemis in Arcadia was *Stymphalia*, Our Lady of Stymphalos. Stymphalos gave its name to the Stymphalian Birds, the man-eating monsters whose claws and wings and beaks were of bronze, and whose feathers were shot out like arrows, and who were ultimately driven from their native haunt by Herakles.[4] Coins of Stymphalos carry the representation of one of these Birds,[5] and, says Dr. Frazer in his note upon the passage in Pausanias, 'it is the head of a waterfowl, not of a monster.' On an amphora in the British Museum they appear as long-necked waterfowl with variegated plumage—very like Alcaeus' penelopes in fact. These 'fearful wildfowl', who devour men and yet retain the shape of birds, point to the worship of some primitive divinity in form of a waterfowl or, as one ought rather to say because it is less ambiguous, to the worship of a waterfowl regarded as divine. The ivory *fibula* recovered from the sanctuary of Orthia or Bortheia at Sparta[6] allows us to follow an almost identical process with that through which our Penelope must have passed. It shows the goddess, herself half bird, grasping two great marsh birds by the neck. Later she became entirely anthropomorphic, the Maiden Artemis. Now at Stymphalos Pausanias saw in an old sanctuary there

[1] So F. Solmsen, *Kuhn's Zeitsch.* xlii. 1909; *Odysseus u. Penelope*, p. 232 f.

[2] Vat. schol. Ar. *Birds* 292.

[3] Alcaeus 48 (53). The punctuation is uncertain. Ibykos 8 a. Cf. Stesich. 89.

[4] Paus. viii. 22. 7.

[5] Imhoof-Blumer and P. Gardner, *Num. Comm. on Pausanias*, *J. H. S.* vii, p. 99.

[6] See R. M. Dawkins, *Laconia*, *Sparta*, B. S. A. xiii, p. 78, fig. 17 b; *Themis*, p. 144, fig. 20. Penelope, it is worth remembering, had a *heroon* at Sparta.

certain marble figures of virgins with the legs of birds, and upon the roof of the temple a representation of the Stymphalian Birds. Clearly, the marble virgins were only more idealized forms of the Birds upon the roof, and they help us to realize still more clearly that the goddess of the shrine must have been at heart a mere Stymphalian Bird herself. More of her we cannot say, for, like so many other local Korai in Arcadia, she was identified with Artemis and her house made the shrine of 'Stymphalian Artemis'. But here was one Waterfowl Kore in Arcadia. Why should not Penelope be another?

The ancient Bird of Stymphalos was absorbed in the Olympian Artemis, who had all these mountain lands of Central Peloponnesos for her hunting-ground. When Nausikaa is compared to her, the poet thinks of the quivered goddess racing on some Arcadian or Laconian height, 'towering Taygetos or Erymanthos.'[1] For him of course Artemis is that 'queen and huntress, chaste and fair', who has so dominated the tradition of art and literature. Yet for him too, we have seen, she is specially Arcadian, and in Arcadia she was, from the earliest time to which our knowledge reaches, a mighty goddess. It may have been that she was a goddess there from the beginning, for she can be shown to belong to that type of the divine Mother-Maid, who under so many names, and often with no distinctive name at all, seems to have drawn to herself the earliest worship of men in Greek lands. But we cannot tell. Neither can we say why she, who was herself perhaps at first the divinity of some little clan or community, won at last so great a place in the national religion. The process by which she won it, however, is obvious enough. Her cult had the power of swallowing up the cults of other divinities, like herself local forms of the Earth-Mother, as Aaron's rod could devour the rods of the magicians; and so the edifice of her honour was built upon the ruin of theirs. Yet the survival of a temple legend or some peculiarity of ritual will reveal in many a consecrated place behind the dazzling presence of the

[1] ζ 103.

Olympian the shadowy form of some more ancient Holiness—or if not more ancient, at any rate of longer standing there—some cantonal Mother rather eclipsed than extinguished by the brilliant new-comer. I am thinking especially of Arcadia, for nowhere were these survivals commoner than there, where we constantly find Artemis in possession of some local shrine and called by some local title not originally her own; so that one may even say that wherever in Arcadia there are traces of any Kore of the familiar kind—not necessarily thought of as a 'goddess' in any very definite sense of the term—there is a presumption that she will be identified, or in some way brought into relation, with Artemis. Penelope indeed has preserved her identity. Yet when it is shown that her story upon analysis reveals her in essence one with Artemis, we shall be able to draw from that certain conclusions helpful for the discussion of her origin and religious significance, and for the study of the Odyssey also very illuminating.

The type of Artemis of the Wild, *Agrotera*, is embodied with singular completeness in the figure of Atalante, the virgin huntress on Arcadian hills and the companion of the goddess. Every one recognizes that Atalante is but a replica, a human other-self of Artemis. She was the daughter of Iasos son of Lykourgos of Tegea, but grew up in ignorance of her parents. For Iasos, because he had wished for a son, exposed her at her birth by a well at the mouth of a cave in the 'Mountain of the Maid' Parthenios.[1] But a she-bear who had been robbed of her young suckled the child, until at last some hunters found it and brought it home with them. When Atalante grew up, she kept her virginity and passed her days in hunting ἐν ἐρημίᾳ, upon the lonely hills. Afterwards she took part in the Hunting of the Boar at Kalydon and won the spoils of the monster. But, says the pseudo-Apollodoros who tells the story out of older authorities, 'she found her parents afterwards and, when her father would have her marry, she went to a suitable place and planted there a stake three

[1] This may be an echo of female infanticide in Early Greece. Cf. *Rise of Greek Epic*, p. 186.

cubits long, driving it in up to the middle; then she set this course for her suitors and raced them in full armour. And he who was beaten in the race had to die; but he who won was to marry her. But when many had now died for her sake, Melanion'—Meilanion is the usual form—'who had come to love her, entered the race with golden apples in his hand, the gift of Aphrodite; and as Atalante sped after him, he threw them away, and as he threw them, she picked them up, and thus was beaten in the race. So Melanion married her.'[1] But Hesiod said that she was the daughter of Schoineus of Boeotia, and that she married Hippomenes, a descendant of Poseidon, and that the contest was at Onchestos.[2] That must be the original story, for even in the Arcadian version Atalante is called the daughter of Iasos or Iasios or Iasion and 'Klymene the daughter of Minyas'. And the Arcadian tradition preserved in Pausanias held that she came from Boeotia to Methydrion, where her race-course was pointed out, and gave the name of *Schoinous* to that neighbourhood.[3] Now Schoineus, her father in the Boeotian story, is so called from a little patch of land called Schoinos, where the brook Schoinous fell into the Lake of Hyle, and he was accounted a son of Athamas the Minyan king.[4] Schoineus then is definitely Boeotian, and yet Apollodoros in naming the hunters of the Kalydonian Boar can speak of 'Atalante the daughter of Schoineus, from Arcadia'.[5] After all, that is substantially accurate, because it suggests that the story of Atalante spread from Orchomenos to Methydrion, carried there by the same agency which introduced so many other legends of Central Greece into Arcadia. Indeed it is worth remarking that all the great achievements of Atalante are performed outside of Arcadia, in Kalydon, at the funeral games of Pelias where she wrestled with and threw Peleus, and among the Argonauts. Her son Parthenopaios was slain among the Seven at Thebes.

[1] Apollod. *Bibl.* iii. 9. 2. Cf. Callim. *Hymn to Art.* 221 f.

[2] Philodemos, περὶ εὐσ., p. 60 G, schol. Townl. Ψ 683. Cf. Eustath. 1324, 18; Apollod. iii. 9. 2.

[3] Paus. viii. 35. 10. [4] Apollod. *Bibl.* i. 9. 2, 3. [5] Ibid. i. 8. 2.

In Arcadia she became more and more representative of the great goddess of the land, and that is why the study of her legend helps so much to define for us a conception of Artemis at once more primitive and more consonant with what we know of her character in Greek religion generally than the ideal of Homer and the sculptors. The story of the maiden princess and her wooers is found in the folk-literature of I suppose every people, and recurs in Greek mythology, in the legend of Hippodameia for instance, above all in the legend of Helen; while the pleasant tale of Agarista, daughter of Kleisthenes tyrant of Sikyon, is an historical or semi-historical example. Now it is certain that these stories reflect a tribal custom, for the imagination of primitive men is entirely moulded by the conditions under which they live. For Greece at least the custom seems proved by the anecdote in Herodotus.[1] And the normal sequel of the stories, in which the suitor who is successful in the trial of skill marries the princess and becomes thereby king of the land, finds its explanation, as is now generally admitted, in the custom of inheritance through the female, which is believed to have obtained among the older peoples of Greece 'before the Sons of the Achaeans came'. Thus Agamemnon married Klytaimnestra, and Menelaos married Helen of Sparta. But if the story is told, not of some princess of romance or actual life, but of a maiden divinity who avoids the paths of men and whose lovers are put to death, we must seek the full explanation in something deeper than a mere tribal custom, although the custom has coloured the story; we must seek it in religion. Penelope and Atalante, Helen and Hippodameia, are princesses of saga, but in their original and more real nature they are divine, even when they are not like Helen and Penelope independent divinities, but like Atalante and Hippodameia evidently mere types, representatives, functionaries in a ritual. The Contest of the Suitors is now a myth, but it was once a ritual also. More accurately, the practice of the ritual has ceased, its theory or explanation

[1] vi. 126 f.

survives. And not only is the Myth the explanation of the rite, it is at the same time—and I doubt if this has been sufficiently allowed for by some students of religion—in part at least the explanation of the god. To primitive minds it is a matter of such transcendent importance to get the ritual exactly right (for the slightest deviation from the rules will ruin everything), that the worshippers will not proceed one step without authority. And who is their authority? In normal circumstances the oldest man in the tribe, the worshipper who has been most frequently through this particular ceremony before. And *his* authority? Well, the oldest tribesman within his memory. And so the tradition goes back and back—*οὐκ ἐμὸς ὁ μῦθος*. But it must end somewhere, and it ends, as a thousand instances show, in an imaginary divine founder of the rite, who becomes the centre of the Myth. Again, since according to tribal ways of thought the founder will be regarded as an ancestor, he will come back to his people on these solemn occasions and take part, the leading part, along with them in the rite, unseen perhaps but none the less felt to be there in the midst of them. Something like this I think must often have happened in the process by which the god is generated or projected from the ritual. He is the Founder of the Sacrament.[1]

As for the myth of the Contest of the Suitors, it can be studied to most purpose in the legends of Atalante and Hippodameia, just because these owe their whole existence and meaning to the ritual, and the myth has not to be detached from other discrepant ceremonies and myths, as in the case of more complex legendary figures. The story of Hippodameia is in all essentials like the story of Atalante. There are the Suitors, the contest for the bride, the putting to death of the

[1] I have admitted that this is not the whole truth. But it is perhaps half the truth. The Ritual creates the need of the god, but the Myth formulates him. (See *Themis*, p. 47.) The tendency in Greek Religion evidently was for the Myth to develop rapidly, to break away from the Ritual, and acquire an independent existence. The Olympians of Homer, for instance, are almost purely mythological beings, however carefully their mythology has been selected and manipulated by the poets.

unsuccessful competitors, the marriage of the princess to the successful wooer. Hippodameia was the daughter of Oinomaos son of Ares and Sterope the Lightning Flash, and Oinomaos was king of Pisa in Elis. Many suitors came to woo his daughter, but, because he would not have her marry, he set them to contend with him in a chariot-race from Pisa to the altar of Poseidon at the Isthmos. The horses of Oinomaos were as swift as the wind and always outran the horses of the Suitors, and as he overtook his opponent in each race, he transfixed him with a spear; and in this way thirteen were slain. But at last Pelops came with a golden chariot and winged unwearіable horses, the gift of Poseidon who loved him, and by their means, and by bribing Myrtilos, the charioteer of Oinomaos, he won the race. Oinomaos was killed by falling from his chariot, or by his own hand, and Pelops married Hippodameia and succeeded to her father's kingdom at Pisa. It is only the story of Atalante in a new setting. To be sure, the trial of skill in one case is a foot-race, in the other a race of chariots. But no one will think that a vital difference, and in fact there is every reason to believe that the chariot-race in the legend of Hippodameia, although it became the mythical prototype of the chariot-race in the Olympian Games, was not in its original meaning a race at all, but simply the carrying off of the bride by the bridegroom, who had won her by victory in a previous foot-race.[1] Again, although it is nowhere expressly stated that Atalante's father was slain after the victory of Meilanion, and that the latter succeeded to his throne, who does not feel that this is implied in the story?

Penelope too has her Wooers; to win her in marriage they have their trial of skill; the successful Suitor is her husband, who is then recognized as King; finally, the defeated competitors are slain. So close is the parallel between her story, even as we read it in the Odyssey, and the legends of Atalante and Hippodameia. And the resemblance is not superficial, but becomes more distinct and deep reaching on a more

[1] F. M. Cornford in *Themis*, p. 218 f.

critical examination, when certain points obscured or distorted by the exigencies of the epic plot reveal their true character. If, for instance, we take the Trial of the Bow (*Toxou Thesis*) narrated in the twenty-first book, we may be disconcerted at first by an apparent discrepancy between the situation in the Odyssey and the situation contemplated in the parallel myths. In them the prize of victory is marriage with the princess, who in Homer is already married; and again, in them the victor is a stranger youth, while in Homer he is her returned husband. But the truth is, we have in this part of the Odyssey two saga motifs in combination, the formula of the Princess and her Wooers and the formula of The Husband Returned. The result has been a kind of displacement in the logical order of events, and a story originally told of Penelope in her maidenhood is now told of her after twenty years of marriage. The story is in Pausanias.[1] He says that when Penelope was still a girl in the house of her father Ikarios at Sparta, her suitors ran a race for her hand, and Odysseus was victor. There is of course nothing of this in Homer. It is a Spartan tradition connecting itself, no doubt, with the *heroon* of Odysseus and Penelope at Lacedaemon.[2] As for its genuineness, no one will deny that who compares it with the essentially identical legends of Atalante and Hippodameia, of the daughter of Antaios and the daughters of Danaos.[3] But granted that it is genuine, that the story itself is very ancient, may it not have attached itself to Penelope in 'post-Homeric' times? No, because at heart it is the same story as the *Toxou Thesis*.

Apart from this, it may be argued that the long tarrying of Odysseus, now universally believed to be dead, has in effect reproduced the situation in which Penelope stood before her marriage. At least, no one questions her right to marry again. And as she promises to leave the house of Odysseus and go forth with the Suitor who shall most easily string the great bow and send the arrow through the row of axes.[4]

[1] iii. 2. 1. [2] Plut. *Qu. Graec.* 48. [3] Pind. *Pyth.* ix. 111 f.

[4] φ 74 f. Van Leeuwen regards the axes as Cretan. See *Mnemosyne*,

Here the contest is in archery. There is a wonderfully close parallel to the version of the Odyssey in the *Mahabharata*, which relates how Draupadi, daughter of the king of the Panchalas, was only to be won in marriage by him who could bend a certain great bow and shoot five arrows through a revolving wheel so as to hit the target beyond the wheel. After many wooers had vainly essayed the task, Arjun, who was disguised—this is very like Homer indeed—performed the feat, and carried off the princess to be his wife.[1] The oldest legends concerning Odysseus clearly represent him as an archer. Indeed the bow used in the contest of the Suitors is the famous bow of Odysseus himself, inherited from Eurytos of Oichalia. Since Odysseus was characteristically a bowman, it was natural that the contest in which he defeated the Suitors should be represented as a trial of archery.

I think that the bow is characteristic of Odysseus for the same reason that it is proper to Apollo, because it is the weapon of the Sun who shoots his rays from afar. Odysseus, in his original nature evidently a mere fertility spirit like other 'Heroes', an Eniautos Daimon as Miss Harrison says, comes for that very reason to be in some degree identified with the Sun who rules the seasons; not completely identified, as indeed a large part of my purpose has been to show, but in a certain part of his nature, almost, one might say, at a certain stage in his evolution from Daimon to epic hero, an embodiment of Helios.[2] It is as Helios (according to the familiar paradox of primitive religion) that Odysseus incurs the enmity of Helios, just as he incurs the wrath of Poseidon

vol. xxxviii, 1911, *Homerica*. He thinks that Nausikaa comes out of a tradition in which the hero married a foreign princess. The story of Nausikaa would in that case be so far parallel to the story of Penelope.

[1] Quoted by Dr. Frazer in *The Early History of the Kingship* from the epitome of *Romesch Dutt*, p. 15 f. Cf. Gruppe, *Gr. Myth.* i. 713, n. 9.

[2] There is an admirable remark in *Themis*, p. 370, which is applicable here. '. . . Herakles takes on the form of an Eniautos-daimon, and therefore has solar elements, but these do not exhaust his content. The same is true of Apollo, Odysseus, Orpheus and Dionysos, and indeed almost all gods and daimones . . .'

because he stood very near Poseidon in actual cults of the god. As Helios then he slays the sacred cows of Helios, and as the Setting Sun descends at the western verge of the world into the kingdom of the dead, and as the Sun in his renewed splendour kills the Suitors on the festal day of Apollo and with Apollo's bow.[1] That in the *Toxou Thesis* Odysseus represents the Sun-god is made still more probable, and indeed I think quite certain, by Mr. Cornford's analysis of the myth of Hippodameia. Behind this and the similar myths lies a symbolic or ritual marriage representing the union of the Sun and Moon, that is to say, of the Fertility Spirit and his Mate. The object of the contest is to decide who shall win the bride, and so perhaps the original conclusion of the Odyssey came, as has been believed upon quite other grounds, with the words: *οἱ μὲν ἔπειτα ἀσπάσιοι λέκτροιο παλαιοῦ θεσμὸν ἵκοντο.*[2] It is the rule also in these myths that the old king, usually the bride's father, is put to death or deposed, or somehow conveniently disappears to make way for the victorious Suitor his successor. The Old Year makes way for the New Year, the Winter Sun for the Spring Sun. As it happens, Ikarios the father of Penelope plays no real part in the Odyssey, he is only a vague shadow moving somewhere in an unrealized background; it is Penelope herself who proposes the Trial of the Bow. The actual Old King in the Odyssey is Laertes the father of Odysseus, not Ikarios, perhaps because Homer is so vehemently patrilinear in his sympathies. All through the epic Laertes is represented as living in retirement, as in fact deposed. As the parallel cases of Aigeus and Oineus show, that was one way of disposing of the Old King. But now, if Odysseus is the Young King and the Sun Bridegroom, Penelope must be the Moon Bride.

In this there is nothing inconsistent with our previous conclusions. Penelope is not, simply, the Moon; one could

[1] υ 276, φ 258. Eurytos challenged Apollo to a contest in archery and was slain by the angry god, θ 226 f. Eurytos is but a replica of the Archer Apollo and his bow, which Odysseus inherited, a copy of Apollo's bow.

[2] ψ 296.

never explain her legend on so bare an hypothesis. But we may say of her that she is capable of becoming the Moon. Exactly the same is true of Artemis. And the reason for this is exactly the same in both cases. Artemis and Penelope are alike at bottom Fertility Spirits, Daimones of a very simple and uniform kind, 'Mothers' as they called them in Anatolia, though not at all necessarily conceived of as in human form. Penelope, for instance, was evidently the divine Penelops of Arne. Kallisto, whom an interesting notice in Athenaeus[1] calls the sister of Odysseus, was a divine Bear, the Bear Artemis *Kalliste*.[2] I cannot find that Penelope was anywhere identified with Artemis, and one may be glad that she repelled the intruder more successfully than the Bird-divinity at Stymphalos. But they came very near each other. Olympian mythology indeed represented Artemis as maiden, while Penelope is the mother of Telemachos. But the earlier conception of Artemis preserved in the local cults and the non-Homeric legends (Homer speaks of her rarely) is not of a virgin so much as of an unmarried mother, the word *parthenos* being capable of this twofold meaning. So Atalante and Kallisto and Auge, all forms of the Arcadian goddess, bear Parthenopaios and Arkas and Telephos. In the same way Telemachos is the son of Penelope. And it cannot be without significance that he is her *only* son, just as Parthenopaios is the only son of his mother; and so with Arkas and the rest. For the human relation in which Penelope stands to Telemachos undoubtedly represents the relation of the Mother Goddess of the Anatolian type to the subordinate male divinity constantly appearing at her side as son or consort or lover—Telemachos or Adonis or Hippolytos. But all this has been forgotten in Homer,[3] and its discussion is foreign to our immediate purpose. To that I now return.

[1] iv. 47, p. 158 d.

[2] Prof. Murray writes to me: 'There seems to be (1) a contest of beauty (I. T. 1147 ff.), the winner of which got the καλλιστεῖον (I. T. 23) and became ἡ καλή or ἡ καλλίστη: (2) then she is identified with or grows into Artemis.'

[3] There seems, however, to be a lurking consciousness that some significance does lie in the fact that Telemachos is an only son, for the

Odysseus and Penelope met at Mantineia. We shall have to explain why, that being so, the Odyssey has no knowledge of the fact. But first we may remark on something that looks like an unconscious memory of the truth. The Suitors of Penelope have for the most part either obviously typical names or no name at all; and so these can have no historical associations. But the leading Suitor Antinoos bears a name which may be traditional, and clearly, if any of the Suitors has historical significance, it is likely to be he. Well, Antinoos is a specially Mantinean name. It was the name, one remembers, of Hadrian's favourite, whose legend seems the most romantic thing in the prosaic age in which it grew. This Antinoos indeed was a native of Bithynion on the Sangarios. But Bithynion was accounted an Arcadian colony and, as it seems, definitely Mantinean; for at Mantineia Hadrian established a cult of Antinoos and games in his honour.[1] The legendary founder of the historical Mantineia was Antinoe, the daughter of Kepheus. At the bidding of an oracle, following the guidance of a snake she founded Mantineia from the older site called Ptolis.[2] The snake must have been the Luck of the old settlement passing to the new. In the historical town the Common Hearth of the Mantineans was at the same time the Tomb of Antinoe.[3] But, although she was buried there, she came from the ancient Ptolis, where was the tomb of Penelope. Is it not significant that among the Suitors the least shadowy is called Antinoos?

fact itself is curiously insisted upon. See π 117 f. Odysseus too was an only son, and so was Laertes, and in all this some hidden purpose of God is being fulfilled upon the race of Arkeisios.

[1] Paus. viii. 9. 4. Coins of Mantineia show Antinoos, with a horse on the reverse. Imhoof-Blumer and P. Gardner, *Num. Comm. on Pausanias*, *J. H. S.* vii, p. 99.

[2] Ibid. 8. 2.

[3] Ibid. 9. 2. The antiquity of the name is further evidenced by the statement of Pausanias that one of the daughters of Pelias, whose grave-monuments were shown near Mantineia, was called Antinoe by Mikon the painter, viii. 11. 3.

CHAPTER IV

MINYANS AND IONIANS

αἰπεῖ⟨άν⟩ τε Πύλον Νηλήιον ἄστυ λιπόντες
ἱμερτὴν Ἀσίην νηυσὶν ἀφικόμεθα.

If we knew a little more of the history and manners of the people to whom tradition attached the name of 'Minyans' at the time when these dwelt upon the Kopaic Plain of Boeotia, we should learn a good deal, I think, about the beginnings of epic poetry in Greece. But the clouds are too thick above so remote a past; and now of that old civilization only the faintest picture is possible, all the light and colour gone from it, as they have vanished from the dismal heights of Akontion that look down so frowningly upon the desolation of Orchomenos. To help the imagination there is nothing but the fragments of prodigious walls and the great ruin which was named the Treasury of Minyas. Pausanias, standing before its broken cone of dark grey marble, thought of the Pyramids of Egypt. But the kings who were buried in it with gold masks upon their faces had seen a yet more wonderful sight, Orchomenos in its full glory, 'all the causeys, bridges, aqueducts'—one still finds traces of great engineering works designed to drain the marsh—and all the wealth which made the poets call it Rich in Gold. Yet it was not merely of their Boeotian realm that the poets of the Minyans sang, but also of their more northerly home or colony, Iolkos, at the head of the Pagasaean Gulf, under the long ridge of 'leaf-shaking' Pelion with the sea-wind in its forests where the Centaurs dwelt and the good ashen spear-shafts were cut. It is something more than conjecture if we infer that the sea entered largely into the thoughts of the Minyans, for the traditions of a people invariably reflect its ways of life; and the Sailing of

Argo is the legend of a sea-faring race, making adventurous voyages as far perhaps as Lemnos and the Hellespont, nay even to some distant vaguely named 'Aia' (Land), tradition said, somewhere beyond the gates of the Pontus. Thus one may find a certain significance in the zeal which impelled the men of Iolkos to carve the nautilus and murex upon little tables and collect the shells of the sea-snail called the *conus*. The Minyans have been called, no doubt too enthusiastically, the carriers of the Mycenaean culture. It is at least certain that the civilization revealed by excavation at Dhimini and Orchomenos is in its general character definitely 'Mycenaean': the 'Treasury of Minyas' is almost a replica of the 'Treasury of Atreus'. Whatever elements of a 'Northern' culture the Minyans may have combined with that which they shared with Mykenai, we cannot doubt that the Mycenaean elements predominated.[1]

It was in Boeotia that the tale of Argo first took definite shape. That I think follows from the circumstance that, while Iolkos is in the foreground of the narrative as we have it now, the background, corresponding to an earlier stage of the saga, is unmistakably Boeotian. Phrixos and Helle were the children of Athamas from Mount Laphystion, Tiphys the original steersman of Argo was the hero of Siphai,[2] and it would not be hard to show that of the undoubted Minyans in Jason's crew nearly all are Boeotian. Jason himself is apparently an exception, and one very difficult to explain; for, although in the versions of the Argo legend preserved to us he is the leader of the Argonauts and becomes king in Iolkos, evidence still stronger than that of myth, the evidence of an actual and certainly ancient cult, connects him with Corinth. An *Argonautica* without Jason is unthinkable; an *Argonautica*

[1] A convenient summary of the archaeological evidence then (1898) available is given in Frazer's *Pausanias*, iv. We have now *Prehistoric Thessaly* by Wace and Thompson, Cambridge, 1912. See espec. pp. 241–9. Boeotian mythology (Europa-Kadmos-Rhadamanthys) points to an early connexion with Crete. But we cannot on that ground alone infer the existence of a 'Minoan' culture in Central Greece before the 'Mycenaean'.

[2] Or Tiphai. See Fick, *Personennamen*, p. 367.

without Medea is not easy to imagine. Medea was worshipped as a goddess in Corinth[1] with Jason for her consort. It seems most reasonable then to suppose that Corinth contributed the figures of Medea and Jason to the story. It will be remembered that there was a great cult there of Poseidon *Hippios*, and that the Minyan Leukothea and Melikertes were worshipped at the Isthmos, and that Sisyphos was the brother of Athamas. At least we cannot be wrong in assuming that the Argo legend in any form in which we should recognize it contained elements drawn from various sources, from Iolkos and Corinth as well as Boeotia. We may imagine a 'Minyan' sphere or spheres of culture extending from Pelion to the Isthmos, and radiating as a rule from centres where the ships touched. If we do that, we must regard Orchomenos, whose ancient greatness has been revealed, as the natural centre of all this sphere; and the archaeological evidence seems to prove this.[2] To the end the Argonauts remained 'Minyans', and Greek tradition constantly maintained that the earliest home of the Minyans was in Boeotia (not Iolkos). Certainly it was in Boeotia, in 'Minyan' Orchomenos, that their culture came to flower. Here also in all probability came the first important stage in the development of their saga. And we are entitled to infer that the saga reflects, in the imaginative way of early poetry, amid much that is purely mythical, something of the actual way of life followed by these Minyan folk, especially the adventures of their mariners upon seas at that time remote and perilous.

These tribal names are a constant source of difficulty in early Greek history. They have fallen into a confusion which seems now quite inextricable. The reason must be that the races and fragments of races who bore them were greatly scattered and intermingled in the troubled times of the Migrations. Yet it seems scarcely possible to make oneself understood at all, unless one is permitted to make some use of the current names. Accordingly it seems desirable at this point to explain as clearly as possible what meaning is here attached to 'Minyans' and 'Ionians', in order that the

[1] Schol. Eur. *Medea*, 10.

[2] *Prehistoric Thessaly*, p. 241, &c.

reader may make the necessary qualifications and misunderstanding be avoided. Let me say first that I lay no stress upon the names themselves. My main purpose is to prove the fact of a migration on the part of a people originally dwelling in Central Greece to Arcadia, and thence to Pylos in Elis. If I can do that, it is a matter of comparatively little importance what name they were given or gave themselves. So when I speak of them as 'Minyans' I do not wish to assert more than that they came, in the main at least, from a land where the Minyan name was especially famous, and that their religion and legends were, again in the main, what tradition assigns to the Minyans. The name 'Ionians', on the other hand, I shall be found using, for the sake of clearness and simplicity, in a somewhat extended sense. Primarily I wish to show that the migrating people (who, it may be admitted, must have picked up a good many alien elements on the way) ultimately formed an important section of the Ionian colonists. Therefore I venture to speak of them as in this sense Ionians before Ionia; and as a matter of fact we shall see that there is some justification for believing that the name is really older than the Anatolian Colonies and was given to some people living in prehistoric times side by side with the Minyans in Boeotia.

Orchomenos (*Ἐρχομενός*) lay at the mouth of the Kephisos where it entered Lake Kopais. Homer, who speaks of its great wealth,[1] calls it 'Minyan Orchomenos';[2] and 'Minyan' Orchomenos it remained into historical times.[3] In the Boeotian traditions it played a famous part. Under its king Erginos it levied tribute from Thebes, until Herakles came to the aid of his native city and conquered and shamed the Minyans[4]—a tale which is like the echo of an actual conflict between Thebes and Orchomenos in which the city of Kadmos had the better; as we know that in later times there was ever bitter enmity between the two.[5] In close neighbourhood to

[1] I 381. [2] B 511, λ 284. Both texts are Boeotian.
[3] Her. viii. 34; Thuc. iv. 76. [4] Eur. *Herakl.* 220.
[5] For details one may still refer to K. O. Müller's *Orchomenos und Minyer*,

the Minyans in Boeotia lived Ionians in the time before Ionia. Herodotus, in relating how Kadmos taught them letters, says expressly that in these days the greater part of this region was inhabited by Ionians.[1] The Iliad in a somewhat perplexing passage brings Ionians and Boeotians into juxtaposition: 'Boeotians and Ionians with trailing chitons'.[2] The sentence at once gains in clearness and point if we think of the two peoples dwelling side by side in their Boeotian homes, as they appear side by side in this passage.[3] A tradition preserved in Nikolaos of Damascus told of a war between Ionians and the men of Orchomenos.[4] The use of the name Ionian to denote one of the three great divisions of the Greek race in the historical age undoubtedly began in Asia, the native peoples of Anatolia applying to the whole Greek nation the tribal name of certain settlers on the coast lands about Mykale. We need not doubt that it was simply one of the obscure tribal names so numerous in the cloudy background of Greek history and did

1820. Müller's conclusions of course often require modification. See Ed. Meyer, *Gesch. d. Alt.*, ii. 126.

[1] v. 58. 2 *περιοίκεον δέ σφεας τὰ πολλὰ τῶν χώρων (τῆς νῦν Βοιωτίης καλεομένης) τοῦτον τὸν χρόνον Ἑλλήνων Ἴωνες.* See Additional Note, p. 236.

[2] N 685 *ἔνθα δὲ Βοιωτοὶ καὶ Ἰάονες ἑλκεχίτωνες . . . σπουδῇ ἐπαίσσοντα* (*sc.* Ἕκτορα) *νεῶν ἔχον.*

[3] This little catalogue in N seems to deserve more discussion than it has received. It is in flat contradiction of the *Boiotia*. In line 686 we have *Λοκροὶ καὶ Φθῖοι καὶ φαιδιμόεντες Ἐπειοί.* The *Φθῖοι* are never mentioned again in Homer, but they can only be the men of Phthia. Their leaders Medon and Podarkes are named in B as the commanders of the forces of Philoktetes and Protesilaos respectively (727, 704). That is to say, they came from this very district of S. Thessaly. The leaders of the Epeioi here are wholly different from their leaders in B. The Epeians seem to be thought of as living beside the Phthians and Lokrians, not in Elis (cf. Gruppe, *Gr. Myth.*, &c., i, p. 144. Epeios, builder of the Wooden Horse, dwelt on Parnassos). The orthodox view takes *Ἰάονες* as equivalent to *οἱ μὲν Ἀθηναίων προλελεγμένοι* (689), but, as Mr. Allen observes, the isolated *μέν* is a difficulty. He suspects that there has been an omission in the passage and that the omitted line mentioned the Athenians (T. W. Allen, *Cl. Qu.* iii, *Argos in Homer*, p. 81 f.). My own feeling is that the reference to Menestheus has been interpolated, the interpolator taking advantage of the name *Ἰάονες* to identify them with the Athenians. The natural order of the words requires a full stop at *Ἕκτορα δῖον.*

[4] ch. 53. See Additional Note, p. 236.

really exist in Hellas before it was carried across the Aegean. Kallimachos speaks of a river Ἰάων in Arcadia,[1] and we hear of Ἰωνίδες or Ἰαονίδες νύμφαι in Elis.[2] Yet, it seems, the name could never have been in very general use in Greece before the colonization of the Asiatic shore.

We have seen that the worship of a Horse-god under the title of Poseidon *Hippios* was characteristic of the Minyans. But Poseidon was not only in a special sense the god of the Minyans; the Ionians also were his peculiar people. This of course is well known. The common worship of Poseidon *Helikonios* at Mykale was the religious expression of the political unity of the Twelve Cities;[3] while in the leading states accounted definitely Ionian we find the service of Poseidon prominent. Why was it that the Ionians in Asia found a symbol of their political solidarity in the cult at Mykale? The answer must be, because so many—we must not say all—brought this very worship with them when they landed on the Asian coast. This solution of the question is in harmony with the little we know about the colonization of Ionia. The prevailing tradition among the Ionians themselves derived them from Athens immediately, but ultimately from the Peloponnesian Achaia, from which they made their way to Attica. This looks like the invention of a literary age, when Athens had come to be regarded as the *metropolis* of Ionia. At any rate, whatever truth may underlie the tradition can scarcely be accurately measured now, and has almost certainly been distorted. For when one comes to consider the traditions and foundation-legends of the separate states—stories which must be older than any account of the origin of the Dodekapolis as a whole—one finds a quite different tale. They have been collected and discussed by Wilamowitz-Moellendorff,[4] who shows that the princely families of Ionia derived their ancestors

[1] *Hymn to Zeus* 22.

[2] Nicander in Athenaeus xv. 683; Strabo, p. 356; Paus. vi. 22. 7. Ἰαωλκός may mean 'Haven of the Ionians'; but this is disputed.

[3] Her. i. 148; Strabo, p. 639; Diod. xv. 49.

[4] 'Über die Ionische Wanderung', *Sitz. Berl. Akad.*, 1906, i, p. 63 f.

from all parts of Greece, but especially from three places: Crete, the Argolid, and Boeotia. Boeotia indeed has the credit of Miletos, of Teos, of Kolophon, of Priene; while Lebedos points to Lebadeia. Herodotus says that among the settlers were Abantes, Minyans, Kadmeians, and Phokians;[1] and with this Pausanias agrees: 'Thebans under Philotas, a descendant of Peneleos, and some Minyans of Orchomenos.'[2] With significant uniformity Ionian genealogies trace themselves back to one great saga figure, Neleus king of Pylos, Neleus who was the son of Poseidon and a Minyan, indeed the brother of Pelias. It is hard to appraise the value of the confused evidence, but it is clear that an important body of the Ionian settlers came, according to their own belief, from Pylos and Boeotia. Now it was never forgotten that the Triphylians of Pylos were Minyans and had come from Central Greece. Consequently, while not denying that settlers may have gone directly from Boeotia to Ionia, I incline to think that a considerable emigration of Pylians to the new colony at a time when memories of their Boeotian origin were still fresh among them will account for many traditions of a Boeotian origin among the Ionian states also. But it is enough for my special purpose if an emigration from Pylos is accepted as a fair inference from the Ionian traditions, with their curiously emphatic insistence upon the Neleid ancestry of the Ionian princes, and from certain positive statements which we may consider later; for then it becomes clear who carried the Odysseus legend to Ionia.

This, however, is to anticipate; and it is necessary now to deal with the evidence for a migration from Boeotia to Pylos of a people carrying the Minyan traditions.

In the very portal of the Peloponnese, in the Isthmos and Corinth itself, the Minyans left clear traces of their presence. The worship of Poseidon of Horses in this region has already been touched upon. Poseidon strove with Helios, the Corinthians said, and Briareos composed the quarrel, adjudging to

[1] i. 146.
[2] vii. 1 f. Strabo speaks to the same effect.

Poseidon the Isthmos and Akrokorinthos to the Sun.[1] If we were right in thinking that the cult of Poseidon *Hippios* originated in the horse-plains of Thessaly and Boeotia, we may interpret the Corinthian legend as a mythological way of expressing the fact that *Hippios* was an invader from Onchestos, who came into conflict with the old god of the land. There is no question at all of the Minyan strain in ancient Corinth, 'Aeolian' Corinth, as Thucydides calls it.[2] There in old days dwelt Sisyphos 'son of Aiolos',[3] brother of the Minyan king Athamas. The great Corinthian hero Bellerophon was, according to one account, the grandson of Sisyphos; according to another, the son of the Horse-god himself. The importance of Bellerophon comes from his possession of Pegasos, who was subdued to him by Athena *Chalinitis* and Poseidon *Damaios*.[4] From any point of view Pegasos is vitally connected with *Hippios*. If, therefore, we can trace the origin of the winged horse, we shall learn something about the god. According to the myth, Bellerophon flew to Heaven on the back of Pegasos, being ambitious to enjoy the converse of the gods. But, stung by a gadfly sent by Zeus, Pegasos threw his rider. The myth is very ancient and reappears in the story of the Babylonian hero Etana, who vainly sought to reach the gods on the back of an eagle, and in the story of Gilgamesh. In what seems the oldest form of the legend, then, it is a bird which carries the hero towards Heaven. Now the really significant thing about Pegasos is not that he is a swift but that he is a flying horse. His wings are not given him to symbolize or aid his speed, as in the case of the winged steeds which Poseidon bestowed on Pelops, but that he may soar with them like a bird. He is very like the τετρασκελὴς οἰωνός, the winged quadruped on which Okeanos enters the stage in the *Prometheus Bound* of Aeschylus.[5] With these instances before us, we cannot doubt that the wings are an organic part of him; and in fact the earliest representations of Pegasos, which appear on the archaic coinage of

[1] Paus. ii. 1. 6. [2] iv. 42. [3] Z 154.
[4] Pind. *Ol.* xiii. 65 f. [5] 395.

Corinth, dating in all probability from the reign of Periandros (625–585 B.C.), show him winged.[1] He was the offspring, Hesiod tells us, of Poseidon and the Gorgon Medousa and was born beside the springs of Okeanos (Ὠκεανοῦ περὶ πηγάς), wherefore he was called *Pegasos*.[2] Hesiod certainly thinks of him as winged, for he says that after his birth from the mutilated body of his mother he 'flew away' (ἀποπτάμενος) from earth, and 'came among the Immortals. And he lives in the halls of Zeus bringing the thunder and lightning to Zeus the Counsellor'.[3] A horse carrying thunder and lightning is not very convincing to the imagination, nor is it all clear how Hesiod imagined it. The very doubt is instructive, but perhaps, if he had been pressed, he would have solved the difficulty in the manner implied in the line quoted in the *Peace* from the *Bellerophon* of Euripides: 'Yoked to the chariot of Zeus he carries the lightning.'[4] But clearly this is not a very primitive conception; Pegasos in harness is an absurdity. Yet his connexion with thunder must be authentic, else it would not be brought in so clumsily. It becomes perfectly intelligible the moment we remember that he is at least as much a bird as a horse. Pegasos is in fact a Thunder Bird, first no doubt in his own right, then as the servant of the Thunder-god. That is why, as Hesiod tells us, his true home is in Heaven. Pindar knew it also, for he says that after the fall of Bellerophon Pegasus was received 'in the ancient stalls of Zeus upon Olympos'.[5] The statement that he was born beside Okeanos may possibly date from the time when Okeanos meant Ouranos,[6] and in that case it would fit in with our view of Pegasos as an Ouranian Bird. In any case, as the quoted passages show, he properly belongs to Olympos and the Thunderer; it is his temporary possession by Bellerophon which makes the latter an earthly rival of Zeus and so brings upon

[1] Also certain Melian gems. Furtwängler, *Die ant. Gemmen*, 1901, Pl. V, 17; Pl. LXI, 5.

[2] *Theog.* 274 f., Rzach.

[3] Ζηνὸς δ' ἐν δώμασι ναίει βροντήν τε στεροπήν τε φέρων Διὶ μητιόεντι.

[4] Ar. *Pax* 722 ὑφ' ἅρματ' ἐλθὼν Ζηνὸς ἀστραπηφορεῖ.

[5] *Ol.* xiii. 92.

[6] See Additional Note, p. 236.

him the Olympian jealousy. But how has Pegasos become, all but the wings, a horse? In the same way, I think, as the bird of Okeanos became half a horse.[1] Poseidon, being originally a form of Zeus, has an equally good title to Pegasos. So, when he descends from heaven to earth and becomes the Horse-god, Pegasos becomes a horse conformably. Corinth then loses its claim to be the original home of the winged horse. It might, however, be his first home on earth. But there are indications which make against that view also. Perseus, who cuts off the Gorgon's head, has a name which points to Northern Greece.[2] Bellerophon himself is an Aiolid.[3] The Horse-Medousa, who must be the mother of Pegasos, is evidently of Boeotian origin; for she appears on an archaic vase from Boeotia,[4] and is clearly akin to the Erinys of Tilphossa. Hesiod, as a Boeotian, must have known this Medousa. Moreover, as a native of Helikon, he must have known that Pegasos by a stroke of his hoof (equivalent in its effect to a blow from the god's trident) created the well of Hippokrene[5] there. It is instructive that, in his account of Pegasos, Hesiod makes no mention of Bellerophon and Corinth. Still more instructive is the comment of the scholiast on the *Acharnians* 243. He tells us of a certain Pegasos who received Dionysos at Eleutherai. Dionysos was then on his way from Boeotia to Athens. This Pegasos may well be a Thunder Bird priest receiving the Child of the Thunder: he cannot be a Corinthian or Libyan thoroughbred. Even the legend that the spring of Peirene on the Akrokorinthos was produced by Pegasos was challenged by a rival tradition, according to which it was created by the River-god Asopos at the instance of Sisyphos.[6] Accordingly it seems on the whole probable that

[1] See *Themis*, p. 457.

[2] Cf. Usener, *Götternamen*, pp. 11, 12. According to Lykophron 1175, 'Perseus' was the father of the Thracian goddess Brimo. Πέρση is one of the names of Hekate.

[3] Αἰολίδα βασιλεῦ, Pind. *Ol.* xiii. 67.

[4] In the Louvre. Reproduced in Miss Harrison's *Prolegomena*, p. 179, fig. 22.

[5] Ἵππου κρήνη, *Theog.* 6.

[6] Paus. ii. 5. 1.

Pegasos came, with so many figures of Corinthian legend, from the North, perhaps brought in by the Horse-god himself. —The Minyan Neleus was buried in a taboo grave at Corinth.[1] In the Isthmos, Ino and Melikertes were worshipped, becoming in an unusually obvious way identified with a similar divine pair, Leukothea and Palaimon, who were evidently there before them. And the whole body of Minyan saga, as reflected in the *Argonautica*, took fresh root and a new development at Corinth.[2]

From Corinth to Arcadia. The importance of the worship of Poseidon *Hippios* in Arcadia has already been considered in some detail. Almost more significant, because their identity is so unmistakable, are the strange cults of the Horse-goddess at Phigaleia in Arcadia and Mount Tilphousion in Boeotia. Then—although legends often seem to travel upon the wind —the Arcadian stories have a kind of evidential value, since they corroborate less deceptive indications, and it is hard to believe that any casual wind blew so many from Boeotia. Of them all, two, as perhaps the most striking, may simply be named: the story of the birth of the divine horse Areion, and the story of Atalante. To these we must add the story of the coming of Odysseus to Arcadia and his marriage with Penelope of Mantineia . . . But we are not confined to the evidence of cult and myth. There are many Arcadian place-names recalling Boeotia: the canton *Eutresia* like-named with a place near Thespiai, the spring *Arne* near Mantineia, and, hard by, another spring, πηγὴ Ἀλαλκομενειάς,[3] reminiscent of the Boeotian Alalkomenai. Then how significant to find an Arcadian *Orchomenos* (here also properly *Erchomenos*), the very name of the golden city of the Minyans! And, lest that should be thought a mere coincidence, we find two neighbouring Arcadian mountains named, the one *Sepia*, the other *Skiathis*,[4] just as near Iolkos Mount Pelion stretches out into the promontory or beach of Sepias, while over against it lies

[1] Paus. i. 2. 2.

[2] This development was associated with the name of Eumelos.

[3] Paus. viii. 12. 7.

[4] Paus. viii. 16. 2; 14. 1.

the island of Skiathos. Again, to us remembering Arkesilaos of Lebadeia, the statement of the Boeotian Plutarch that the Lebadeans enjoyed the right of 'equal citizenship' with the Arcadians[1] will seem of great importance, for it points to more than a legendary connexion between Boeotia and Arcadia, and provides as well a new and essential link in the chain of evidence which binds the Battiadai of Kyrene to Lebadeia. Recall the intimate relations which we know to have subsisted between Kyrene and Arcadia: community of cults, such as that of Zeus *Lykaios*[2]; the divine figure of Aristaios, son of the nymph Kyrene and a god in Arcadia; the mission of Demonax—Demonax of Mantineia—to reform the Kyrenean constitution[3]; the ultimate origin in a Mantinean mystery-cult of much of the Egyptian Hermetic lore, which came by way of Kyrene.[4] Between Mantineia and Kyrene the link is Sparta. Now all along the coast where Taygetos comes down to the sea, and on the shores of the Messenian Gulf, are so many names and associations reminiscent of Boeotia that the local traditions of a Minyan settlement there must apparently be accepted. In the interior also we find names like *Leuktron* and *Arna* and *Therapnai*; and even in Strabo's time the inhabitants of Thalamai were called 'Boeotians'.[5]

The case of Sparta itself is very notable. For who can the great Spartan clan of the Aigeidai be but the Sons of Aigeus? And who can 'Aigeus' be but Poseidon? Accordingly we hear that there was at Sparta a temple of their Father-god, *Poseidon Genethlios*.[6] They came, as tradition held, with the Sons of Herakles, leaving their native Thebes, where also the Aigeidai formed a clan; so that Pindar, who belonged to it, can speak of himself as in some sense a Spartan.[7] Thus we can understand how there came to be at Lacedaemon a shrine to 'the Erinyes of Laios and Oidipous'.[8] It seems, then,

[1] *Qu. Graec.* 39. Lebadeos and Eleuther εἰς Βοιωτίαν ἔφυγον, καὶ Λεβαδεῦσίν ἐστιν ἰσοπολιτεία πρὸς Ἀρκάδας.

[2] Studniczka, *Kyrene*, 15. [3] Her. iv. 161, 162.

[4] See Zielinski, *Archiv f. Religionswiss.*, 'Hermes u. d. Hermetik', 8, 9, esp. 9 (1906), p. 33 f.

[5] 360. [6] Paus. iii. 15. 10. [7] *Pyth.* v. 75. [8] Her. iv. 149.

that we must take into account the existence of a Minyan-Boeotian element in the older population of Laconia, having as the visible symbol and memorial of its persistence through the harsh days of Dorian repression the worship of Poseidon on the promontory of Tainaron; for it is here that the Minyan legends are most vivid and precise. When we remember that this Poseidon of Tainaron was peculiarly the god of the Helots,[1] the conquered pre-Dorian race, certain interesting possibilities begin to dawn upon us. Beyond Laconia, the Minyan legend takes us to Thera, and from Thera to Kyrene. Behind Laconia, we discover many proofs of ancient association in the traditions of Sparta and Arcadia, in the story of Orestes, for instance, whose bones were found so strangely hidden away in Tegea,[2] in the story of Penelope, who becomes the daughter of Ikarios and has a shrine at Sparta. One sees how it all may have come to pass. Boeotia to Arcadia, Arcadia to Sparta, Sparta to Thera, Thera to Kyrene—these are the stages by which the Minyan legends evidently travelled, for at each stage one finds clear traces of their presence.[3]

Elis. In his tale of the wanderings of the Minyans, children of the Argonauts, Herodotus says that the greater number of them went eventually to Elis, 'against the Paroreatai and Kaukones', and founded there the cities of Lepreon, Makistos, Phrixai, Pyrgos, Epion, and Noudion; 'the majority of these were sacked by the Eleans in my time'.[4] The tale is an extraordinary one, and in some of its details quite incredible. Yet, although it is I think a pure invention, it is plainly designed to account for two things regarded as historically certain: that Minyans did go to Thera, and that Minyans did live in Elis. It is with the second tradition that we are here concerned. M. Victor Bérard has shown that the

[1] Schol. Ar. *Knights* 1322, 'He is imitating the Helots when they crown Poseidon'. Cf. schol. Ar. *Acharn.* 509.

[2] Her. i. 67. Cf. Eur. *Orestes* 1643 f.

[3] Confirmatory evidence will come later. The influx of Boeotian cults and legends into Arcadia and Laconia is exhaustively treated by Gruppe, *Griech. Mythol. u. Rel.* i, p. 195 f., &c.

[4] iv. 148. Cf. viii. 73.

Homeric Pylos, the Pylos of Nestor, was in Triphylia, the district of Elis just south of the estuary of the Alpheios, the very district in which, according to Herodotus, the fugitive Minyans settled.[1] So too Strabo thought.[2] Of this Pylos Doerpfeld claims to have found the site near Zacháro, a little north of Samikon; and on this promontory of Samikon was the temple of Poseidon *Samios*, which formed the religious centre of the Minyan community in Triphylia.[3] Here then lived the Pylians of Nestor, conscious of their Minyan origin, and at enmity with the 'Dorian' Eleans in the time of Herodotus. In this case at least tradition has been justified.[4]

Now Ithaca was colonized from Pylos. This also we can hardly doubt. The linguistic evidence, admittedly scanty, yet allows Hoffmann to conclude that the Ithacans came from Triphylia[5]; and although Doerpfeld will have it that not Thiáki but Leukas was the Ithaca of the Odyssey, his excavations in Leukas have revealed there buildings of a character similar to that of the prehistoric palace-ruins discovered by him at Kakóvatos (the Homeric Pylos), thus supplying direct or indirect proof of the presence of Nestor's people in Homer's Ithaca according as one does or does not identify it with the Leukadian peninsula. If Ithaca was really Leukas, then the archaeological evidence favours the hypothesis of a Minyan settlement there from Pylos. If on the other hand it was the modern Thiáki, there is at least a presumption that a migration from Triphylia to Leukas would pass through Thiáki. With regard to Zakynthos, Thucydides relates that at an early date in the Peloponnesian War the Peloponnesians and their allies sailed to the island with a hundred ships, and he adds that the islanders were 'colonists of the Achaeans in the Peloponnese'.[6] This accords with the inscriptions, which

[1] *Les Phéniciens et l'Odyssée*, i, pp. 83–105.
[2] p. 337.
[3] *Vierter Brief über Leukas-Ithaka*, p. 25 f.; Strabo, p. 343.
[4] Mr. T. W. Allen (*Argos in Homer*, 81 f.) thinks that Ἴασον Ἄργος meant the plain of 'Hollow Elis' and Triphylia, and that Ἴασον has perhaps the stem of Ἰάονες. There were Ἰωνίδες νύμφαι, we remember, in Elis.
[5] Collitz, *Dial. Inschr.*, ii. 166. See, however, A. Thumb, *Handbuch d. griech. Dial.*, 1909, p. 166 f.
[6] ii. 66.

appear to be in the Achaean dialect rather than in the speech of Triphylia. But what was the dialect of the islands before they were colonized from Achaia, we do not know.—With respect to Kephallenia, the case is somewhat complicated by the circumstance that the island is not so named in Homer (although we hear of Kephallenians), and that it is not clear what name he does give it. Hellanikos was for identifying it with the Doulichion of the Odyssey. If he was right, we may recall how Meges the son of Phyleus appears in the Iliad as chief of Doulichion and the Echinades islands; Meges son of that Phyleus who, in wrath against his father Augeas, king in Elis, went to sojourn in Doulichion.[1] If, however, Kephallenia is the Homeric Same or Samos, the name at once recalls Samia and Samikon in Triphylia.—Then, for Ithaca, there was at least one tradition which made Ithakos, the mythical founder of the state, come from Kephallenia.[2] It must be admitted that the natural course for Triphylian settlers in Ithaca to take in these early days was just along this bridge of islands; and in fact we do find that in the *Catalogue* Kephallenia, Zakynthos, and Samos, as well as Ithaca, have Odysseus for their overlord.[3]

'All are Ionians', says Herodotus, 'who are of Athenian origin, and celebrate the festival of the *Apatouria*'.[4] The test is certainly too exclusive, as Herodotus himself afterwards implies. Yet it was constantly believed that Athens was in some special sense the mother-city of Ionia; for by 'Ionians' in this context Herodotus means the inhabitants of Ionia and Attica, although conceivably he may have believed that the Ionians of the Argolic *Akte*, for instance,[5] came from Athens also; just as Aristotle evidently believed that Epidauros

[1] B 629. One hardly knows what to make of the statement in Stephen of Byzantium that Aristarchos said the Doulichians were called 'Epeians', s.v. Δουλίχιον.

[2] Schol. ρ 207 quoting Akousilaos.

[3] 631 f.

[4] i. 147.

[5] Cf. Paus. ii. 32. 8; 37. 3 (Trozen); Strabo, p. 374 (Hermione).

was occupied by Ionians from the Attic Tetrapolis.[1] Even Solon called Attica 'the eldest land of Ionia'.[2] The whole Athenian claim cannot be allowed, and, as we saw, the original traditions of Ionia do not support any hypothesis which would derive the entire body of the settlers from any single district in Greece. Yet that Attica was regarded in historical times as Ionian is of course certain. That it played a leading part in the colonization of the Central Asiatic coast is exceedingly probable. The somewhat singular fact that the *Apatouria* was apparently confined to Ionia and Attica (with Trozen) cannot be disregarded, especially in the light of another singular fact—that the presiding deities of the *Apatouria*, Zeus and Athena, with whom is associated Apollo *Patroos*, are also conjoined and regarded with special reverence in the Iliad.[3] Yet the Ionian chroniclers did not exactly assert that the first settlers in their land came from Athens. What they did say was, that they came from the Peloponnesian Achaia by way of Athens. In answer to the question, how Ionians could have come from the land of the Achaeans, they said that in ancient days the land was called Aigialos, and was inhabited not by Achaeans but by Ionians. Afterwards, when the Sons of Herakles returned, the Achaeans retreating before their Dorian conquerors occupied Aigialos (henceforward called *Achaia*) and drove out the Ionians, who went to Athens, and thence, two generations later, to Asia.[4] All this, it cannot be denied, has an appearance of unreality; and the impression is confirmed by the difficulty of reconciling any view that the Ionians as a whole came from Achaia with the various local traditions of the Ionian communities themselves.[5]

[1] Strabo, p. 374. The Ionian Gulf was formerly called Κρόνιος καὶ Ῥέας κόλπος, Tzetzes on Lykophron 630. Cf. Aesch. *P. V.* 837. This helps out the suggestion of a colonization from Elis with its Kronos-Rhea cult at Olympia. And Ἰόνιος κόλπος is taken to mean 'The Gulf of the Ionians'.

[2] πρεσβυτάτην γαῖαν Ἰαονίας, *Ath. Pol.* 5.

[3] *Themis*, p. 501.

[4] Her. i. 145.

[5] Wilamowitz, *Ion. Wand.*, thinks the Ionians, as preservers of Homer, wished to be thought Achaeans. But the tradition as given by Herodotus implies just the contrary.

Yet it is true that Poseidon *Helikonios*, who became the League-god of Ionia, was worshipped with peculiar devotion in Achaia, as Homer himself attests, when he speaks of the many gracious offerings made to him at Helike and Aigai.[1] The twelve states of Achaia curiously correspond to the twelve states of Ionia. So there may be something in the tradition after all. . . . But the foundation legends serve us better, and certain scraps of recorded history. 'We left steep Pylos,' says Mimnermos, 'the city of Neleus, and came in ships to Asia of our desire, and settled in lovely Kolophon with overweening violence,'—no doubt!—'showing the way to cruel outrage.'[2] The Ionians in Asia Minor, says Herodotus, 'set to be kings over them, some, Lycians of the race of Glaukos son of Hippolochos, others, Kaukones from Pylos of the race of Kodros Melanthios' son, yet others, kings of both dynasties.'[3] Glaukos was descended from Sisyphos, Kodros was descended from Neleus. So closely are Minyans and Ionians related; so clearly amid all the confusion is the connexion of Ionia with Pylos remembered.[4]

[1] Θ 203. Cf. N 21. ε 381. [2] *Fr.* 9 (12). [3] i. 147.

[4] The origin of the Ionians has, naturally enough, been greatly discussed, and there is no pretence to thoroughness in my treatment of the question. Dr. Farnell, to whose account of the religion of Poseidon in his *Cults of the Greek States* I am much indebted, thinks that the earliest home of the Ionian race in Greece was in Boeotia, and almost identifies Ionians and Minyans. Kretschmer, in an important article in *Glotta*, vol. i, pp. 9–34, 'Gesch. d. gr. Dial., 1. Ionier u. Achäer', argues that we have no ground for asserting that the Ionic group of dialects is less ancient than the Achaean—what other scholars have called the Aeolic—or the West-Greek; and therefore we must seek an Ionic-speaking race in European Greece independent of Achaeans and Dorians. Hence he is led to the conclusion that anciently the Ionian race was spread over Central Greece and the Peloponnese, forming a 'layer' over which in process of time spread a second layer of population consisting of its Achaean conquerors.—The interesting suggestion made by Prof. Burnet (Proceedings of the Classical Association of Scotland, 1911–12, p. 91 f., '*Who was Javan?*'), that the Ionians were 'Minoans' from Crete, involves the rejection of the great body of Ionian tradition and of the two accepted criteria of Ionian race, viz. the worship of Poseidon of Helikon and the celebration of the *Apatouria*, neither of which can have a Cretan origin. An even stronger objection to my mind is that the Ionian spirit—a very

At best it is but a confused picture that we can ever hope to win of the world in which the Homeric Poems began to gather shape. It is better to leave it so than to reduce it to an unwarranted symmetry. But we must not spare ourselves the effort of reconstruction, and to make this we must know the evidence. Part of the evidence—that which bears upon the fortunes of a people with Minyan traditions, who migrated from Boeotia by way of the Isthmos and Arcadia to Pylos in Triphylia, and from there overflowed into the Ionian Islands, and ultimately, starting from Pylos, took a prominent part in the colonization of Ionia—has been considered in detail, because it supplies us with an historical explanation of the rise and development of the Odysseus legend. We have tried to follow the progress of this people from their earliest discoverable seats in Central Greece, first to Corinth with its Minyan memories, then to Pheneos and Mantineia, then to Olympia with its story of the Minyan Salmoneus, then to Pylos under the rule, it was said, of the aged Nestor, whose life is the history of his folk—the youthful fighting with the Centaurs of Pelion, the burying of his father Neleus in Corinth, the forays against half-conquered Arcadians and Epeians. We have found the worship of Poseidon *Hippios*, with which they were so much concerned, at Corinth, at Mantineia, at Olympia—where the, perhaps Boeotian,[1] Pelops won Hippodameia with the winged steeds of the god and whence Oinomaos used to drive to the altar of Poseidon at the Isthmos,—at Pylos where the Horse-god taught Antilochos the art of chariotry. Then he takes to the sea and becomes a Sea-god, crossing the Aegean

definite thing, however hard to define—is radically antipathetic to the spirit of Minoan custom and religion. To those who share my point of view the Homeric Poems are historical evidence of this. I myself believe that Cretan influences were at work in Ionia before the coming of the settlers from the Greek mainland, and that these when they did come were thoroughly permeated by at least the more external effects of the ancient culture. Mr. Hogarth has shown that in *Ionia and the East.* It must also be admitted that many Ionian traditions speak of Cretan colonists.

[1] Gruppe, *Gr. Myth. u. Rel.*, i. 653.

with his worshippers to Mykale, where he unites them in his service as he had united them at Samikon. I cannot think of any tribal migration in the background of Greek history which has left clearer or more consecutive traces of its course.[1] Certainly many things may have happened which, if we knew them, would give us a considerably different impression of what actually occurred; and it may be that even this minor movement which we have been trying to follow had less continuity, and the people who made it less homogeneity, than we have been imagining. Yet if the movement took place at all, and if the general course of it was what has been suggested, that will be enough for our purpose. For I hope to show that the Odyssey embodies the legends of this people.

[1] It explains, for instance, the tradition in Pausanias (viii. 24) that Zakynthos was an Arcadian colony. In the island reappear the names *Psophis* and *Arkadia* (Diod. xv. 45).

CHAPTER V

THE BOEOTIAN ODYSSEY

WITH so large an infusion of Minyan blood in them, with at least so rich a treasure of Minyan traditions, the people whose advance from Boeotia to Ithaca we have been seeking to follow had of course, as one of their most cherished possessions, the great saga of Argo, which was to form material for so much splendid poetry, until it reached its last important and not least beautiful expression in Greek in the *Argonautica* of Apollonios of Rhodes. Now a great part of the Odyssey also tells of adventures upon dangerous seas, and (what is specially to be remembered here) these adventures are very often repeated in the *Argonautica*. That these poems are both of the greatest antiquity, that they grew up side by side through long ages of development, may be conceded even by those who think of Homer as the last of a long series of poets who had treated the story of Odysseus before it was made into our Odyssey. As it happens, we can confidently define the region in which the Argo legend must have taken its first substantive and recognizable form: we have seen that this was, speaking broadly, Boeotia. And we have in a tentative way traced the beginnings of the Odysseus legend also to Boeotia. If it can now be shown that the Odyssey and the *Argonautica* have in the very groundwork of their structure (for merely external similarities prove nothing) a common basis of Minyan-Boeotian tradition, that will be an additional, and surely very strong, argument in favour of the Boeotian origin of the Odyssey or, to speak more precisely, of the Odysseus legend.

We may begin with a simple instance. When Odysseus made the passage of the Wandering Rocks, no ship before his had sailed between them except Argo on its voyage back from Aietes.[1] That tale had made the hearts of all men beat before the poet's day. The Wandering Rocks are in fact nothing else than the *Symplegades,* the Clashing Rocks of the Argo legend as Euripides knew it.[2] But now comes the strange conclusion: if the Wandering Rocks of the Odyssey are only the Clashing Rocks of the Argo Epic in a new context, they have been transported from the waters of the East to the waters of the West. For, as we know, it was the land of the Colchians, where the Phasis falls into the south-east corner of the Pontus, that was the goal of the Argonauts; and, although so definite a localization of the vague 'Aia' of the earliest legend can only date from a time when the Black Sea had been explored along its southern coast, yet it shows that the Greeks looked for Aia in the farthest East. Homer knows of Euneos the son of Jason in Lemnos[3]—sufficient proof that for the Iliad also the Argo sailed eastward. Then the name *Hellespont,* the Sea of Helle as the Greeks took it to mean, is another indication of the direction taken by the Argonauts in the original legend. But indeed the point is scarcely worth labouring; no one, so far as we know, ever dreamed that Aia was not east of the Hellespont. So when the Odyssey speaks of the Argo as 'sailing from Aietes' (the king of Aia) when it threaded the Wandering Rocks, the poet is clearly remembering, perhaps even quoting from, some older *Argonautica* which placed them in the east.[4] When Milesian navigators followed on the fabled track of the Argonauts, they found the Wandering or Clashing Rocks in two promontories upon the European side of the Bosporus, at the Black Sea end, called from their colour *Cyanean.* The simple audacity of the Greek imagination has something lovable in it, and it has certain obvious advantages for the student as well. We know now where the early Greeks conceived the Symplegades to lie. But certainly Odysseus could never have passed them after the North wind drove him beyond Malea and Kythera. Ought we then to conclude that

[1] μ 70. [2] *Medea* 2. [3] H 468. Cf. Φ 41.
[4] See Additional Note, p. 236.

the passage of the *Planktai* in the Odyssey has been incorporated there, with certain necessary qualifications and accommodations to its new setting, directly from the Argo saga, to which alone the episode originally belonged? Not necessarily, I think. The story of the floating rocks may have been told of Odysseus as early as of Jason, and the rest of the evidence appears to me to support that view. But what no one can deny is, that the language of the Odyssey at this point has been strongly coloured by the language of an Argo epic treating of a similar adventure. It is not difficult to prove this, and the proof carries with it at least this result, that there can be no question of the *Argonautica's* borrowing the episode from our Odyssey, and, secondly, that the story of the Planktai-Symplegades is originally a Minyan legend.

When once we have realized that the Wandering Rocks were first thought of as in far eastern waters, and that their passage was one of the adventures of Jason as well as of Odysseus, many other parallels between the *Argonautica* and the Odyssey begin to reveal themselves. The Wandering Rocks are reached after no long voyage from the island of Kirke, which in Homer is called 'the isle of Aia', *Αἰαίη νῆσος*. And it is situated 'where Morning the child of Dawn has her house and dancing-places and the Sun his uprisings',[1] that is to say, at the north-eastern verge of the world, where the Greeks imagined Aia to be. And Kirke herself is 'very sister of ill-plotting Aietes',[2] since both are children of the Sun and of one mother, Perse daughter of Okeanos. Aietes was the king of Aia who had the Golden Fleece in his keeping, till Jason recovered it. Then comes the further thought: Kirke the sister of Aietes, Medea his daughter—are they not, essentially, one and the same? Medea is the great enchantress of Greek legend, typical witch and sorceress, who has an antidote against the fiery breath of the fearful bulls and can charm the sleepless lids of the dragon; while Kirke also is *pharmakis*, one who with her medicines transforms men into swine and wolves and lions, and again restores them to their

[1] μ 3, 4. [2] κ 137.

proper forms. Kirke indeed has a certain graciousness we do not find in Medea. But then our thoughts of Medea have been coloured by Euripides' play and by Apollonios' hardly less subtle and sympathetic portrayal of the same woman before Jason had quite destroyed the image of him in her heart: 'questa fù tal nella sua vita nuova'; it is I think the chief glory of Apollonios to have shown us the girlhood of the dreadful heroine of the *Medea*, whom we could scarcely help hating, unless we remembered all she might have been. But the result has been that the divinity Medea must have retained in the earlier forms of the saga, in the *Korinthiaka*, for instance, ascribed to 'Eumelos' of Corinth, in which city Medea was honoured as a goddess, has disappeared in this intense humanity with which the poets have endowed her. Yet any form of the *Argonautica* that can have been known to the Odyssey at the stage when κ was forming is likely to have retained the older conception of Medea, when she was still what Kirke is in Homer, a 'dreadful goddess',[1] not merely a subtle and passionate woman. Thus Kirke as she is represented in the Odyssey may come nearer than we imagine to the Medea of the Argo epic in its older forms, in which she must have been to Jason very much what Kirke is to Odysseus, a favourable goddess whose love is something of a condescension and nothing at all of an infatuation. And now we are confronted with the question, Is the figure of Kirke a mere creation of her poet modelled upon the figure of Medea, and is her relation to Odysseus imagined after the relation of Medea to Jason? It may be pointed out that the association of Medea and Jason in the Corinthian cult almost certainly created their association in the myth, and on this ground it might be argued that the *Argonautica* has the priority. But such an argument would not be very relevant, for it is possible, and indeed to my mind far more likely, that Kirke is not a mere copy of Medea, but Medea herself in another form. No doubt she had won an independent existence in the popular imagination before she entered the epos, while her

[1] κ 136.

love for Odysseus is not borrowed from, but is parallel to, Medea's love for Jason. In the end the conclusion is pretty much the same. If this part of the Odyssey is not copied from the Minyan epic, it is the Minyan epic in a new frame. We have to do here with variant forms of the same story.

Kirke and Aietes are the children of Helios and the Oceanid Perse, and Perse is an old name of Hekate, who, according to the *Theogony*,[1] was the daughter of Perses, while the *Hymn to Demeter* calls her the daughter of Persaios.[2] Medea, the daughter of Aietes, is the special votary of Hekate, so that Kirke and she have this further relationship, that they are both forms in some sort of the goddess Hekate. Again, Medea was worshipped in Corinth, but she reappears in transparent enough disguise in that *Agamede* with the yellow hair 'who had knowledge of all the simples that the broad Earth nourishes', and was the eldest daughter of Augeias, who was the son of Helios and ruled in Elis.[3] And Agamede must be very nearly related to the cunning *Agamedes*, who with his brother Trophonios built the Treasury of her father Augeias, and was the son according to one legend of Erginos king of the Minyan Orchomenos; according to another, king of Stymphalos in Arcadia.[4] Boeotia, Corinth, Arcadia, Elis —that follows the course of the Minyan migration. We even hear of a sister of Penelope called Mede.[5] Jason was the son of Polymede, the daughter of Autolykos,[6] and according to Natalis Comes was called *Dolomedes* before his name was changed to Jason.[7] Now Odysseus also was the son of a daughter of Autolykos and is called *δολόμητις*, which is the same thing as Dolomedes.[8]

[1] 409 f. [2] 24. [3] Λ 740 f.

[4] Schol. Ar. *Clouds* 508, quoting Charax.

[5] Μήδη, called Μέδη in Asios *ap.* schol. δ 797. See Usener, *Götternamen*, p. 163.

[6] Apollod. *Bibl.* i. 9. 16. [7] *Mythol.* vi. 8, 2nd ed., Venice, 1581.

[8] Σίνωπος is a companion of Odysseus in Pherekydes *ap.* schol. M 257. Now Autolykos had a *μαντεῖον* in Sinope. Strabo xii. 546 ἐτίμων . . . ὡς θεόν. ἦν δὲ καὶ μαντεῖον αὐτοῦ. Cf. Plut. *Lucull.* 23; Apoll. Rh. ii. 955 f.

The parallelism goes farther than one had expected. How far can it be traced in the Odyssey? At least one step more. When Odysseus was sailing from the Isle of Aiolos to the Isle of Kirke he put in at the haven of the Laistrygonians under the shelter of the great cliff-wall on the summit of which their stronghold was built, 'the fort of Lamos'. The Laistrygones, as was soon to appear, were giants and cannibals, and Odysseus lost many of his men before he escaped from that inhospitable coast. . . . Of the Argonauts we are told that when they came to Arktonnesos in the Propontis they found there certain Earth-born giants, whom they fought against and exterminated. Odysseus to be sure may have his own adventure with giants as well as Jason or any other wanderer in fairyland; and if there were nothing more than this quite general similarity between the episode in the Odyssey and the episode in the *Argonautica*, it would not in any way prove their original identity. But the Odyssey says that when the three companions of Odysseus, whom he had sent to explore the place, came near the city of the Laistrygonians they found a girl going down to a spring to draw water, and the name of the spring was *Artakie*.[1] Now there was a real spring called Artakie beside Kyzikos; and Kyzikos was in Arktonnesos. Here again, it would seem, the *Argonautica* has the priority. Yet we must go on to ask, In what sense has it the priority? The Laistrygones lived in perpetual daylight, in a land of the midnight sun, where a sleepless man might earn double wages, for day-labour and night-labour[2]; so that one must imagine Laistrygonia in the far north, if this indication is to be followed. Nor is it the only one of the kind; for when Odysseus sails to the River Okeanos to consult the soul of Teiresias, he beaches his ship on the farthest shore of the world, where dwelt the Kimmerians 'shrouded in mist and cloud', unbeholden of the sun.

If one could trust the statement that Jason was an adopted name, it might be conjectured that a Minyan hero more or less a double of Autolykos and Odysseus was identified with Jason of Corinth.

[1] κ 108. [2] κ 82 f.

The land of eternal night, like the land of eternal day, must be sought in the extreme north. In fact, the historical people whom the Greeks called the Kimmerians dwelt it appears in Southern Russia (where they gave their name to the Crimea), before they invaded Asia Minor about 700 B.C. We can only conjecture that some rumour of this people and of a land with longer summer days and winter nights had travelled downwards into Greece when the epic of Odysseus' wanderings was taking shape. Where then did the story originally place the Laistrygonians, in Kyzikos or the undefined North? Did some poet, finding in an older form of the Odyssey the Laistrygonians vaguely located in the land of continual daylight, think of those other giants in the *Argonautica* and borrow from it the name of the well Artakie? In the Odyssey the Wandering Rocks, which we found to be identical with the Clashing Rocks of the Argo epic, in some inexplicable way resolve themselves into Skylla and Charybdis, a cliff and a whirlpool that do not move at all. Has a later poet inserted the description of the Wandering Rocks into an older Odyssey in which they did not appear? I do not know how we are to answer these questions, or to say of any particular passage in the Odyssey that it has been taken from the *Argonautica*, or of any passage in the Argo epic that it has been suggested by the Odyssey, without more definite proof of this than we have found. What every one, however, must recognize is, that both poems draw upon a common stock of epic tradition telling of a hero who wandered in strange seas, and fought with giants, and passed between floating rocks, and won the favour of a witch descended from the Sun. That they had a common stock of verses also seems to me equally certain, although I do not wish to insist upon that point here. Yet it is perhaps a necessary corollary to the broader view, and it explains the verbal similarities in the two poems, the recurrence for instance of that well of *Artakie* in the Odyssey.[1]

[1] Although the *Argonautica* brings the Minyans by way of the Danube and the Eridanos into the Tyrrhenian Sea and so to the island of Kirke,

What follows from this? Not that the Odyssey is necessarily a Minyan poem; we must prove that on other grounds. But if we succeed in proving it, if we succeed even in making it very probable, then here is a great body of additional testimony drawn from an admittedly Minyan source to confirm our persuasion. If we incline to believe that the Odyssey, like the *Argonautica*, received its first substantive form in the ancient epic schools of Boeotia, the fact that it is in parts a mere replica of the Minyan epic becomes a very important argument. And surely no one need wonder that the loveliest part of the Odyssey has been wrought out of the same material as the Argo epic, which has so much, more even than the Odyssey itself, of a kind of wild beauty we are apt to think of as mediaeval or modern rather than characteristic of ancient poetry. It is a poem full of pity and terror, with weird reflections, very alluring to our imaginations which have fallen in love again with man's earliest dreams, of a picturesque barbarism—the horror of the midnight forest, the miracle of the Fleece coloured like a cloud at dawn.[1] Certainly the subject which inspired three masterpieces so different as the *Fourth Pythian* ode, the *Argonautica* of Apollonios, and *The Life and Death of Jason,* has its wonderful possibilities, unexhausted even in the tense and gorgeous narrative of Pindar, in Apollonios' poem with its wistful, only half-achieved beauty, and in *Jason* with its special charm of showing us, as it were, a familiar landscape

and thereafter makes them pass in reverse order through many of Odysseus' adventures; and although Scheria was very early identified with Corcyra, and the *Naupaktia* represented Jason as going there after the death of Pelias and not to Corinth (Paus. ii. 3. 9 = *Fr.* 10 Kinkel); I assume that all this was directly suggested by the Odyssey. Yet that does not follow, there may have been here also a common body of tradition from which, and not from our Odyssey, the two other epics derived this matter. If it be so, it is a very striking confirmation of the view that the tradition is Minyan, since the *Naupaktia* was largely concerned with the adventures of Jason and had strongly the character of the old Lokrian-Boeotian genealogical epic. Apart from this, it may be thought something of an argument that the Greeks felt so vividly the spiritual relationship between the Odyssey and the saga of Argo.

[1] *Argon.* iv. 124 f.

through Gothic windows 'innumerable of stains and splendid dyes'. If the same genius had been expended upon the Argo legend as upon the Odyssey, we should have had three supreme Greek epics instead of two; for indeed the poets who sang of the Argo had an epic motive as profound and fascinating as that of the Odyssey and even more varied.[1]

Well, the Muses lived on Helikon, the hill of Poseidon of the Minyans, dancing about the violet-bordered Well of the Horse. Where the Muses were worshipped, poetry was held in honour, and we must take account of the fact that Helikon was the chief seat of their worship in Greece,[2] although they are so often called 'Thracian'.[3] It was from Helikon, no doubt, that the knowledge of them disseminated itself through Southern Greece at least; and so for us it is specially interesting to find in a Boeotian poem the story of Thamyris and his contest with the Muses localized in Dorion in Triphylia, whither the myth had been carried quite evidently by our migrating Minyans, to whom Dorion is in this passage of *B* definitely assigned.[4] If the Muses are found in Boeotia, there also we find the earliest epic poetry in Greece. For the *Argonautica* and the great Theban sagas treat of an age anterior to the Trojan War; are more local in their interests; above all, have no knowledge of the Trojan saga, while the Trojan saga knows them and is brought, so far as the discrepancies admit, into harmony with them. The oldest school of epic poetry which we can assign to a definite centre and associate with an apparently historical name is Boeotian, its representative poet Hesiod of Askra. Although it is impossible to date with any precision the several parts, of very different ages and perhaps origin,

[1] The parallelisms between the Odyssey and the *Argonautica* are discussed by Wilamowitz in his *Homer. Untersuch.*, p. 163 f.

[2] Miss Harrison reminds me that Mnemosyne the mother of the Muses is connected with the Trophonios oracle at Lebadeia. See *Themis*, p. 511 f.

[3] The question of Thracians in Early Boeotia is still completely obscure, and it is hardly safe to infer that the Muses did come from Thrace.

[4] 594 f.

which compose the *Works and Days* and the *Theogony*, yet these poems, even as we have them, embody masses of epic tradition demonstrably very ancient and demonstrably Boeotian. Then, for the art of Hesiod,—which it is very important in his case to distinguish from his *style*, the difference in character between the two being just what makes Hesiod with all his great merits so unsatisfactory—who does not feel that it is not only a less masterly but a less developed thing than the art of Homer? It is not so much an 'effort to adapt the form of Ionian epos to a different genius and to material of a different order'[1] as a really heroic attempt to preserve or revive a kind of poetry older than Ionia itself and qualitatively different from Homer. It is some feeling of this which suggests the words of the Muses to Hesiod when they appeared to him as he kept his flocks upon Helikon: 'We can tell false things that seem like true; and we know also, when we please, how to recount true things.'[2] This distinction of Homer as the singer of false things that look like true, from Hesiod whose words are all truth—for this is what the Muses mean—is based no doubt upon the matter rather than the manner of the Homeric and Hesiodic poets, the ideally treated saga-stuff of the former being contrasted with these long lists of mnemonic precepts for the farmer and generations of gods and heroes in the latter. It is also necessary to admit that the language of Hesiod has been powerfully affected by the language of Homer, that it is indeed the diction of the Ionian epos in degeneration. But the mere kind of Hesiod's poetry is cruder and older than the kind of the Odyssey. It has that effect upon us when we reach a 'Hesiodic' passage in Homer, the Catalogue of the Ships for example, the other name of which was *The Boeotian Poetry*.[3] The Catalogue forms a critical problem by itself, and there is no agreement among scholars about the date of its insertion in the Iliad, or its own internal homogeneity, or whether it was composed originally for its present context or

[1] Jebb, *Growth and Influence of Classical Greek Poetry*, p. 105.

[2] *Theog.* 27 f.

[3] Βοιωτία (πόησις). Cf. Ἰλιάς.

has been borrowed from another.[1] But very few can now doubt that in substance it is an extremely ancient document; for not only does it, in the opinion of most scholars, contemplate a different preponderance and marshalling of the Greek forces before Troy from what we find in the rest of the Iliad, but it has a geography and ethnology of its own referring to an age quite other than that generally assumed throughout the rest of Homer. Even if it exactly fits its present place, the Catalogue will still be as old as anything in the two epics. If it is taken from the *Kypria*, as there is much reason for believing, the view that it is in fact what it purports to be, 'Boeotian poetry' representing Boeotian tradition, will be considerably strengthened; for the *Cyprian Verses* told of the assembling of the Achaean host at Aulis in Boeotia. We may accept this view with the greater assurance because such Catalogues were characteristic of the Boeotian 'Hesiodic' school. Now, since we find such early traces of this kind of poetry in the Greek epos (as indeed such metricized lists of its divine and heroic names are probably about the first things a tribe cares to have recorded), we may assume that the Hesiodic type of epic was indigenous in Central Greece, an inheritance from an earlier age, from an age surely earlier than that in which an elaborate poem like the Iliad or even the *Argonautica* or the *Thebais* could have been constructed. With this in mind and remembering the importance of Boeotia in the pre-Homeric epic tradition, one is led to believe that the Minyan people had their own bards capable of at least a rudimentary form of the epos. The *Argonautica* itself is one proof of this. But the Odyssey is another.

I have sought to make it probable that Odysseus is ultimately identical with Autolykos of Parnassos, whose name and nature he inherited[2]; that his grandfather the progenitor

[1] The latest study of the question is Dr. Leaf's *Troy* (1912).

[2] Cf. Dieterich, Kleine Schriften xx, *Volksglaube*, p. 315, 'Der vielfache Brauch, dass das Kind den Namen des Grossvaters bekommt, ist in manchen Fällen als Glaube an den eigentlichen Übergang der "Seele" nachzuweisen.' For the reincarnation of grandfather in grandson see further J. G. Frazer, *The Belief in Immortality* (1913), vol. i, p. 417 f.

of the race, whom the epos calls Arkeisios, is in fact the hero Arkesilaos buried in Lebadeia; that the visit to the dead related in the eleventh book of the Odyssey is a Boeotian legend, since its purpose is to consult the soul of the Theban Teiresias, and the catalogue of famous women dead is in the manner of the Boeotian epic, while the names themselves are chiefly of Minyan and Boeotian heroines; that the wanderings of Odysseus on strange seas and his adventures in wonderful lands correspond, sometimes in detail, with the wanderings and adventures of Jason; that Odysseus stands in the closest relation, in the non-literary as in the literary tradition, to Poseidon the tribal god of the Minyans and Ionians. Other Minyan elements in the Odyssey need not be recapitulated here. Those which have been named are organic to it, without them there can be no Odyssey. Therefore it must be to this extent a Minyan poem. Whether Odysseus himself is originally a Minyan hero is not so evident. His legend may have been drawn within the sphere of the Minyan traditions from a non-Minyan source; and this is not unlikely, if his earliest home was Parnassos or even Lebadeia. There is nothing Minyan, so far as I know, about Arkesilaos or Laertes, although it seems as if the Battiadai thought there was, and although Laertes as the father of a great hero of the Trojan poetry came to be reckoned among the Argonauts. Neither is Autolykos considered a Minyan, although he went with the Minyans to Sinope. But what is certain, and the important thing for us, is that Odysseus at least *became* a Minyan-Ionian hero, brought indeed into an especially close connexion with the Minyan Horse-god.

We are now in a position to suggest what the first great stage in the development of the Odyssey, the *Boeotian Odyssey* one may call it, was like; what materials went to its composition. We must expect, however, to find that the necessity of reconciling the later developments with this earliest one has coloured and in parts transformed the Boeotian poem. If the completed Odyssey was to have organic unity, such modifications were inevitable; and in fact I think it can be shown that they took place. If, for instance, we reason that in the earliest version of Odysseus' visit to the dead he must have consulted Teiresias in the way one did consult such a buried prophet in Greece, by descending into a hole in the ground, or by some means placing oneself in direct communication with the hero in his grave, this version, which must have been localized in Boeotia—for where but in his own land could Teiresias be consulted, where else would he listen?—could not be harmonized with those other adventures of Odysseus in the remote places of the earth. And so in our Odyssey Teiresias is consulted, not in Boeotia, but at the world's end by the River Okeanos. Yet Odysseus feeds the ghosts with blood in a trench and vows to sacrifice a black ram to the seer. That was the ritual in Boeotia.[1] Is not this then a reminiscence from the older version? The poet who knew that one might consult Trophonios so in his Boeotian home under the ground could never have imagined that Odysseus must travel to ultimate Ocean to question him. Why should he think it necessary in the case of Teiresias? Well, when the Visit to the Dead had to find its place among the other strange sufferings of the hero, when indeed it had for the satisfaction of the imagination to be made strange and terrible beyond what was possible at any actual oracle of the dead in Greece, it had to be set in some vague region of the 'outer geography', at the earth's western margin therefore, which perhaps was always thought of as yielding one way down to Hades. Doubtless an actual change of belief concerning the dead among the people who cherished the Odyssey may have helped to effect this result. That point will be considered later. But in the meantime observe that when Odysseus vows to sacrifice the ram to Teiresias it is on his return to Ithaca that he will make the offering[2]; it was hard for him to find a pure black ram in Kirke's island. Is there not some strange confusion here? By the far western beach Teiresias is content with mutilated rites and an incomplete sacrifice. The appropriate offering is made in Greece. In

[1] Paus. ix. 39. 6. And of course elsewhere in Greece. [2] λ 30.

Ithaca, the Odyssey implies. But if the Visit to the Dead is a Boeotian legend told of Odysseus before he was thought of as an Ithacan (that is, before his tribe went to Ithaca), then the completed sacrifice was made in Boeotia. And where would the ram be slaughtered except over the prophet's grave, how else could he drink the blood? And if it be said, all this religion of the buried dead and their blood-drinking is quite un-Homeric, one can only answer, Is it not all the more extraordinary that here in the Odyssey we find a buried hero (distinguished from the burned dead by the retention of all his wits[1]), and the drinking of the blood? Has not a legend of the older chthonian religion been wrought upon and almost, yet not quite, entirely harmonized with the Homeric religion?

Even as we read it now, the eleventh book of the Odyssey is a composite thing falling even into self-contradiction. For it first represents Odysseus as standing on the beach of Ocean by the grove of Persephone, and then suddenly we find ourselves in the Asphodel Meadow, and then in the Hell of the great sinners. A certain confusion of thought regarding the place and condition of the dead is possible enough in the mind of an early poet, or a modern poet for the matter of that, but scarcely a confusion which involves the holding at one and the same time of two fundamentally opposite creeds. Yet this is the kind of confusion we find in the *Nekyia*. The dead in Homer are burned, and there, for all effective purposes, is an end of them; for the Homeric religion the world of the dead hardly exists any more than it did for the religion of Israel. But we know now that it was intensely real and near to the Greek people throughout their history, among whom the normal method of disposing of the dead was burial, and who felt themselves surrounded even in life by friendly and by malevolent ghosts. This is hardly the place for even the briefest discussion of Orphism and the so-called 'Orphic Interpolation' in the *Nekyia* describing the punishments of Tityos

[1] *φρένες ἔμπεδοί εἰσιν*, κ 493. One might almost translate his *mana*. Cf. Sophocles' *πάμψυχος ἀνάσσει* of Amphiaraos whom the earth swallowed up alive, *El.* 840.

and Tantalos and Sisyphos, Minos with gold sceptre in his hand sitting in judgement upon the dead, the shadowy hunting of Orion, and the phantom of Herakles not yet weary of strife. When we have reached this point it is evident that we have now passed into a new circle of beliefs about the future life, which have their source in a religion that Homer otherwise consistently ignores and rejects. Almost certainly the whole passage is a rather late interpolation. That does not prevent it from being on the whole much more primitive in its conception of the life after death than Homer, or, if that is begging the question, not less primitive. The notion of future punishment may be comparatively late, although I do not know how we can prove that. In any case it presupposes a theory of death at least as old as Homer's. And the clash of two incompatible theories has clearly led in this 'Orphic' passage to some misconception. The myth of Sisyphos and his stone has been explained by M. Salomon Reinach[1] as the result of a misunderstanding. Sisyphos was regarded as the builder of the Akrokorinthos, and was represented in art carrying a great stone on his shoulders up the slope. The Feast of Tantalos can be explained as a tribal initiation ceremony.[2] Orion the Earth-born, beloved of the Dawn, married to Side who was cast into Hades, cured of his blindness by the first rays of the morning sun, slain at last by the Moon-goddess Artemis, is probably like Herakles a Daimon of the Sun-Year. Minos is a more complex figure. Most of these damned are in Hades, not because of any real impiety committed by them, but in virtue of their very nature, which forces them to travel for ever between the two poles of darkness and light, death and re-birth. Behind the Orphism which has been found in this part of the Odyssey dimly appears the pre-Achaean religion of Greece.[3]

Once more, if the legend of Odysseus was at first inde-

[1] 'Sisyphe aux enfers et quelques autres damnés' in *Cultes, Mythes et Religions*, ii. pp. 172 ff.

[2] *Themis*, p. 243 f.

[3] For the different conceptions of the future life in Homer and popular Greek belief, see further Lawson, *Modern Greek Folklore*, &c., chs. v, vi.

pendent of the story of Troy, the episode in which he speaks with the shades of Agamemnon, Achilles, and Aias has been added to the original Teiresias episode; and one is the readier to believe this because Odysseus confers with Teiresias by the trench full of blood from which the dead man must drink before he can speak, or at least before he can prophesy, but with Agamemnon and Achilles and Aias in the Meadow of Asphodel, and without giving them of the blood. But 'the original Teiresias episode'—what exactly did that contain? Here again, no doubt, we have to make certain deductions. The prophecy of Teiresias, as we now read it, implies knowledge on the poet's part of a *Nostos* which related the accomplishment of all the prophecy contains; it has obviously quite outgrown its original proportions; for it is composed out of a full knowledge of all that happens in the Odyssey and of much else that does not happen there. Yet it does not follow that the Visit to the Dead was not part of the original Odysseus legend, although we cannot tell how large a part. Many poets have worked at the episode, until it has come to mirror all the rest of the poem. And that the Visit is original is as certain as anything of the kind can be. Odysseus as Eniautos Daimon must descend to Hades. Since this is so, we are dispensed from considering the objection that, since Kirke is able to tell Odysseus all he needs to know of the future, he has no adequate motive for consulting Teiresias at all. Odysseus is not obeying a motive but a law of his nature.[1]

Whatever else is original in the myth of Odysseus, the Visit to the Dead is so. And since in one aspect of his nature as a Daimon of the Year he is regarded as the Sun, we must also admit as original the tale of Helios' wrath against Odysseus for the slaughter of the sacred cattle in Thrinakie. It seems indeed clear enough to me that the wrath of Helios is an earlier *motif* in the complex legend of our Odyssey than the wrath of Poseidon, which has come to play so large a part

[1] The *Nekyia* is discussed by Wilamowitz in *Hom. Unt.*, pp. 140–62, 199–226, and by Rohde in *Psyche* i, p. 49 f.

in it. The quarrel with Poseidon is not a necessary part in the *Dromenon* of the Season-Daimon; in some form or other the quarrel with the Sun-god is. It is significant that in the prophecy of Teiresias, the *nekyomanteia* proper, it is against Helios in the first instance that Odysseus is warned; the Sun-god is the real enemy. However, in reconstructing the Boeotian Odyssey it is not necessary to decide this question of priority, for the quarrel with Poseidon is certainly very ancient, and nothing is gained by too relentless an application of the analytic method to the growth of saga. It is interesting to observe, and it is a kind of proof of the ancientness of their association in the story, that Odysseus follows in his evolution somewhat closely the evolution of the god, who began with being something very like a god of fertility [1]—at least a god of the fertilizing waters, and at last became chief god of the sea, as Odysseus became the typical mariner. There may be something in this beyond a mere analogy.

A fascinating speculation of Welcker regarding the Phaiakians calls for at least a passing notice on account of their importance in the Odyssey both as directly influencing the course of events and as occupying, on a mere counting of lines, so much space for the description of their delightful manners and ways of life. Welcker observed that the word *Φαίαξ* is derived from *φαιός*, 'grey', 'dusky', and so was led to the conclusion that the Phaiakians were at bottom no other than the dark Ferrymen of the Dead, familiar personages in folklore. They convey the slumbering Odysseus after all his labours and wanderings (including, we must remember, his visit to the underworld) back to his earthly home in Ithaca. 'Sweet sleep', says the poet, telling how at last the Wanderer

[1] Was not the oar that Odysseus fixed in the ground a holy symbol, not an oar in men's earliest thoughts of it but, as the wayfarer guessed, a winnowing-fan indeed, such as was set up in honour of the fruitful Demeter, while she stood smiling with sheaves and poppies in both hands? Theocr. *Id.* vii, *ad fin.* Poseidon stood in close relation to Demeter in many places of Arcadia. The nature of Odysseus' oar was first explained by Miss J. E. Harrison in two articles entitled *Mystica Vannus Iacchi*, *J. H. S.*, vols. xxiii (1903) and xxiv (1904). See esp. vol. xxiii, pp. 301 f. and 306, vol. xxiv, pp. 241 ff.

was borne in the wondrous Phaiakian ship to his native shore, 'A sweet sleep fell upon his eyelids, an unawakening sleep, very pleasant, scarce distinguishable from death, θανάτῳ ἄγχιστα ἐοικώς . . . and like a hawk the ship in her light speed cut the waves carrying a man whose lore was like the wisdom of the gods. So he who in the old days had suffered many and many a pang in his heart as he drave through battles of men and cruel billows slept now without a stir and all the pain forgotten.'[1] An imaginative reader may feel, under the quite sufficient human loveliness of this strangely moving passage, the suggestion of something mysterious or allegorical in that profound slumber of Odysseus, 'very like unto death.' Neither perhaps ought we to forget that the ships of the Phaiakians were magical. 'The Phaiakian ships have no steersman or rudders like other ships, but have, themselves, the thoughts and wisdom of men, and know the cities and fruitful fields of men everywhere, and most speedily cross a spacious sea, hidden in a misty cloud.' And the Phaiakians 'give all men hurtless convoy'.[2] One may think of the story in Procopius of the mysterious ferrymen who carried over the souls of the dead to the island of Brittia,[3] and of the Frisian legend, at heart identical with the other, told by Heine in the essay on Gods in Exile. And yet the whole Phaiakian episode in our Odyssey is related with such entire unconsciousness of any significance in it beyond its significance for art—there is no part of Homer with so much luxury of detail—and with so perfect an illusion in the art itself, that I myself should have no confidence that Welcker's suggestion is right, and should be inclined to accept the view of so great an authority as Rohde that it is all a groundless fancy,[4] if it were not for the fact that it is altogether appropriate that Odysseus as Eniautos Daimon should be ferried between the shores of Life and Death by mysterious Grey Men. We must conclude, I think, that Welcker is right.[5] And the Phaiakians must have come into the earliest form of the Odys-

[1] ν 79 f. [2] θ 553 f. [3] *Bell. Goth.* iv. 20.
[4] *Psyche*, i, p. 81, n. 2. [5] *Kl. Schr.* ii, pp. 1–79.

seus legend. Beyond this we can scarcely hope to penetrate. What evidence there is that might help us to connect them with a definite locality points to Trozen and, beyond Trozen, to Anthedon in Boeotia as the original centre of their mythology.[1]

The Boeotian Odyssey then probably told of Odysseus how he blinded Polyphemos, a name with Boeotian associations,[2] and so incurred the wrath of Poseidon; the peril of the Laistrygones; the enchantments of Kirke; the visit to the world of the dead to consult the soul of Theban Teiresias; where he meets the ghost of his mother Antikleia the daughter of Autolykos, and sees the vision of the heroines, who may have told him more fully in this older poem, round which our Odyssey has grown, the story of their fortunes, for the Odyssey says: 'One after one crowding they came; and each told me her race to the end, and I questioned them all'[3]; the peril of the Wandering Rocks; the sojourn with Kalypso; the departure from her 'Ogygian' isle—another Boeotian name—the wreck of the raft and escape to the land of the Phaiakians, where he was fated to reach the end of his sufferings.[4]

On the whole, then, the earliest Odyssey, of which this is a tentative reconstruction, would seem to have been nearly coextensive in matter with the *Alkinou Apologos.* It therefore makes so natural a division in the completed Odyssey as we read it with an introductory *Telemacheia* and the Ithacan scenes which fill the last twelve books, that one finds it easier to believe that this central part—told, it has long been observed, in the first person—is indeed in substance the oldest of the three. But doubtless only in substance. The original poem has lost and gained.

I have deliberately left the outlines of the Boeotian Odyssey

[1] Gruppe, *Griech. Myth.* p. 398, n. 4.

[2] Polyphemos the Argonaut, husband of Laonome the sister of Herakles, is an obvious double of Euphemos. This Polyphemos also was the son of Poseidon. Schol. Ap. Rh. i. 40—a version going back to Socrates and Euphorion.

[3] λ 233 f.

[4] ε 288 f.

as I conceive it vague and uncertainly defined. Homeric scholarship has already suffered hurt from theories too rigidly held or too precisely formulated. There will always be something, and this the most important element of all, finally inexplicable in the growth of a great poem. If it were otherwise the poetry would never have come there at all. Some theory of course the critic must have. But he is wise to be content with broad outlines, if at least these are very clear and significant. I believe that the Odyssey first took shape in Boeotia, and that the matter of it then was substantially the matter contained in the narrative of Odysseus to Alkinoos in Scheria. But whether, in respect of its form, we should have been justified in speaking of it as an 'epic', no one can say. It seems likely that the poets who gave its first shape, however rude, to the *Argonautica* were in some sense capable of epic poetry and, by inference, could have given some sort of unity to the legends which clustered about Odysseus. For after all, Odysseus is only another Jason with one new great adventure, the visit to Teiresias. I am speaking of course of the hero in the Boeotian Odyssey. The adventures related in the *Alkinou Apologos* are in the main adventures which attached themselves to Odysseus doubtless long before he left Boeotia. But the Boeotian poetry about him was certainly different in all kinds of ways from our *Apologos*. I am not concerned to deny that. I am merely arguing for the existence of a Boeotian *stratum* in the legends which have gone to the building-up of our Odyssey. If now it can be shown that the Odyssey in its further developments reflects the subsequent history of the people among whom it arose, my theory of the origin and evolution of the epic of Odysseus may claim to be generally established.[1]

[1] Odysseus as Sun- and Year-Daimon is the subject of two learned studies by Carl Fries, *Studien zur Odyssee* (Mitteil. d. Vorderasiatisch. Gesellschaft), I *Das Zagmukfest auf Scheria*, 1910, II *Odysseus der bhikshu*, 1911 (Leipzig). The Phaiakian Episode, he thinks, describes an ancient Spring festival of the familiar kind celebrating the Return of the God, here Odysseus, who, however, in the *Apologos* adopts a new rôle and becomes the reciter of his own adventures. The beggar-disguise in

Ithaca, again, has a symbolical meaning and is to be understood by comparison with the ascetic practices common in most religions. The author supports these positions with an impressive array of parallel instances. But I think he attempts to prove too much. The principle, 'Der Hauptinhalt aller Mythologie ist die Himmelsreise des Tagesgestirns und seine Entsprechung im Jahreslauf und der Wiederkehr des Frühlings' (i. 3), surely requires modification, or at least very careful handling. In my opinion he makes the mistake of dwelling too exclusively upon a single aspect of Odysseus. But much that he says is suggestive, and his material interesting and valuable.

CHAPTER VI

ODYSSEUS IN ARCADIA

When the Minyans came to Mantineia, they found a new divinity and a new legend, Penelope and the story of her Wooers. In the Odyssey she is the wife of Odysseus; the hero of the invading people has been married to the Kore of the land, the marriage expressing in a symbol, although it was much more than a symbol, the fact of their invasion and settlement there. It is indeed characteristic of primitive races, partly from the mere tyranny of the personal over all their ideas, partly from that inadequacy of language which necessarily accompanies their confused and emotional modes of thinking, to describe the circumstances in which it finds itself placed in its dealings with other tribes and races in terms of the human relationships. Certain chapters in the early history of Israel aptly illustrate this tendency. The special relation of husband and wife, of king and queen, was commonly used in early Greece to express a situation which must have recurred again and again, the coming of a race or fragment of a race of Northern origin into a district still held by an older population, and the final amalgamation of the two peoples. Thus the chiefs in Homer are 'Achaeans'; their wives, when they too have a real part to play in the legends, are seen to be princesses of the pre-Achaean dynasties. So Penelope is the daughter of Ikarios, who was in tradition (although Homer is silent on this point) a brother of Tyndareos and therefore of the royal house which held rule in Sparta before the coming of Menelaos, and even in Homer is a strangely impersonal, almost disembodied figure, not really in the story, the survivor of a past already becoming vague—clearly no Achaean. Penelope, however, was no mortal princess, and Odysseus, however early the poets rejected his divinity, never lived on earth. Yet this, which at first seems to shake all our conclusions, really gives them greater certainty and precision. A tribe may marry its queen to a stranger coming alone with nothing but his sword, and an air of mystery about him perhaps, such as leads primitive minds to look on a stranger as divine. And if the pre-Achaean societies of Greece were, as seems most probable, matrilinear, we may explain these traditions of marriage between foreigners and the native princesses as memories of an actual custom of exogamy and *beena* marriage, as Dr. Frazer explains the traditional history of the Latin kings.[1] If we do this, there is no need to invoke an immigration of conquering foreigners; to do that is in fact to misunderstand the custom. But the case of Odysseus is made different by the fact that he is divine. A people will hardly marry its native goddess to a foreign divinity, unless his worshippers have come with him; the old Arcadian race would not have married Penelope to Odysseus, if his tribe had not settled in their land. Of such a settlement, of which evidence has already been given, the legend of their marriage is at once a result and a proof. And it must have arisen at Mantineia; that is a necessity of the case, as one may see from the parallel instance of Menelaos and Helen. The tradition of their marriage could have arisen only at Sparta; to be quite accurate, at Therapnai, where was her grave and the *Menelaion*. And indeed Homer knows that they came from Sparta.

We have seen how the point of view thus gained affects our impression of the Odyssey as a whole and our theories of its development. By comparing the myth of Penelope's Suitors with other myths of the same kind, especially with the myth of that other Arcadian, Atalante, we arrived by this comparative method at the conclusion that in the original form of the story Odysseus himself was one of the Suitors, the successful Suitor, who marries the princess for whose sake the rest had given their lives. Then another motive inter-

[1] *Early History of the Kingship*, p. 231 f.

vened. Odysseus' people were incomers, invaders; and it was a pretext for their invasion that in reality Odysseus was only returning to his native land, from which for so many years he had been wandering. It was the pretext of the Dorians when they too came to the Peloponnese; 'they were the Children of Herakles restored to his rightful kingdom.' So in the new development of his myth Odysseus became the Returned Wanderer, and, since he was the husband of Penelope, the Returned Husband. And thus it has come about that in the Odyssey we have a fusion of these two most ancient and widespread legendary *motifs*, the legend of the Princess and her Wooers and the legend of the Husband Returned. That this should have happened is after all natural enough. Only, for Ithaca we must substitute, as the earlier scene of the story, Arcadia.

In Arcadia, then, the Odyssey attained the second important stage in its development. To the older Boeotian poetry telling of the wanderings of Odysseus was added a new body of legend: how Penelope was beset by many wooers in the absence of her lord; how at last after many years he returned, unrecognized of all but his faithful dog and swineherd—for this is part of the *motif*—and in the end slew the Suitors and was reunited to Penelope. All this, by far the greater part of the saga as we find it complete in our Odyssey, now gathered shape. We may call it the second or *Arcadian* Odyssey.

I shall not attempt to delimit the content of the Arcadian, any more than the content of the Boeotian, Odyssey, or to sever it from its context in the completed epic. In the main it corresponds to the last twelve books; for, while the *Telemacheia* is clearly dependent to a great extent upon these books, it is not at all clear how much genuine saga is embodied in it. The fact is that every part of the Iliad and Odyssey now reflects every other part, and fragments of Boeotian and Arcadian tradition have become, as it were, displaced. One is tempted, for instance, to think of the Sirens, who of course appear in the *Alkinou Apologos*, as somehow connected with the Bird Penelope; and the same connexion may help to account for the frequency with which Athena throughout the Odyssey assumes the form of a bird. The Prophecy of Teiresias illustrates on its smaller scale what is true of the Odyssey as a whole. It is one of those predictions which are wise with the knowledge of the event. Whoever composed the speech of Teiresias knew of Odysseus' coming to Mantineia, because it can only be the cult of Poseidon there and its fabled foundation by Odysseus that is in the mind of the seer when he bids his consultant go, after the death of the Suitors, among a people ignorant of the sea, and there offer sacrifice to the god. The Prophecy must have had this meaning and this solution for the poet who first recited it and for his hearers. It must have been part of the poetry about Odysseus dealing with his adventures after the killing of the Suitors, the episode with which to all intents our Odyssey ends. Why does our Odyssey end at just that point? It is artistically the right, the effective point. But did the poet who composed the Prophecy compose it for an Odyssey which closed with the killing of the Suitors? Did he not rather compose it for one which contained the fulfilment of the Prophecy? At least he knew, and his audience knew, how it was fulfilled. An ancient tradition, let us say boldly an ancient poem, the sequel to our Odyssey, has been lost.

If we only knew how much of it was incorporated in the *Telegoneia*! Some scholars indeed have spoken of this Kyrenean poem as if it were an attempt of Eugammon to construct, like an historical novelist, out of his own imagination an original story conformable to the hints contained in the prediction of Teiresias. That in effect is what Monro says. But what was the subject, actually, of the *Telegoneia*? The argument in Proclus is so brief that it can be quoted at length. I give it in Monro's own translation.[1] 'After the burial of the suitors Ulysses sacrifices to the nymphs and then goes to visit his herds in Elis, where he is entertained by Polyxenus.

[1] *Odyssey* xiii–xxiv, Appendix, p. 382.

The stories of Trophonios, Agamede, and Augeas are related.[1] After returning to Ithaca to perform the sacrifices prescribed by Teiresias, Ulysses goes to the country of the Thesprotians, marries their queen Callidice, and leads them in a war against the Brygi, in which Ares takes part on behalf of the Brygi, and Athene for Ulysses, while Apollo intervenes as a mediator. On the death of Callidice, Polypoetes, son of Ulysses, becomes king, and Ulysses returns to Ithaca: then Telegonus son of Ulysses by Circe, who had been seeking for his father, makes a descent upon Ithaca. Ulysses comes to repel the attack and is killed by his own son. Telegonus finds too late what he has done, and takes his father's body, with Telemachus and Penelope, to his mother Circe, who makes them immortal. Finally, Telemachus marries Circe, and Telegonus Penelope.'

Teiresias in the Odyssey bids Odysseus go carrying the oar among the inland people and sacrifice among them to Poseidon, and thereafter return home and sacrifice hecatombs to all the gods; and then a gentle death will come upon him out of the sea. But in the *Telegoneia* after the burial of the Suitors[2] Odysseus goes to Elis. Then, says the argument in Proclus, 'after returning to Ithaca to perform the sacrifices prescribed by Teiresias, Odysseus goes to the country of the Thesprotians.' The sacrifices are the 'hecatombs to all the gods' which in Homer follow the incident of the oar. Consequently, if Eugammon followed the order of events in Homer, he must have placed the incident of the oar somewhere between the burying of the Suitors and the return of Odysseus to Ithaca. He must, if he followed Homer, have imagined it as taking place somewhere in the heart of the Peloponnese, since in the interval we are discussing he went there, to Polyxenos, namely, in Elis. Did Eugammon then definitely think of Mantineia as the scene of the offering to Poseidon and the planting of the oar? It is an alluring conjecture,[3] especially in view of the very close connexion in these days between

[1] Monro should have said *Agamedes*. The stories were of Augeias and the brothers Trophonios and Agamedes.

[2] Cf. ω 417.

[3] Made by Svoronos.

Kyrene and the Arcadian town. Yet it is no more than a conjecture and on the whole perhaps, after all, an improbable one. For the Greek commentaries on Homer, whose information may go back ultimately to the *Telegoneia* itself, say that it was in Thesprotia that Odysseus planted the oar, and we are told further that Eugammon embodied in his poem some older poetry attributed to Mousaios and called *Thesprotis*. The natural inference from these two facts—the existence of a tradition that the incident of the oar happened in Thesprotia, and the certainty that the scene in part of Eugammon's epic was laid in the country of the Thesprotians—is that, if the incident occurred at all in the Kyrenean *Telegony*, which Proclus does not say, it must surely have taken place when Odysseus went to Thesprotia. But in that case Eugammon contradicts the Odyssey.

If the *Telegoneia* is an imaginary sequel to our Odyssey, it is a singularly maladroit one. For not only does it apparently displace the affair of the oar from its proper order in the course of events, but its account of the death of Odysseus is also at variance with the words of Teiresias. For the prophet says that the death which is to come from the sea will be gentle, and indeed, by the emphatic idiom he uses,[1] seems to lay a particular stress upon this aspect of the end which is to befall Odysseus as a sort of culmination to the happiness destined for him in these latter days. But in the *Telegoneia* the son of Odysseus and Kirke having landed in Ithaca and ravaged it met his father in battle and slew him. That is perhaps a death that came 'out of the sea': it would be strange to call it a gentle one, even if the spear of Telegonos was not tipped, as certain poets said, with the poisonous spine of the *trygon* or sting-ray.[2] Neither Eugammon nor another

[1] ἀβληχρὸς μάλα τοῖος, λ 135.

[2] The legend of the sting-ray is called in the schol. on λ 134 an invention of οἱ νεώτεροι. Aeschylus gave his own version in the *Psychagogi* (*Fr.* 275). The story has the appearance of an ancient *Märchen*; indeed Aeschylus would never have *invented* so foolish a tale. The loss of the *Psychagogi* is particularly regrettable, as it must have told us much about Odysseus we cannot recover now and much about ancient wizardry, for the Ψυχαγωγοί

has given us the true answer to the prophet's riddling words. Yet the fatal combat between father and son is no invention. Of that, remembering Rustum and Cuchulain, and Hildebrand, we can have no doubt. It is a story much older than any possible 'age of Homer', and, since it does not seem to have been told of any other hero of Greek mythology except Odysseus, it may have been told of him from the first; in which case Homer must have known it. But it is exactly the kind of story Homer cannot tolerate. A story of parricide, nothing less than that! It would be quite in accordance with the usual practice of Homer in these matters if he deliberately avoided direct allusion to the known fate of Odysseus, or, rather, deliberately used an expression, significantly emphatic, which was an implied contradiction of the terrible current tradition. He has the final justification of being right poetically. Not that the slaying, by an unhappy error, of the father by the son may not be made the theme of great poetry; but it seems a still finer stroke of imagination which leaves us dreaming of a soft mysterious death for Odysseus from that sea on which he had endured so much and which, our modern sentiment would fain believe, he had come to love.

Yet, although the poet of the *Telegoneia* has quite clearly not found the true answer to the Prophecy, we are not forced to reject the tradition which placed the incident of the oar in

raised the ghost of some one from the dead, evidently Teiresias, because *Fr.* 275 (Sidgwick) corresponds to his prophecy:

> ἐρωδιὸς γὰρ ὑψόθεν ποτώμενος
> ὄνθῳ σε πλήξει νηδύος κενώμασιν·
> ἐκ τοῦδ' ἄκανθα ποντίου βοσκήματος
> σήψει παλαιὸν δέρμα καὶ τριχορρυές.

Van Leeuwen thinks the *Psychagogi* must have been a Satyric play, to judge from this fragment. It is extremely interesting to find that the Arcadian Phigaleia was especially famous for its ψυχαγωγοί. To them the great Spartan king Pausanias resorted to cleanse him from the stain of blood (Paus. iii. 17. 7). That story must have deeply impressed his contemporaries, including Aeschylus. Was the scene of the *Psychagogi* then Phigaleia? In that case Odysseus would of course recall Pausanias. —It was an ἐρωδιός that Athene sent to comfort Odysseus in K 274. It was a kind of moorfowl, and one cannot but think of the πηνέλοψ. But the evidence is quite insufficient to admit any certain conclusion.

Thesprotia as the invention of Eugammon or some earlier bard. The original scene of the incident was Mantineia, and this earlier form of the tradition had already settled the order of events in the saga when the incident was transferred to Thesprotia, so that the *Telegoneia* was involved, as we saw, in something very like self-contradiction. This is the way of the saga. Romances change their frontiers like nations. It is not impossible that the people of Odysseus, who once placed the affair of the oar in Mantineia, afterwards, when their wanderings had carried them to Ithaca and, as it seems, to Leukas, placed it in Thesprotia. That is at least conceivable and, if it happened, it illustrates a principle which has been made cardinal in all this argument upon the history of the Odyssey: that a tribal legend reflects the fortunes of the tribe, 'its exiles, its flights across the sea,' as Renan said of the Celtic Race in words which apply equally well to the Greeks of the Migrations; that it is in fact an imaginative version of its history (although it is much more than that too); as indeed it is usually the only history the tribe possesses. . . Because it marks the advance of the Odysseus tribe from Arcadia, another illustration of the principle may be appropriately given here. The theft and slaughter of the cows of Helios by the companions of Odysseus finds an analogy in the theft and slaughter of Apollo's kine by Hermes.[1] Now Hermes put the stolen beasts in stall at Pylos by the Alpheios,[2] that is at Pylos of the Minyans. The very route the driven cattle take has evidently its significance, for they come from Pieria past Onchestos into the Peloponnese, and so at last to Pylos, the port for the Western islands.[3] The Minyans knew that road. Thus we can realize a little more definitely than before the relation of Odysseus to Hermes when we know that the people who had Odysseus for their hero told substantially

[1] The recently discovered fragments of Sophocles' *Ichneutai* show that the play dealt with Hermes' theft. But the *Hymn* is of course our main authority.

[2] *Hymn* 101.

[3] Sikes and Allen, Introd. to *Hymn*, p. 131 f. They suggest a Boeotian origin for the Hymn.

the same story of him and of the god. The relation then is ancient and authentic.

If it seems now that a case has been made for the hypothesis of a migration from Boeotia into Arcadia, we shall find that hypothesis useful in explaining certain difficulties in the tradition regarding Odysseus, of which the solution is not at first sight so obvious. We have made great use in this discussion of the *Telegoneia*. We are indebted to the scanty notices of it extant in Greek for the information that it mentioned a son of Odysseus and Penelope named Arkesilaos. The *Telegoneia* was ascribed to Eugammon of Kyrene. Kyrene ranked as a Spartan colony, although its kings, among whom the name Arkesilas was hereditary, claimed Minyan descent. All this we have already discussed. But now what authority ought we to assign to the *Telegoneia*? What were its sources? We know something of these also. There seem to have been at least two. One of them was a poem called the *Thesprotis*, attributed to the mythical Mousaios, for Clement of Alexandria quotes a statement that Eugammon 'stole' the whole of his Thesprotian book, that part of the *Telegoneia* which deals with the adventures of Odysseus in Thesprotia, from Mousaios;[1] and the title *Thesprotis* we get from Pausanias.[2] The other source was evidently an older *Telegoneia* ascribed to Kinaithon the Lacedaemonian.[3] Now, apart from the fact that Kyrene was regarded as a Spartan colony, the intimate relations between it and Sparta have been illustrated by recent excavation. Nothing is more probable than that Eugammon made use of this older Lacedaemonian poem. It has been conjectured that the title *Telegoneia* in the Eusebian Chronicle is corrupt. But the evidence is in favour of its genuineness, for tradition did in fact at a very early period associate Odysseus, or at least Penelope, with Sparta, and we remember that they

[1] *Strom.* vi, p. 266 (628 B). Clement's authority is the Jew Aristoboulos (*flor.* c. 170 B. C.).

[2] Paus. viii. 12. 5.

[3] Euseb. *Chron., ad Olymp.* iv. 2: Cinaethon Lacedaemonius poeta qui Telegoniam scripsit agnoscitur.

had a *Heroon* there. That part of the tradition which represents Ikarios as the father of Penelope and brother of Tyndareos has indeed somewhat the air of a literary fiction, and, if it is one, Kinaithon's poem may well have given it currency. If, on the other hand, it is genuine popular tradition, a Spartan epic is sure to have recognized it. In either case we may regard the *Telegoneia* of Kinaithon (of whom we can say nothing except that he was 'of Sparta', that is, that he wrote of Spartan things, no doubt consciously for the glory of Sparta) as in part an attempt to claim for Lacedaemon as much as he could of the Odysseus legend. Not very much indeed could be done in that way; the Odyssey no doubt even then held the field. But the Odyssey was rather curiously reticent about the ultimate fate of Odysseus and Penelope and Telemachos. Here then was a subject, although a subject certainly without any obvious connexion with Sparta. But in indicating, perhaps in some cases inventing, connexions of saga and locality the early so-called 'post-Homeric' epic poets were all adepts; from the Odes of Pindar alone we could be sure of this. One principal method was genealogy, and ἐγενεαλόγησε γὰρ καὶ οὗτος ἔπεσι, says Pausanias of Kinaithon, 'this poet also genealogized in verse.'[1] If a son of Odysseus settled in Sparta and became the ancestor of a famous race there . . . then the problem was solved. The Odyssey indeed knows only of Telemachos. According to Hesiod Telemachos married Polykaste, the youngest daughter of Nestor, and their son was Persepolis;[2] a story perhaps designed to connect Odysseus with the Neleid princes of Miletos and other Ionian communities, although I think the evidence we have had to consider will make us cautious of rejecting as untrue a tradition of such considerable antiquity linking Odysseus with Pylos. It may not be without significance that the *Telegoneia* of Eugammon, presumably following the old Spartan poem, differed from Hesiod, and seems to have related that, after the death of Odysseus, Penelope and Telemachos were made immortal by Kirke and lived in

[1] ii. 3. 9. [2] *Fr.* 17 (Rzach).

her island—others said in the Islands of the Blest. The extraordinary complication of intermarriages with which Eugammon's poem ended must surely have belonged to a genuine tradition; it is so absurd. Still for him the significant figure in the genealogy of Odysseus was not Telemachos, but Arkesilaos. Now this Arkesilaos must have been a Spartan, or at least his descendants were Spartans, for the Arkesilaoi of Kyrene were derived from Theras of Sparta. There is no reasonable way of connecting Arkesilaos son of Odysseus with Theras, except by making the former a Spartan too, or at the very least connecting him with Sparta; and it is perhaps worth remarking that Arkesilaos is found as a Lacedaemonian personal name.[1] It is altogether likely then that Eugammon found Arkesilaos in the old Spartan *Telegoneia*, even if he sought to enhance his prominence in the story. The likelihood increases with every test applied to it. Arkesilaos of Sparta leads us back to Arkesilaos of Lebadeia, just as Theras of Sparta leads us back to Euphemos of Lebadeia. That cannot be accidental. The line from Lebadeia through Mantineia to Sparta and Kyrene is so clear. Neither, in the circumstances, can it be accident that Odysseus like Euphemos is a hero of Minyan legend.

We learn from the abstract that Eugammon told 'the story of Trophonios and Agamedes'. What the story was we learn from other sources. It closely resembles the Egyptian *Märchen* of King Rhampsinitos and the Thieves as we read it in the second book of Herodotus. Accordingly Professor von Wilamowitz-Moellendorff made the attractive suggestion that the tale of Trophonios and his brother was a Kyrenean contribution to the legend of Odysseus, was in fact the Egyptian story transplanted to Greek soil, Kyrene being the obvious channel for the transmission into Greece of Egyptian influences and beliefs.[2] The legend of Trophonios, however, is not a copy of the Rhampsinitos legend, but a variant of it,

[1] Thuc. v. 50. 4, 76. 3; viii. 39. 2.

[2] *Hom. Unters.* p. 186. Parts of the Odyssey, however, do appear to show some acquaintance with the Kyrenaic coast.

one out of many independent versions of a popular folk-tale[1]; and it appeared in the *Telegoneia*, not because it was current in Egypt, but because Trophonios and Agamedes were heroes of Lebadeia. Charax said that Agamedes, whom he called king of Stymphalos, married Epikaste, and their son was Kerkyon. Trophonios was the son of Epikaste by a former marriage. Agamedes, Trophonios, and Kerkyon together plundered the treasury of Augeias in Elis. Agamedes was caught. But Trophonios cut off his head and fled with Kerkyon to the Boeotian Orchomenos. There they parted, Trophonios proceeding to Lebadeia, Kerkyon to Athens.[2] Here are Trophonios and Agamedes in Arcadia. Another version made Trophonios and Agamedes brothers, sons of Erginos, king of the Minyan Orchomenos. And Pausanias adds that they built the old temple of Poseidon at Mantineia.[3]—We can see how all this would interest a Kyrenean audience.

Pylos to Ithaca: this is the final step in the movement we have sought to trace, and, just because it is the final step, it is that which the epos most clearly remembers. Odysseus is now king in Ithaca; that is how the saga represents the settlement of Ithaca by his people. In the Iliad, Diomedes is king of Argos; that is how the saga represents the coming of his people from Aetolia to the Argolid. The case of Odysseus is not singular, it is normal; it follows one of the rules which governed the growth of the Greek traditions and explain their character. Then he was a wanderer in far lands and seas, and that conception of him, apart from the fact that a god or hero so often migrates with his worshippers, would help men to think of him as prince of some remote island—*πανυπερτάτη εἰν ἁλὶ κεῖται πρὸς ζόφον*—beyond which there is nothing but the sea.[4] Certainly it was a profound artistic instinct working unconsciously within the imagination of the race, or half-consciously within the imagination of its poets, which enclosed within the limits of the little isle, as within the four walls of a house, the drama unfolded, almost too

[1] Many parallels are given in Frazer's note on Paus. ix. 37. 5.
[2] Schol. *Clouds* 508. [3] viii. 5. 5; 10. 1. [4] ι 25.

deliberately for modern readers, in the second half of the Odyssey. We are made to feel with almost painful intensity the loneliness of Odysseus. He is face to face with his enemies now, with no escape and no aid for him or for them. Setting aside the mere telling of the story, which, while admittedly incomparable, is perhaps not always at the same level of mastery, I think this must be accounted one of the most dramatic situations in literature. Yet Odysseus is not king of Ithaca because some poet was pleased to make him so, but because his people conquered it.

That is why Ithaca forms the setting of our Odyssey. From Central Greece the saga of Odysseus had travelled through the Peloponnese to its western coast and so to the islands beyond, gathering fresh additions on the way (being then still capable of growth), never losing much perhaps of the older material but gradually, more or less unconsciously, transforming it. Transformation of this kind was inevitable, and there are many quite certain instances of it. One, which is not quite certain, has been already suggested. It would be a very striking thing if the wanderings of Odysseus in the Boeotian Odyssey were placed in the east like the wanderings of Jason, and were only changed to the west when his people came to Western Greece. We have seen that there is evidence for this which cannot be lightly dismissed. If this theory of a change of scene is accepted as a fair inference from the language of the Odyssey, the migration from Boeotia to Pylos will give the historical explanation. The folk who once dwelt by the Euripos and the Gulf of Pagasai lived now on the shores of a westward-stretching sea; their eyes were turned from the Phasis to Corcyra.

Ithaca itself has added curiously little to the actual content of the saga. A possible faint memory of tribal warfare, in which Laertes captured the stronghold of Nerikos, presumably in the Leucadian peninsula[1]; a certain amount of local colour in the Odyssey drawn, it may be, from personal knowledge of the island: that is all.

[1] ω 377.

Outside the epos there was the tradition, very significant for us, that Odysseus was born near the temple of Athena at Alalkomenai in Boeotia. The *Boiotia* enumerates among the followers of Odysseus at Troy not only Ithacans but Kephallenians and the men of Zakynthos and Samos and, finally, the inhabitants of 'the mainland and the parts opposite',[1] that is, opposite the islands. 'This means', says Strabo, 'that the poet includes Akarnania generally as well as Leukas'[2]; and in effect it must be so. The *Alkmaionis* epic knew of a brother of Penelope called Leukadios, who was the 'founder' of Leukas.[3] This suggests an explanation of the appearance of the seer Theoklymenos in the Odyssey. His genealogy is given at length. He was the son of Polypheides, who was the son of Mantios, who was the son of Melampous.[4] The passage is thought to be an interpolation; but, whether it is original in the Odysseus legend or not, it owes its place to the interest of the poet and his audience in the famous lineage of Theoklymenos. Alkmaion has his place in it as well, for he was the son of Amphiaraos, who was the son of Oikles, who was the son of Antiphates, who was the son of Melampous.[5] Theoklymenos, then, was a Melampodid. Now

[1] B 631 f. [2] p. 453. [3] Strabo, p. 452, quoting Ephoros. [4] *o* 225 f.

[5] The family tree is this:

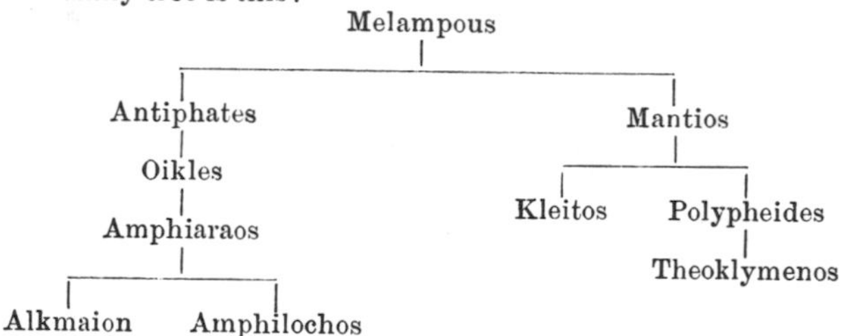

Theoklymenos thus belongs to the generation of Amphiaraos, the age of the Theban War. He could not then be a contemporary of Odysseus. Humanly of course it is possible, but we are not dealing here with historical persons. These genealogies were meant to be, so far, scientific, if we may use so bold a term. They supplied the only chronology of the Heroic Age which the Greeks possessed, and so we are entitled to count the generations carefully. Theoklymenos then seems out of place in the story of Odysseus. Has he been brought in from some other saga, the *Thebaid* or the *Epigoni* or the *Alkmaionis*?

Melampous was the son of Amythaon the son of Aiolos, the ancestor of the Minyan heroes. The *Nekyia* knows the story how Melampous drove the oxen of Iphiklos from Phylake, that his brother Bias might win Pero the daughter of their uncle Neleus.[1] The poet of the fifteenth Book knows it also, and adds that formerly Melampous lived in Pylos,[2] but afterwards ruled in Argos.[3] The legends generally reveal him as a sort of prototype of the missionary priests of Dionysos, and it would be interesting to know what causes worked to produce this conception of him. But what most concerns us here is the fact, admitted in all the legends, that Melampous was a Minyan. The most famous of his descendants was Amphiaraos; he had his oracle at Oropos.[4] The son of Amphiaraos, Alkmaion, the leader of the Epigonoi who conquered Thebes, had a sanctuary in that city.[5] It seems very clear that the history of Melampous and his race began in Boeotia and was part of the Minyan-Boeotian stock of legends. That is why he came to be connected with Pylos the realm of Neleus. Well, Theoklymenos is a descendant of Melampous, and, when he is fleeing from Argos, takes refuge in Pylos, the home of his ancestor. He has every right to appear in the Minyan-Boeotian saga the Odyssey.

Of Alkmaion it was related that after the murder of his mother Eriphyle he fled before her Erinyes, until he came to the little desolate islands at the mouth of the Acheloos called by the Greeks the Echinades, and settled there in obedience to an oracle of Apollo, and in the end became king of the region about Oiniadai, and left a son Akarnan, who gave his name to all this land of *Akarnania*.[6] The brother of Alkmaion was Amphilochos, the reputed founder of Amphilochian Argos and the eponymous hero of the Amphilochians. The *Alkmaionis*, it is assumed, reflected the Corinthian settlements in

[1] λ 285 f. The driving of Iphiklos' cows to Pylos is surely a variant of the Hermes story.

[2] ο 226. [3] ο 239. [4] Rohde, *Psyche*, i. 125, n. 1, 2.

[5] This appears to be the meaning of Pindar, *Pyth.* viii. 57.

[6] Thuc. ii. 102. 5, 6. His authority may have been the *Alkmaionis*; he says τὰ μὲν περὶ Ἀλκμέωνα τοιαῦτα λεγόμενα παρελάβομεν.

Leukas and the neighbouring regions of Akarnania about the end of the seventh century before Christ, and doubtless in its later forms the *Alkmaionis* did reflect these events. But Alkmaion was not a Corinthian hero, neither was his story, although parallel in some of its details to the story of Belleorphon,[1] a Corinthian legend. It must have been current in Akarnania before the Corinthians went there; otherwise it seems inexplicable how it could have arisen at all. The reflection then arises that the settlement of Alkmaion the Melampodid in Akarnania mythologically represents an actual settlement in the lower valley of the Acheloos of the same people who brought the Odysseus legend from Arcadia and Pylos to Ithaca. For the story of Alkmaion connects itself with Arcadia also. He took refuge with Phegeus king of Psophis, who gave him his daughter in marriage; and in Arcadia long afterwards he met his death, and his tomb was shown at Psophis.[2] If then the legend of Alkmaion was carried by the same stream of migration which took the legend of Odysseus to Ithaca, we must think of the stream as flowing on, into the Leukadian island or peninsula and the mainland beyond. This is what the archaeological evidence suggests, and mere probability is quite on the side of the conjecture, which may perhaps explain why Odysseus had an oracle among the Eurytanes, and may be the historical basis of the Thesprotian adventures celebrated in the *Telegoneia*—how he penetrated far into Epiros and fought against the Brygi.

The Odyssey is the saga crystallized at the moment when Odysseus had become king in Ithaca, and had brought with him Penelope and her Suitors, and all the Boeotian and all the Arcadian myths and traditions of which he was the centre.

[1] See *Prolegomena*, p. 220 f.

[2] Euripides wrote a play on the subject, Ἀλκμέων ὁ διὰ Ψωφῖδος.

CHAPTER VII

THE ACHAEANS

Stat magni nominis umbra.

THE conclusion that the Odyssey is an Ionian poem, with only such qualifications of the word Ionian as have been already indicated, is met by two objections, which may seem to invalidate the whole argument we have been elaborating. The first is drawn from the predominance of the *Achaean* name in Homer. The second objection is that the language of Homer is not Ionic, but is, or is based upon, a speech which certainly contained elements definitely non-Ionic. Although they cannot be treated altogether separately, we may begin with the former of these objections. Hitherto I have purposely simplified the argument by speaking of the Odyssey as an entirely Minyan-Ionian poem and of the people whose special inheritance it was as Minyan-Ionians without any mention of Achaean elements in the poem or the people. My intention now is to show, if I can, that the argument does not, owing to this simplification, in any vital way change its character or lose its force.

When Homer has to speak of the Greeks as a whole he calls them the Achaeans or Argeians or Danaans, sometimes 'All the Achaeans', *Παναχαιοί*,[1] and once 'All the Hellenes', *Πανέλληνες*.[2] The usual name is the Achaeans. It has the same meaning and extension as the name Hellenes had in the historical age, or, if not quite the same, it is not the epic use that is the more restricted. We are probably justified in giving a more limited significance to the names in the well-

[1] H 159, I 301, Ψ 236. [2] In the *Catalogue* 530.

known line in the *Catalogue of the Ships* which says of Achilles' men, 'Myrmidons were they called and Hellenes and Achaeans'[1]; and in that other line of the Iliad with which Achilles replies to the promise of Agamemnon's daughter in marriage: 'There be many Achaean women in Hellas and Phthia'[2]; for it was from this district of South Thessaly that the historical Achaeans, according to all the evidence, came. But this use is markedly exceptional in Homer, who when he speaks of the Achaeans means all but invariably the Greek forces as a whole. Consequently scholars have thought themselves entitled to regard the civilization depicted in the Homeric Poems as that of the Achaeans (whether pure Achaean or largely borrowed from the older native culture), and the language of the Poems as substantially or fundamentally the speech of the Achaeans. They think, in short, that the extension of the name Achaeans to cover the entire Greek army at Troy implies the fact of an Achaean conquest of all Greece. But there is exactly the same amount of evidence for this as there would be for concluding from the extension of the name Hellenes in what we call post-Homeric times that all Greece was once subject to the little tribe of the historical Hellenes. The mere use of the name in Homer proves nothing.

If we turn to history for an answer to the question who were the Achaeans, we are involved in a new enigma. There were in historical times Achaeans in three separate parts of the Greek world: in the district of Phthiotis in southern Thessaly, in the district of North Peloponnese called after them Achaia, and in the colonies founded from this Achaia in Lower Italy. That at these three points geographically so far apart they were really the same people, is not doubted by any one. The settlement of the Italian colonies from the Peloponnesian Achaia is matter of history, and that Achaia in its turn had been occupied by an earlier movement of the Phthian Achaeans to Peloponnesos is attested by such evidence as we possess. The recurrence of the name of course would

[1] B 684. [2] I 395.

in itself almost decide the question, the name being here used in its ethnic or tribal sense and not as Homer uses it. But Strabo, following Greek tradition, says definitely of the Achaeans on the Corinthian Gulf, 'They were in origin Achaeans of Phthiotis.'[1] The genealogies made Achaios, the mythical ancestor of these Peloponnesian Achaeans, the son of Xouthos, who was the son of Hellen, who lived in Phthiotis.[2] These then were the Achaeans of history, and history knows of no others. Yet in all three districts—Thessaly, Peloponnesos, Italy—they spoke a language which, if the recovered inscriptions prove anything, was akin to the 'North-Western' group of Greek dialects, which included the Aetolian, Lokrian, and Phokian, and is akin to Doric. It is in no sense the language of Homer in any possible stage of its development. It reveals radical dialectic variations from Aeolic and Ionic. Are we then to conclude from the linguistic evidence that the Achaeans were not an Aeolian race at all?

The distinguished scholars who have made a study of the Greek Dialects have felt the difficulty and have tried to solve it. They point out that, although the inscriptions from Phthiotis are in a North-Western speech, none of them is really ancient, while some of the later were composed in the days of the Aetolian League and would therefore not unnaturally be in the Aetolian dialect; while some scholars think that the evidence warrants the belief that the Phthiotian dialect possessed the Thessalian-Aeolic usage of the patronymic.[3] Originally then, it is argued, this Phthiotian Achaean speech was Aeolic, but at some unknown period, probably at the time of the Thessalian conquest, when, as Herodotus says, 'the Thessalians came from Thesprotia to dwell in the

[1] p. 383.

[2] The interesting suggestion has been made that the name given to Greek Italy ἡ μεγάλη Ἑλλάς originated with the Achaean colonies, who may have thought of the Thessalian Hellas, which was to all intents only another name for Phthiotis, as in some sense their *metropolis*. Ed. Meyer, *Forsch.* i. 111.

[3] Cauer, *Grundfragen*, pp. 213, 214. Cf. Fick in Collitz.

Aeolian land'[1]; or even earlier, when fragments of other tribes of North-Western origin and speech may have invaded Phthiotis, the Achaeans dwelling there adopted the idiom of the invaders.[2] In the Peloponnesian Achaia a quite different set of circumstances, it is supposed, combined to produce the same result. The Achaean inhabitants of the Aigialos also at first spoke Aeolic, but came in time to be so permeated by Dorian and Aetolian influences, that they accepted a dialect very like the Aetolian. If this be granted, it is not so hard to explain the Doric affinities of the inscriptions from the Achaean colonies in the south of Italy. For these, as the name we give them implies, were in the main founded from the Peloponnesian Achaia: Kroton from Rhypes,[3] Sybaris from Helike[4] and Trozen,[5] Kaulonia from Aigion,[6] and so with the rest. Afterwards there seems to have been an influx of Dorian settlers who mingled with the original colonists from Achaia, for Pausanias mentions a Lacedaemonian colony to Kroton,[7] and Antiochos said that the district of the Siritis was occupied by Dorians of Taras as well as by Achaeans of Thurii.[8]

It is probable that the scholars who offer these explanations do not find them very satisfactory. They are in fact so little satisfactory that they will scarcely bear examination. Expert opinion decides that, so far as the inscriptional evidence goes, it is certain the Achaeans of historical times did not speak an Aeolic or Ionic tongue, although it is not so certain whether we ought to class the Achaean speech with the North-Western or the Doric group of dialects.[9] The expert must be allowed to decide the question of fact, but the reasons—which must be in the main purely historical reasons—for this striking fact it is rather the student of history who is entitled to decide: at least the historical evidence must be considered.

[1] vii, p. 176. [2] Cf. O. Hoffmann, *Die griech. Dial.* ii, *Einleitung* 7.
[3] Antiochos in Strabo, p. 262 f. Cf. Herod. viii. 47.
[4] Strabo, p. 263. [5] Arist. *Pol.* viii (v). 2, 10.
[6] Paus. vi. 3. 5. [7] iii. 3. 1.
[8] Strabo, p. 264. Cf. Hoffmann, *Dial.* i. 9. 10.
[9] A. Thumb, *Handbuch d. griech. Dial.*, p. 166, § 178.

To begin then with the Achaeans of Phthiotis, we found that they, if any, formed the original stock. They had always been there so far as our positive knowledge reaches, and there they remained throughout Greek history. The Thessalians came from the West and conquered the land thereafter named Thessaly. Yet even against them the Achaeans maintained a measure of independence, as is implied in the special mention of them in Herodotus side by side with the Thessalians.[1] The latter, themselves speaking a North-Western dialect, adopted the Aeolic speech of the tribes they conquered. Is it likely that they imposed their dialect on the Achaeans whom they did not, or did not so completely, subdue? Is it likely that, with a tenacity contrasting strangely with their previous impressionability, the Achaeans retained the speech of the Thessalians after the Thessalians themselves had lost it? With Peloponnesian Achaia the case is somewhat different. It is not so obviously unlikely that here Dorian and, especially, Aetolian influences were strong enough to convert an Aeolic-speaking race into speakers of a 'Doric' dialect. Yet here also the historic probabilities are strong against this hypothesis. We never hear of any actual settlement of Dorians or Aetolians in Achaia. The political isolation of this part of the Peloponnese is one of the singular things of Greek history. Why should this state, so independent always, so jealous of Dorian influence in times of which we know something, accept an alien idiom? These Achaeans were never conquered as the ancient realm of Nestor was conquered by the Eleans. Yet the Eleans were not able to impose their dialect on the inhabitants of Triphylia. And one would think that, if the Achaeans had indeed lost their ancient speech, the loss could not have been so absolute but some trace of the older idiom would betray itself even in the scanty remains of the Achaean dialect. Yet none has been discovered. The name *Poseidonia* indeed, given to a colony of Achaean Sybaris[2]—Poseidonia is the Roman Paestum—seems like an Aeolism, because it embodies the Ionic-Aeolic form of the god's name with σ for the Doric τ. But we

[1] vii. 132. [2] Strabo, p. 252.

cannot tell how strong Ionian influences may have been in Sybaris. And there are other possibilities. The discovery of a silver plate at Poseidonia with the words: 'I belong to the Girl Goddess (*Παῖς*)', suggests that Arcadians dwelt there, for the worship of Hera *Pais* was a Stymphalian cult.[1] For Arcadians, Poseidonia would be a correct form.—But what seems most unlikely of all in the hypothesis that the Achaeans in their early history spoke Aeolic is just this circumstance that, wherever we find them, in districts widely apart as Thessaly and Peloponnesos and Magna Graecia, they are found speaking essentially the same dialect. If that is a mere coincidence it is a very remarkable one. But when the supposed change of dialect in Phthiotis is ascribed to one set of unattested assumptions, and the change in North Peloponnese, which must have taken place very early, before the Achaean colonization of South Italy, to another and totally different set equally unattested and, as we have seen, not even probable; we can scarcely regard this as a satisfactory explanation of the facts. Coincidences equally strange happen in life, but we ought not to make our hypotheses dependent on their happening. For those who believe that the Achaeans did once speak Aeolic the less heroic course followed by Eduard Meyer is surely wiser—to admit that the facts have never been explained. The alternative view is that the facts require no explanation, that the Achaeans were from the first a 'Doric'-speaking people, and that their affinities by race were what they were by speech.[2]

It must be confessed that the general opinion of those most competent to judge is that the Achaeans were an Aeolian people. This view rests upon more than one ground of belief. These grounds are mainly historical; but one is philological. According to Fick, *Ἀχ-αιϝοί = Αἴϝο-λοι, Αἰολεῖς*.[3] If 'Aeolian' is a by-form of 'Achaean', why then of course Achaeans and Aeolians were one and the same. Only it must be admitted that Fick's equation is not certain; and in philo-

[1] Paus. viii. 22. 2. [2] See Additional Note, p. 237.
[3] *Ilias*, p. 561 f.

logical matters above all others what is not certain is so very likely to be wrong! We ought not then to lay stress upon this argument, unless it can be made very probable for other reasons that Achaeans and Aeolians were identical; although, if that can be done, the philological argument will be very nearly decisive.—Let us then proceed to the historical evidence. The name *Aeolian* connects itself especially with the most northerly of the Greek settlements on the western sea-board of Asia Minor. Now it is certain that the founders of the Aeolian colonies came in the main from southern Thessaly and from Boeotia, countries where the Aeolian name persisted, at least in tradition. But South Thessaly, the cradle of the Aeolian race, was also the ancient home of the Achaeans. And since Aeolians and Achaeans came from the same district, are they not likely to have been the same people? That is the argument. But how little weight it carries must be felt by every student of early Greek history, and it is perhaps especially valueless when we are dealing with just this region of southern Thessaly, which harboured at various times so many different tribes. So we come to the traditions. Now it is true that the Achaean and Aeolian legends are at many points curiously interlaced. For example, although criticism in such material is very precarious, we may for the present assume that, since he reigned in Phthia and led to Troy the people whom we regard as 'true', historical Achaeans, Achilles was an Achaean. It is still possible that he was not himself originally an Achaean at all; he may have been adopted—there is nothing inherently improbable in the suggestion—as their hero or tribal god, by the Achaeans from some other race. But let us assume that he was an Achaean. We can trace the legend of Achilles from Phthiotis to Pharsalos, where there was a *Thetideion*, and to Pelion, where dwelt Peleus his father, the Man of the Mountain, and where Cheiron instructed his youth. From this region of Magnesia he passes to Skyros, and finally we hear of him fighting in Lesbos and Troyland. Well, this progress from the Pagasaean Gulf to Lesbos and the opposing coast may be a reflection, a mythological simplification, of the historical movement or series of movements which culminated in the settlement of Aeolis,[1] and Achilles did in fact become in some sort a marine deity of the Aeolian colonies and a divine director of their own subsequent colonizing enterprises. Yet the circumstance that the Aeolians worshipped an Achaean god would not prove that they were themselves Achaeans; or by the same reasoning we should have to conclude that, because the Lacedaemonians worshipped him, he was a Dorian. Neither is the fabled descent of the Penthilidai of Mitylene from Orestes conclusive of anything. For, apart from the fact that Orestes was not originally an Achaean in the strict tribal sense at all, it was not from the Peloponnese, as the story of Penthilos implies, but from Central Greece that the movement to Aeolis started.[2] Everywhere we test it, the evidence appears thus weak and indecisive. We must add that the Aeolians themselves did not claim to be the Achaeans. When one thinks of the tenacity of tribal memories, at least of Greek tribal memories, in matters of this sort, and the temptation there was to claim descent from Homer's warriors, it seems impossible that, if they were the genuine representatives of these Achaeans, the Aeolians could have been ignorant of their high origin, and almost incredible that, if they knew this, they did not proclaim it with trumpets.

It is not then apparently so much any positive historical evidence which has created the conviction that the Achaeans must have been Aeolians as the seeming probability, amounting, it might be thought, to something like a logical necessity, that the Homeric Achaeans must have been represented in later times by the Aeolic-speaking races of Greece. For those who agree with Fick that the Homeric Poems were originally composed in Aeolic no conclusion could be more welcome. But now it is generally thought that Fick has not proved his case. He has set us on the right track, but he has not proceeded far enough upon it; we must advance beyond Ionic,

[1] The occupation of the Troad is a different and a later event.
[2] Strabo, p. 582; Paus. iii. 2. 1; ii. 18. 7.

beyond Aeolic, to a speech more ancient than either. But even if Fick is right, if the Achaeans spoke Aeolic, and *Aioleis* is equivalent to *Achaioi*, the historian will still have to ask whether the Achaeans did not perhaps acquire Aeolic, or the Aeolians adopt the Achaean name. For, as we saw, Homer does not help us in this matter. For him all Greeks without distinction are Achaeans, and while it is true that the Ionian and Dorian names scarcely occur in him, it is also true that the Aeolian name does not occur at all.[1] What then can we appeal to but the principle, 'Whatever is not Ionian or Dorian must be Aeolian'? Thus Strabo speaks of the Peloponnesian Achaeans as *Αἰολικὸν ἔθνος*.[2] But it does not follow because the Achaeans were neither Ionians nor Dorians that they must therefore be Aeolians. Professor Ridgeway, for instance, thinks they were Celts. Waive this objection, we ought at least to state the problem clearly. If we are using the term 'Dorians' in its narrower signification, we have still to consider whether the Achaeans may have been, not Aeolians, but a people of North-Western affinities. But if, on the other hand, we include the North-Western races as Dorians, we are assuming without proof that the Achaeans were not in this sense Dorians. The linguistic evidence suggests that they were.

We must therefore weigh this suggestion. And, apart from the question of dialect, the evidence altogether favours the opinion that the Achaeans entered Greece from the North-West, vaguely defined regions of Epiros and Illyria. When Achilles at Troy prays to the god of his people, he uses the famous formula: 'Lord Zeus! Pelasgian! God of Dodona thy far-off dwelling-place!'[3] The Achaean chief thinks of the god of his tribe as still abiding in Dodona of Epiros, and we conjecture that at some earlier time the Achaeans of Phthia dwelt in the neighbourhood of that place of ancient holiness, before they threaded the passes of Pindos and

[1] He knows indeed of Aiolos as an ancestor, e.g. Σίσυφος Αἰολίδης, Z 154 and Kretheus, λ 237.

[2] p. 333.

[3] Π 233.

descended upon Thessaly. Pyrrhos-Neoptolemos the son of Achilles is represented in the tradition as going after the fall of Troy to his father's realm in Phthia (where the Odyssey speaks of him as ruling among the Myrmidons),[1] and as taking with him Andromache, who bore him a son in Pharsalos, namely Molossos, who gave his name to the Epirote tribe of the Molossians.[2] Another tradition makes her follow Neoptolemos to Epiros itself, where she became the mother of Kestrinos, who gave his name to the region called Kestrine. The kings of Epiros traced their descent from Neoptolemos, and Pyrrhos was an hereditary name among them; it was through his mother, the Epirote princess Olympias, that Alexander the Great had the right to claim Achilles for his ancestor. It may be that these genealogies have no historical value, although the explanation of them often suggested—that Epirote chieftains in 'post-Homeric' but still very early times were able to persuade Greek poets to pervert the genuine Greek traditions, as here and in the case of the *Telegoneia*, and to get Greek audiences to accept these perversions invented for the glory of such half-civilized 'barbarians', is to my mind quite incredible. In any event there is plenty of evidence from other quarters which might justify this looking back from Phthiotis to the lands washed by the Ionian Sea. It is gathered together in Professor Ridgeway's book, *The Early Age of Greece*. Whether one accepts or not all the conclusions which he draws from the great accumulation of facts assembled there, it is difficult now to reject the hypothesis that the migration of the Achaeans was from the North-West; and I think most scholars now accept this. But if the Achaeans came from the North-West, one must expect their affinities to be with the North-Western peoples. For, so far as our knowledge goes, the Aeolic-speaking tribes did not enter Greece from the North-West. We assumed that they did, because we thought that the Achaeans were the ancestors of the Aeolians. But the actual ancestors of the Aeolians may

[1] δ 9.

[2] Tzetzes on Lykophron 1263, quoting the *Little Iliad* = *Fr.* 18 Kinkel.

have come in rather from the North-East; it is in fact a more probable view than the other.

The advance of the Achaeans has an instructive parallel, as Ridgeway points out,[1] in the advance into Greece of the Thessaloi, the true Thessalians. These, we know, came from the North-West, for Herodotus, having occasion to speak of a prehistoric wall at Thermopylai, mentions that it was built by the Phokians 'when the Thessalians came from Thesprotis to dwell in the land called Aiolis, which indeed they now possess'.[2] The head of Zeus of Dodona appears on the coinage of the Thessalian Confederacy.[3] Well, coming from Epiros, and speaking doubtless a dialect of the North-Western type, these Thessaloi or Petthaloi became the overlords of the land which still bears their name, but settled perhaps in especial strength in that division of it called Thessaliotis. They must have encountered and possibly they broke the power of the Phthiotian Achaeans. Yet the Achaeans retained some shadow of independence, above all they retained their 'Doric' dialect, even after the Thessalians lost theirs. If I am not allowed to argue that the Achaean speech was always thus non-Aeolic, I may at least urge that so close a parallel between the history of the Achaean immigration, so far as it can be reconstructed, and that of the Thessalian invasion altogether supports the view that the two peoples were racially akin, succeeding waves of that great southward-flowing tide of the North-Western tribes which we accept as historical.

Let us turn a new light upon the question. We may do this if we consider the history of the Hellenes and the reasons for the predominance acquired by the name *Hellenes* over other tribal names throughout Greece. In Homer, in the *Catalogue* at least, the Hellenes are counted among the subjects of Achilles, seem indeed indistinguishable except in name from his Achaeans. Yet some distinction there may have been, for in one context at any rate Hellas is different from Phthia, since it says there that Phoinix fled from the former

[1] *Early Age*, i. 340 f.
[2] vii. 176. 4.
[3] 196 B.C. B. Head, *Hist. Num.*, p. 264.

into the latter.[1] Hellas in those days was perhaps south of the Spercheios, reaching down to Boeotia, seeing that Autolykos of Parnassos stole the head-dress mentioned in the *Doloneia*, with its gleaming ring of boar tusks, from Amyntor Ormenides the father of Phoinix.[2] The situation in historical times is only so far different that Hellas is a part of Phthiotis or not distinguishable from Phthiotis itself, and to say Hellenes is in fact to say Achaeans. Although there is some confusion in the testimony, due I imagine to a shifting of population from the Spercheios valley to the more northerly Phthiotis of Herodotus' time, what Homer says agrees well enough with these facts of later history. The main point is that for him also the distinction between Hellenes and Achaeans is almost nominal and tends to disappear. If then we could learn something of the origin and racial connexions of the Hellenes, we should be able to cast a great illumination upon the race and history of the Achaeans. Unhappily here also we must be content with scanty and somewhat indistinct evidence. Yet Aristotle, a sufficient authority, says that the original land of the Hellenes was the region 'about Dodona and the Acheloos', where they were called, not as now Hellenes, but *Graikoi*.[3] The change of name came in the days of Hellen the son of Deukalion, and Aristotle, herein contradicting the more familiar tradition, puts the scene of Deukalion's Flood at Dodona.[4] A fragment of the Hesiodic poem called *Eoiai*[5] gives to Dodona the name *Hellopia*, and this, with some other evidence, has occasioned the conjecture that the true form of the name Selloi, who are known to Homer as the priests who served the Dodonaean Zeus,[6] is *Helloi* and reappears in *Hellenes*.[7] That indeed is no more than a conjecture, but the evidence of Aristotle may stand by

[1] I. 447 f.

[2] 266 f. See T. W. Allen, *J. H. S.* xxx (1910), p. 292 f.

[3] *Meteor.* i. 352 A αὕτη (i. e. ἡ Ἑλλὰς ἡ ἀρχαία) δ' ἐστὶν ἡ περὶ Δωδώνην καὶ τὸν Ἀχελῷον . . . ᾤκουν γὰρ οἱ Σελλοὶ ἐνταῦθα καὶ οἱ καλούμενοι τότε μὲν Γραικοὶ νῦν δ' Ἕλληνες.

[4] Cf. Plut. *Pyrrh.* 1. [5] Kinkel 150. [6] Π 234.

[7] Ed. Meyer, *Forsch.* i. 37 f. Schol. Π 234 says Πίνδαρος Ἑλλοὶ χωρὶς τοῦ σ ἀπὸ Ἑλλοῦ τοῦ δρυτόμου, ᾧ φασι κτλ.

itself. It exactly agrees with the conclusion we have adopted regarding the origin of the Achaeans. We can scarcely be wrong in assuming that Achaeans and Hellenes came together from the regions about Dodona to their new settlements in Thessaly, when even in heroic times, in the days of 'Amyntor Ormenides', we find them living side by side and, according to the *Catalogue,* following a single overlord to war.

There is yet another thread of evidence we may disentangle and follow to some result. In a well-known passage Herodotus tells us that the Dorian race was distinguished from the Ionian by the greater extent of its wanderings. 'In the reign of Deukalion the Dorians dwelt in the land of Phthiotis, but during the reign of Doros the son of Hellen in the region called Histiaiotis beneath Ossa and Olympos. And when they were driven out of Histiaiotis by Kadmeians, they dwelt in the mountain-country of Pindos and were called a Makednian'—that is, apparently, a Macedonian—'race. From here they migrated again, this time into Dryopis, and from Dryopis they came at last into Peloponnesos and were called Dorian.'[1] This account of Herodotus is, as it stands, somewhat perplexing; for that the Dorians pursued so strange a course, first northward and then southward, is difficult to believe. It seems far more likely that their earliest Greek home was the range of Pindos,[2] and that, as they advanced upon their southward wanderings, they occupied successively the regions named by the historian, Histiaiotis, Phthiotis, and 'Dryopis', the land anciently held by the Dryopes, but now to be called Doris. Why Herodotus describes Histiaiotis as 'under Ossa and Olympos' is unknown. Perhaps it is a mistake. But it is a fairly accurate description of the Histiaiotis we read of elsewhere to call it 'under Pindos', and with this correction his account certainly becomes more intelligible. Aigimios king of the Dorians

[1] i. 56.

[2] A place in Doris was called Pindos (Her. viii. 43), and this may have led Herodotus to bring the Dorians by way of the like-named range. I owe this observation to Mr. A. J. Toynbee.

lived, according to the legend, in Thessaly, where he made war against the Lapiths; and Pindar speaks of the Dorians as having dwelt of old on Pindos [1]; while a place in Doris was called *Pindos*: so that it appears safe to conclude that at an early period the Dorians did inhabit the great range which separates Thessaly from Epiros. Subsequently, as we know, they occupied the hilly country of Doris between Oita and Parnassos. The Dorians of the Peloponnese, the Spartans at any rate, always looked back to Doris as their ancient home. 'Zeus himself', says Tyrtaios,[2] 'has given this state to the Sons of Herakles, with whom we left windy Erineos and came to the broad Island of Pelops.'[3] But Herodotus also says that the Dorians once lived in Phthiotis, 'when Deukalion was king.' Historians reject that statement; it was a fiction, they think, intended to connect the Dorians by an especially close relationship with the Hellenes of Phthia, who, as Thucydides remarks,[4] were the original Hellenes.[5] But Herodotus is evidently right. The ancient Hellas may be identified roughly with the valley of the Spercheios.[6] The Dorians settled on the slopes of Oita, whose base is washed by the river. If we perceive that Herodotus is following the topography of the epos,[7] we see that he is substantially accurate in saying that the Dorians inhabited Phthiotis, the Phthia of Achilles. It is a minor matter that his chronology is almost certainly wrong. One suspects an attempt to show that in occupying this region the Dorians were only reconquering their

[1] *Pyth.* i. 66. The epic *Aigimios* was attributed to Hesiod. [2] *Fr.* 2.

[3] Cf. Her. viii. 21 'This country (Doris) is the *metropolis* of the Dorians in the Peloponnese'. Also Thuc. i. 107. That is as much as we can safely assume regarding the wanderings of the Dorians. The suggestion of Prof. J. L. Myres that in Homeric times they were living in the gap of the mainland between the confederacies of Priam and Agamemnon is interesting, *J. H. S.* (1907), p. 177 f. If it is right, it takes us back, as the geography of the *Boiotia* so often seems to do, to an age surely much earlier than that reflected in the Homeric Poems as a whole.

[4] i. 3.

[5] Busolt, *Gr. Gesch.* i, p. 59 f. Cf. E. Meyer, *Gesch. d. Alt.* ii. 171 A.

[6] Still sometimes called the Elládha. *Prehistoric Thessaly*, p. 255.

[7] He probably used some old epic for his sketch of the early history of the Dorians.

Canaan, returning to the land of their fathers. They made that claim, we remember, when they invaded the Peloponnese.

We have found then that the migration of the Dorians from Pindos is in all respects comparable to the migration of the Achaeans and Hellenes from Epiros, so that the one movement is like a reproduction of the other. We have also found that the Achaeans in historical times had a dialect akin to Doric. Then, Achaeans, Hellenes and Dorians of Doris—the 'original' Achaeans and Hellenes and Dorians—remained for centuries in occupation of neighbouring lands and on the same general, comparatively low, level of culture. Now, since the Dorians strongly asserted kinship with Hellenes and Achaeans, claiming to be in some more intimate way than Ionians a 'Hellenic' race, we have already learned enough to make it imperative for us to consider how far the Dorian claim can be substantiated.

It was very ancient. According to the genealogy in Hesiod, Hellen was the son of Deukalion and the father of Doros, Xouthos and Aiolos.[1] But at first perhaps he was the father of Doros only. For Aiolos, as appears from Homer, was really the son of Hippotes, while Xouthos is brought in to harmonize the lineage of Ion with the race of Hellen; for Ion, according to one story, was the son of Apollo, and according to another, the brother of Achaios; a heraldic way of saying that the Ionians of Asia came from the Peloponnesian Achaia. Thus, in order that Achaios and Ion might be affiliated to Hellen, they were made the sons of a shadowy Xouthos, who in turn was called the son of Hellen. If this is the right explanation of it, the Hesiodic genealogy reflects the gradual extension of the name Hellenes from the 'Doric'-speaking races to the Aeolian and Ionian. Nothing could be more significant. It is implied in Herodotus' distinction of the Dorians as a 'Hellenic', the Ionians as a 'Pelasgian' race.[2] Then, the Spartan kings regarded themselves as Achaean. 'O woman,' said Kleomenes to the priestess on the Akropolis of Athena, 'I am not a Dorian I tell you, but an

[1] *Fr.* 25 Kinkel. [2] i. 56.

Achaean!'[1] It does not appear that the claim was disputed, and it is quite distinct from the pretence of descent from Herakles, which is evidently a later literary invention: the priestess merely held it to be irrelevant. 'It was not lawful for a Dorian to enter the shrine of the goddess,' and, whatever Kleomenes might say, he appeared to the priestess to be a Dorian. Why should it appear so strange to us that Kleomenes believed himself to be an Achaean? Only because we have made an inference from Homer. It is an inference unsupported even by his language, and quite unsupported by history, which, to speak plainly, is ignorant of any 'Achaean Conquest' of the dimensions we suppose. It remembers, however, a Dorian Conquest. Yet doubtless the evidence of Homer too would prove helpful, if we could make sure of interpreting it rightly. He knows of Dorians in Crete. There, the disguised Odysseus says to Penelope, are 'Achaeans and Eteokretans and Kydonians and Dorians and Pelasgians'.[2] There is a precision in this language which makes it almost certain that here the name 'Achaeans' has the restricted meaning we do sometimes find in Homer. We may probably take it that these were Achaeans of pure blood. Yet the theory of an Achaean conquest of Crete, if you believe that the Achaeans were a non-Dorian people, is surely untenable. We know a 'Minoan' Crete and we know a Dorian Crete, and archaeologists, who can trace an immense evolution of the old culture, find it pass at last without any intermediate stage, any important traces of a third culture, into the Dorian. Now if Achaeans and Dorians possessed the same type of culture, this difficulty vanishes. And the overwhelmingly Doric character of the Cretan dialects is now more easily explained.

Or we may approach the question from the opposite side by considering whether it is possible to discover a deeply penetrating difference between Achaeans and Aeolians, since, if we can do that, it will destroy the *prima facie* case against the hypothesis that the Achaeans were a North-Western people. . . . The origin of the name 'Aeolian' is obscure. It

[1] *Ὦ γύναι, ἀλλ' οὐ Δωριεύς εἰμι ἀλλ' Ἀχαιός*, v. 72.

[2] *τ* 172 ff.

may have come into prominence first in Asia Minor, as the need for some distinctive appellation for the more northerly colonies in contrast with Ionia accentuated itself. Yet even in that case it is not likely to be an invention of the settlers or their neighbours. It is far more probable that an ancient tribal name to which they had some right survived or re-asserted itself among the colonists. In the main the founders of Aeolis came from South Thessaly and Boeotia; we may take this as perhaps the one certain conclusion to be elicited from the complicated foundation legends whose more exact historical import it is so difficult to elucidate. The dialect of Lesbos and the Aeolian coast of Asia is most nearly akin to Thessalian and Boeotian. Lesbos was first occupied, tradition said, by Gras, who must be the *eponymos* of the Graes living on the lower reaches of the Boeotian Asopos.[1] The starting-point of the colonists was Aulis, men said, perhaps remembering that it was from Aulis Agamemnon set sail for Troy. So many Boeotians took part in the settlement of Aeolis that it was actually called *Boiotike*[2]; while Thucydides more than once refers to the close connexion between it and Boeotia.[3] But although the colonists seem to have come chiefly from Boeotia, some undoubtedly came from Southern Thessaly, or at least remembered a former Thessalian home, for we find at the foot of Mount Sipylos a town called Magnesia, and the mountain-peak which dominates Lesbos was called Olympos. And there may have been men from Phokis among them.[4] Now Herodotus, in a passage already quoted, says that, before the Thessaloi came from Thesprotia, Thessaly was called *Aiolis*. And in a fragment of Theopompos preserved in Stephen of Byzantium we hear of Chalkidians of Euboea making war upon the 'Aeolians of the mainland', Chalioi and Boiotoi and men of Orchomenos and Thebes.[5] Then again,

[1] Strabo, p. 582. [2] Strabo, p. 374, from Ephoros.

[3] vii. 57; viii. 100. Cf. iii. 2.

[4] *α χελληστυς α Φωκεων*, inscription from Methymna. Collitz, *Gr. Dialektinschr.* 277.

[5] *Αἰολεῦσι τοῖς τὴν ἤπειρον ἔχουσι* Χαλίοις *καὶ* Βοιωτοῖς *καὶ* Ὀρχομενίοις *καὶ* Θηβαίοις, *Fr.* 237 Steph. Byz. *s. v.* Χαλία.

Herodotus mentions *Αἰολίδαι* in Phokis,[1] and Thucydides speaks of the Aetolian Plain as 'the Aeolian land now called Kalydon and Pleuron'.[2] Call all this, if you please, a reflection of the name from Asia Minor to Greece; yet, even if it be no more, we have gained an indication of the lands from which in the Greek belief the Aeolians of Asia drew their origin. The probability, however, is that the Aeolian name did first arise in Central Greece. Thus, although Homer never speaks of Aeolians, he knows of Aiolos and his sons, whose fame was celebrated in the ancient epic of Argo. Aiolos was connected in legend and rite with Alos in Phthiotis.[3] And the sons named by Homer are Kretheus, the founder of Iolkos, and Sisyphos of Ephyra, that is Corinth, which Thucydides calls 'Aeolian'. It was from this Aiolos of Thessaly that the Aeolian race, according to the myth, was descended. Of his sons, besides Kretheus of Iolkos[4] and Sisyphos, who represents the Aėolian element in early Corinth, we hear of Athamas and Salmoneus, Deion, Magnes, and Perieres.[5] Athamas was king in Orchomenos. Salmoneus migrated to Elis, where he built a city called after his name Salmone in Pisatis, the land of Nestor's Pylians, while his daughter Tyro was the mother of Pelias and Neleus. That is to say, these by far the most famous of the sons of Aiolos are all, or all but Sisyphos, Minyan heroes. Not one of them is an Achaean. For the rest, Deion represents the older 'Aeolian' population of Phokis before the coming of the North-Western tribes, including the Phokians of history; Perieres begat Aphareus and Leukippos and Tyndareos and Ikarios, who are all pre-Achaean; and Magnes is the name-hero of Magnesia, the land of the Minyans of Iolkos. And if any one cares to follow out the histories of the five daughters of Aiolos who were Kanake and Alkyone, Peisidike, Kalyke, and Perimede, he will find that they are quite obviously invented to account for an ancient domination of pre-Achaean

[1] viii. 35.
[2] iii. 102.
[3] Her. vii. 197.
[4] λ 237. Apollod. *Bibl.* i. 9. 11.
[5] *Bibl.* i. 7. 3. 3 f.

'Aeolians' in Thessaly and Naxos (the Aloadai), in Trachis (Keyx), in Aetolia (Endymion). If it should seem strange that Perimede is the wife of Acheloos, we may remember that Thucydides says that the district of Kalydon was once Aeolian. Peisidike indeed is the wife of 'Myrmidon', and the Myrmidons were Achilles' men. That is no doubt the result of a natural tendency to connect the invading Achaean tribes with the older population of Phthia. Nor does Peisidike in any real sense belong to the living tradition; she is no mother of famous heroes; and after all she is not herself of the blood of the Myrmidons. The evidence of the legends, then, is quite wonderfully emphatic and consistent. The 'Aeolians' were not Achaean but evidently pre-Achaean.

History speaks in the same sense. Neither Aeolians nor Ionians ever claimed to be Achaeans. Herodotus, who knew the old epic literature so well, in his reconstruction of early Greek history has no place at all for an 'Achaean Conquest'. He shows us the interaction of 'Pelasgian' Ionians, inhabiting Greece from times out of mind, and Dorians, descending from the north and gradually expanding over southern Hellas. No doubt this is a simplification of the facts. But the simplification would be intolerable if a race neither Ionian nor Dorian did at one time dominate the Greek world from Oloosson to Cyprus. The truth is that Herodotus, while of course he distinguishes between Dorians and Achaeans, groups them together in dealing with the broad divisions of the Greek nation. Achaeans and Dorians are alike invaders from the north,[1] Ionians are *autochthones*. The Spartan kings were sons of Herakles and Achaeans. As for the ancient 'Aeolian' population of the Greek mainland, Herodotus has scarcely anything to say of them: but he does not speak of them as Achaeans. In describing the ritual at Alos he tells how Athamas 'the son of Aiolos' contrived the death of Phrixos, and 'afterwards' the Achaeans in consequence of an oracle enjoined the curious ceremony upon the descendants of

[1] Cf. the story of Architeles and Archandros. Paus. ii. 6. 5; vii. 1. 6 f. Cf. Her. ii. 98.

Aiolos.[1] Here the Aeolians are the older inhabitants of the land, the Achaeans are invaders. The account given by Herodotus is that of the people of Alos themselves. They were Achaeans; and they did not regard themselves as sons of Aiolos. It was Athamas, they said, who was his son, and Athamas in the usual form of the tradition was the son of Minyas; in either case no Achaean. Athamas, indeed, if any one, is a Minyan, and it has been argued that Aiolos was originally the ancestor of the Argonauts. This perhaps does not mean that Aiolos was a Minyan, but, if it means anything, it must mean that the Minyans were in some sense Aeolians; and in fact where we do seem to find Minyans, in Triphylia for example, they speak Aeolic. The unmistakable trend, then, of the Greek evidence is in the direction of dissociating the Achaeans from the Aeolians and associating them with the Dorians.

The recent excavations in Boeotia and Thessaly have led archaeologists to certain conclusions regarding the early culture and ethnology of these regions which are extremely important for this Achaean question.[2] A surprisingly sharp and distinct line can be drawn between a northern and a southern culture, the former long continuing on a barbarous level, the latter, which centred mainly in Orchomenos, quite different in character and infinitely more advanced. A certain kind of ware found abundantly at Orchomenos has received the name of 'Minyan', because it may be contemporary with the Minyan domination there. Towards the end of the prehistoric period an influx of more definitely Mycenaean influences appears to have arrived from the south, and to have penetrated in some degree into Thessaly. Then almost instantly this new spark of a higher civilization was trampled out, and Thessaly relapsed into barbarism. The first signs of an alien culture appear, quite early, in the valley of the Spercheios. Its exact character and affinities are as yet uncertain. But

[1] vii. 197. Macan's note *ad loc.*

[2] *Prehistoric Thessaly.* The ethnological problem is discussed in the last chapter (xvii).

the indications are that it came through the pass of Tymphrestos from the north-west, and that its pottery is akin to 'the early Iron Age geometric vases from Marmariani, Theotoku, and other sites, which foreshadow the Dipylon style. Thus one of the elements of the later Dipylon style, what may perhaps be termed the geometric element as opposed to the Mycenaean . . . seems to appear first in the Spercheus valley'.[1] This pottery from the Spercheios, Messrs. Wace and Thompson are inclined to regard as Dorian in character; and here was the earliest Greek home of Hellenes and Achaeans. We are probably not justified as yet in basing any argument upon the Spercheios pottery taken by itself. But it does not go by itself, it must be explained with reference to what we know of the Achaeans who inhabited the valley; and these we have been led to regard as akin to the Dorians. In any case we must have some theory to account for the persistence during so long a time of a different and conspicuously inferior type of civilization in the Spercheios basin almost side by side with the quasi-Mycenaean culture of Orchomenos. How can we escape the conclusion that the Achaeans were a rude people, a kind of Picts and Scots, as Mr. T. W. Allen says, on the frontier of the southern civilization, which, if we can trust the traditions at all, must have been Minyan and 'Aeolian'? It exactly accords with this conclusion, that the historical Achaeans, in Thessaly and the Peloponnese, remained below the general level of Greek culture, while their native traditions—and this is surely a very striking thing—have nothing to say of the great 'Achaean' heroes of the epos. We must take the view then, it seems, that, if the Minyan civilization was Greek at all, it was Aeolian Greek, and that it must be markedly distinguished from the Achaean civilization of the Spercheios valley; all of which goes to confirm the belief that the Achaeans were of North-Western race and speech.

It has already been shown that we may think of Ionians as dwelling in Ionia and the Peloponnese before the occupation

[1] p. 254.

of Ionia. Unless it can be proved that the Aeolic and Ionic dialects of historical times were developed out of a common original—and some scholars believe this—, we must argue on the assumption that the speech of these Ionians before Ionia was akin to the Ionic of later days and in certain vital points distinguishable from Aeolic. This is the view of Kretschmer, and it leads him to certain conclusions regarding the Ionians which we cannot leave out of account. He finds what appear to him to be radical differences between Ionic and Aeolic on the one hand, and between them both and Doric on the other; and from these differences of speech he infers a difference of race in the speakers, an Aeolian race with whom the Aeolic dialect originated, Ionians speaking Ionic, Dorians speaking Doric—the accepted division of the historic age thrown back into the pre-historic. The effect of Kretschmer's arguments is to rehabilitate the view of Herodotus that Ionians anciently inhabited great parts of Greece which in later times were no longer reckoned as Ionian at all. Then, when was this 'layer' of Ionian population deposited in the long process from which emerged at last the Greek people? Kretschmer sees that it must have been before the coming of the Aeolians, the speakers of Aeolic, and he accepts as in substance true the traditions which tell of Ionians in Peloponnesian Achaia and elsewhere in the Peloponnesos and Boeotia. The speakers of Aeolic therefore, coming, we must suppose, from the north, formed the second layer of population in Southern Greece. The Dorians formed the third. Kretschmer himself identifies the Aeolian immigrants with the Achaeans. The identification is not necessary, as he admits; and reasons have been given against it. It does not affect the validity of his argument if for 'Achaeans' we substitute the less ambiguous 'Aeolians' in the sense of speakers of Aeolic.[1] With this qualification Kretschmer's hypothesis is entirely in accord with the point

[1] Prof. Ridgeway protests against the recent adoption of the terms North Achaean and South Achaean in dealing with the Aeolic dialects. See the chapter on the Homeric Dialect in the *Early Age*. The scholars who say Achaean are certainly begging the question.

of view taken here. It is quite possible, it may even be necessary, for us on other grounds than language to accept his belief in the conquest or overlapping of an older Ionian population by an Aeolian; if that is the only way in which one can reasonably explain certain features in which the Aeolic of Arcadia differs from the Aeolic of Thessaly and conforms to Attic-Ionic, it is also the only way in which the historical situation, on the quite different lines we have for the most part been following, can be reconstructed.[1]

We must now try to combine the results we have obtained into some intelligible scheme and suggest some logical sequence of events to explain them. It seems possible to do this in the broad outlines of the scheme and the critical moments of its development. . . . Imagine then, in the Plain of Boeotia, a 'Minyan' population with an ancient civilization of the Aegean type concentrated at Orchomenos. The existence of this culture is no longer in question; naturally enough, its origin is, although the indications are that it came from the south.[2] We are justified in connecting it in its developed state with the Minyans in the guarded sense in which we have used that famous name. Whether this race was originally an Aeolian or an Ionian or indeed a non-Greek race we do not know, nor, for any practical purpose, does it now matter. Our authorities speak of Minyans, Ionians, and Aeolians dwelling together in this part of early Boeotia, and, so far as we can make out, they shared the same culture and used the same language. This language was the speech from which the historical Aeolic, perhaps also the Ionic, dialect was developed. It must have been so because, first, Boeotia was from the earliest time we know an Aeolic-

[1] See the well-known article, already quoted, in the first volume of *Glotta*, p. 9 f. The linguistic evidence is there given in detail. But if Kretschmer is wrong, and Aeolic and Ionic had indeed a common ancestor, matters would become, superficially at least, much simpler. Since his view of the evidence will not allow him to accept this easier solution, neither should it allow us, until his arguments have been answered.

[2] *Prehistoric Thessaly*, ch. xv.

speaking district; and, secondly, because the people of Triphylia, who were by descent Minyans from Boeotia, spoke an Aeolic dialect in the midst of a 'Doric'-speaking population. This ancient speech, the mother of Aeolic, preserved nearest to its ancient purity in historical Arcadian and Cyprian, and doubtless, although we have not material enough to judge by, in the speech of the Triphylians, which must have been very like Arcadian, is the language in which the Homeric Poems are, apart from superficial modifications, composed. The fact that Nestor's Triphylians are found speaking Aeolic, the daughter of Homer's speech, is of course very helpful to our argument, although only so far as it shows that the Pylians used a language once spoken throughout Hellas. To resume; if it is certain that Aeolic and Ionic are not derived from a common ancestor, we must suppose that the Ionians in Boeotia learned Aeolic from the older inhabitants of the land—a result not in itself improbable. If, on the other hand, both dialects developed out of one speech, we do not require to make this assumption.

When the Orchomenian civilization was at its height, now rapidly becoming characteristically 'Mycenaean', and spreading its influence northward into Thessaly—perhaps the importance of Iolkos dates from this time—, it was overtaken by sudden calamity. Quite early, Achaeans and Hellenes had penetrated, probably over Tymphrestos, into the Vale of Spercheios. These formed the vanguard of other 'Dorian' invaders from the north-west, who ultimately thrust a wedge of semi-barbarous population between Boeotia and South Thessaly, and conquered the lands west of Oita and Parnassos. Under the pressure of this movement, which for the inhabitants of Boeotia culminated in the occupation of their territory by the Boiotoi, the pre-Dorian peoples of Central Greece were driven out to seek new homes south and east. Some, setting sail, it appears, from Aulis, the harbour of Orchomenos, fled across the Aegean to found the colonies of Aeolis. About the same time another body of them made their way into the Peloponnese by way of the Isthmos, penetrating into Arcadia and Elis and, beyond, into the Ionian Islands. This latter movement indeed may have been only one of a series which resulted in something like an Aeolian conquest of Southern Greece, for which there certainly appears to be some evidence. I content myself with the vagueness of outlines.

Finally, the North-Western tribes descended upon the Island of Pelops. In the van came the Achaeans crossing the Gulf of Corinth, it would seem, in ships and conquering the southern shore of it, the Aigialos, which was henceforward to be known as Achaia. The older Ionian inhabitants took to sea, and sailed away to the middle coast of Asia Minor, where, along with other broken men and refugees from all parts of Greece, they helped to create a new Ionia. The conquest of Achaia was evidently thorough, for these Achaeans remained, like their Thessalian kindred, all through the great period of Greece a backward people who plainly had acquired but little of the ancient culture they did so much to kill, although like true Greeks they spread the old religion of the land, the worship of the Ionian god Poseidon. Behind the Achaeans came other North-Western tribes, Aetolians who settled in Elis and fought with the Minyans of Triphylia, and perhaps made many of these also take to their ships and bring that influential contingent to Ionia whose fortunes we have already described. Last came the true Dorians, who eventually conquered the rest of the Peloponnesos with the exception of Arcadia.

I have chosen to put my hypothesis in this dogmatic form for the sake of clearness. If it seems to explain the facts, it will have all the justification that can be asked of any hypothesis. But it may be thought, we have still one important question to answer, why Homer calls the Greeks as a whole Achaeans. Has not the question in effect already answered itself? Just as we cannot discriminate between Achaeans and Hellenes, the original Hellenes; so we cannot logically explain the dissemination of the Achaean name except as an aspect or duplicate of the dissemination of the name Hellenes. So the *Catalogue* says 'Panhellenes and Achaioi'. Of the two names in their extended use 'Achaioi' evidently was at first most in favour, and this earlier period is reflected in the epos. Then, from some obscure cause, the other name 'Hellenes' came to predominate, such changes in the naming of a people forming a curious problem in the early history of many nations besides the Greek. In Homer himself other 'panhellenic' names compete with Achaioi—Argeioi, namely, and Danaoi. We must not conjure too much with one of them.

CHAPTER VIII

THE ACHAEANIZATION OF THE EPOS

THE argument now takes this form: that the Odyssey is in substance a pre-Achaean poem dealing with pre-Achaean legends and a pre-Achaean hero and heroine; but at a particular period of Greek history the prestige of the Achaeans, a people with 'North-Western' affinities, was so great as to effect a profound modification of the original saga of Odysseus, introducing a wholly different set of beliefs to the exclusion or obscuration of those implied in that. Already an attempt has been made to prove that the Odyssey embodies the traditions and reflects the wanderings of a Minyan-Ionian race, which migrated from Boeotia through the Peloponnesos by way of Corinth and Mantineia to Pylos in Elis, and from Elis to the Ionian Islands. The next step will naturally be to demonstrate, if we can, that, while the poem is fundamentally pre-Achaean, it has submitted to penetrating Achaean influences, which have in effect transformed it. This will accordingly be attempted in the present chapter, but only in outline. Nothing is gained by a pedantic rigour in the application of an historical hypothesis to a work of art. At most I desire to illustrate a process; I do not propose to follow it in minute detail.

The Iliad and Odyssey are Greek poems. Whatever pre-Hellenic elements—customs, beliefs, traditions—are included in them must have been adopted from an earlier population by the Greek tribes when they settled in Greece.[1] But our hypothesis imposes upon us the task of making a distinction within the purely Hellenic elements as well. We must try to discover what is Achaean and what pre-Achaean. The only possible method is one of elimination. Whatever is not 'Mycenaean' will be regarded as Achaean, until the contrary is proved. This will not be objected to by those who believe

[1] Mr. Toynbee remarks that they must have settled very early and in great numbers, before they could have hellenized so thoroughly a country with a civilization superior to their own.

that the Iliad and Odyssey are purely Achaean poems, since it is in fact the method they themselves follow. In the result, the Achaean contribution is not likely to be underestimated.

Of the Homeric heroes who are certainly Achaean? . . . If we begin with Agamemnon, the overlord of the rest, we find that, while the epos locates him in 'Argos' and Mykenai, in popular religion and legend he belongs rather to Sparta and its neighbourhood. As Zeus-Agamemnon he was worshipped at Sparta[1]; he was brother to Menelaos, who in Homer is king of Sparta; his tomb was at Amyklai; nay he was himself, according to Stesichoros[2] and Simonides,[3] king of Sparta. Homer knows him to be of the race of Pelops, who was no Achaean but, if we believe the legends, a Phrygian or Lydian. The legends may be mistaken, for Pelops had his grave at Olympia, and may have been an ancient divinity of that region. In that case he will be pre-Achaean all the same. It is true that he has been affiliated to Zeus, who is perhaps regarded as the great Achaean god. The *Handing Down of the Sceptre* in the second book of the Iliad evidently follows a tradition according to which he was the son of Hermes, while Hermes is the son of Zeus; and in any case, since Agamemnon like the other Homeric kings is descended from Zeus, Pelops must have been held to be so too. But this rule, by which every king is of the blood of Zeus, is in Homer largely formal and heraldic. It is, as instance after instance will show, very often a mere device for asserting Achaean descent for heroes demonstrably non-Achaean. In the case of Pelops it is not with Zeus but with Poseidon that he is most legitimately connected. The first *Olympian Ode* of Pindar indicates that, and the association of the hero with Poseidon at Olympia seems clearly older than his association there with Zeus[4];

[1] Also for somo roason in Attica. *Schol. vet.* Lykophr. 1369 *Λαπέρσαι δῆμος τῆς Ἀττικῆς, ἔνθα Ἀγαμέμνονος Διὸς ἱερόν ἐστιν.*

[2] *Fr.* 39.

[3] *Fr.* 20.

[4] The priestly family of the Iamidai at Olympia claimed descent from Poseidon through his daughter Euadne the mother of Iamos. See the sixth *Olympian.* Note that the Iamidai were originally an Arcadian family.

while some scholars even regard *Pelops* as an epithet of Poseidon himself. There is at any rate some evidence for regarding him as really a Minyan hero :—this intimate connexion with the Horse-Poseidon, who lends him his wonderful steeds; the name *Πέλοψ* suggesting *Πελίας*, who indeed had a daughter Pelopia;[1] the name of the Theban patriot Pelopidas, seeming to imply the existence of a family of Pelopidai in the old Minyan land; the worship at Chaironeia of the sceptre of Agamemnon, which was the sceptre of Pelops; above all, the discovery at Olympia of a culture identical, so far as the somewhat scanty remains permit a conclusion, with that revealed at the Minyan settlement of Pylos. At least there is nothing in all this which suggests the Achaean in Pelops. And the genealogies which do suggest it are transparently fictitious. He was, says one of them, the son of Hermes. This means that Pelops, who was buried at Olympia, was regarded as the son of Hermes *Kyllenios*, the old god of the land, for Mount Kyllene looks down upon the Plain of Elis. But this Hermes was a pre-Achaean divinity, and his transformation into a son of Zeus is part of a process which we may call the Achaeanization of the gods, which has an exact parallel in the general Achaeanization of the epic heroes. Undoubtedly Pelops was regarded as the son of Hermes before the latter became an Achaean divinity; that is the only plausible explanation why Hermes appears in the genealogy at all. Therefore Pelops also was pre-Achaean. According to the more usual account, however, he was the son of Tantalos, who lived upon Mount Sipylos in Phrygia in the morning of the world. This Tantalos the genealogists boldly called the son of Zeus. But he is manifestly no Achaean and indeed appears in Homer among the great sinners of an earlier race and age. Thus, in whatever way we test the evidence, we discover that Pelops cannot have been truly an Achaean; neither then can Agamemnon nor Menelaos, if the genealogies are to count for anything. It might indeed happen that an Achaean hero was affiliated by a political fiction to a non-

[1] Apollod. *Bibl.* i. 9. 10.

Achaean ancestor. But if we deprive Agamemnon of his Pelopid lineage, we are left with nothing but the tradition of a great king vaguely attached to Mykenai, to 'Argos,' to Corinth; and the cult at Sparta. The Spartan cult and the tomb at Amyklai, the only solid things to which we can cling in this haze of legend, strongly suggest that he was originally an indigenous Laconian divinity; therefore pre-Achaean.

Menelaos, as a Pelopid and brother of Agamemnon, is also non-Achaean by descent. He is the husband of the native Spartan goddess Helen and himself a god. There is nothing here to make us regard him as Achaean. True, he seems to be the founder of a new dynasty at Sparta, but it is the Pelopid dynasty. His relation to Helen might be explained as similar to that of Herakles to Hera at Argos. There does not appear to be, in his case, any sign of connexion with Northern Greece; he belongs first and last to Lacedaemon. Being a god, perhaps he too is indigenous and pre-Achaean. Agamemnon and Menelaos are constantly called by Homer the Sons of Atreus, and unquestionably this short genealogy is the oldest and most legitimate of all. But Atreus himself is a very shadowy figure. Homer is silent regarding him, not necessarily from ignorance, for the legends about him are peculiarly savage and unpleasing. Their primitive character, however, is a guarantee of their genuineness. That Atreus is so unsympathetic in them is surely an indication that he was regarded as belonging to a dispossessed race. Few, I imagine, naturally think of him as an Achaean. Far more probably he was a legendary 'wicked prince' talked of from time immemorial by Peloponnesian shepherds.

With Achilles it is perhaps different. He if any should be an Achaean, since he leads the Achaeans to Troy. His kingdom lay in the valley of the Spercheios. His sister Polydora bare to the River-god a son Menesthios,[1] and to Spercheios Peleus vowed a lock of Achilles' unshorn hair, if he came home safe from Troy.[2] The etymology of the name Ἀχιλλεύς can scarcely supply us with an indication of his origin,

[1] Π 176. [2] Ψ 141 f.

even if it is rightly connected with Ἀχελῷος.[1] So much then is the evidence in favour of regarding him as genuinely Achaean, unless we care to add his yellow hair, which, however, can hardly be taken as characteristic of Achaeans only among the Greek invaders. On the other hand, when history speaks, Achilles is an Aeolian hero. Two things may have happened: he may have been an Aeolian from the first, the hero of an Aeolic-speaking people driven out by the Achaeans from the Spercheios district into Phthiotis, from Phthiotis, where the Achaeans succeeded them, into the promontory formed by Pelion, from thence to Skyros and Lesbos, ultimately to Aeolis, while all the time he remained in the memory of his worshippers the prince of Phthia; or he may have been an Achaean hero adopted by these Aeolians. Either account will explain why his mother is Thetis, who had her shrine at Old Pharsalos,[2] and his father Peleus named of the mountain. But we should consider that Peleus is pretty clearly a local Daimon of the hill and pre-Achaean, while Thetis is certainly a very ancient goddess. And what is still more striking is that the historical Achaeans are not known to have worshipped Achilles or to have brought him into their native legends. Our information about the specifically Achaean cults and myths is indeed admittedly scanty, but Achilles, one would have thought, they must have held in especial honour, if he was truly an Achaean. It is but another of the contradictions between Homer and history that are perpetually meeting us. The Homeric Problem is in great part the problem of resolving these.

The case of Idomeneus is also doubtful. Since it seems quite possible that the Achaeans reckoned by Homer among the inhabitants of Crete were Achaeans of pure blood, it is possible that Idomeneus was one of these. Homer indeed calls him the son of Deukalion, and Deukalion in the Thessalian legend was the father of Hellen. Deukalion the father of Idomeneus is called by Homer the son of Minos the son of Zeus, but although Professor Ridgeway has argued that this

[1] For a different explanation see Kretschmer, *Glotta*, 1913, p. 306.

[2] Strabo, p. 431.

Minos was an Achaean in the sense in which he uses the name,[1] the genealogy has surely a somewhat fictitious air. The *name* Minos, as so many ancient settlements called Minoa indicate, is evidently pre-Achaean; and, if it be, as Professor Murray conjectures, a royal title like Pharaoh, it becomes all the more probable that a Minos would belong to the old Cretan race.[2] Moreover, the Zeus who is father of our Minos was clearly the ancient Bull-god of Crete, whose identification with Zeus is part of the Achaeanization of the gods. But although this would seem to destroy the claim of Idomeneus to be the grandson of Minos, it does not really touch his claim to be the son of Deukalion. So we may allow him for an Achaean. And what is said of Idomeneus applies to his half-brother Meriones.

But what of the others? They are not Achaean, and their affiliation to Zeus, which, however, is not always directly asserted in Homer, is often patently fictitious. Thus the grandfather of the pre-Achaean Odysseus, Arkeisios-Arkesilaos, was called the son of Zeus; and although the Odyssey does not say this, perhaps it implies it. Arkesilaos of Lebadeia was of course, to begin with, no son of Zeus but a hero of the old chthonian religion. Nestor the son of Neleus is derived from Zeus by the fiction which represented the great Minyan chiefs as sons of Aiolos, and Aiolos as the son of Zeus; whereas the true genealogy, followed by Homer, made Neleus the son of Poseidon. His mother Tyro was the daughter of Salmoneus the son of the Minyan Kretheus. Nestor, then, was a Minyan. The case of Diomedes is somewhat peculiar. The genealogists called him also an Aiolid, tracing his descent through many generations from Kalyke the daughter of Aiolos. We should remember in this connexion what Thucydides says of the Kalydonian district, which was Diomedes' earlier home, that it was anciently Aeolian territory. Diomedes, then, must have been regarded by genealogists as an Aeolian. But the relations of the legendary Kalydonian princes are

[1] *Minos the Destroyer*, &c. Brit. Ac. Proc. iv, p. 14 f.

[2] Cf. E. Bethe, 'Minos' in *Rhein. Museum*, vol. lxv (1910), p. 200 f.

rather with the native goddess Artemis and the Thracian Ares and Dionysos. Bethe has shown that Diomedes of Argos is ultimately identical with Diomedes king of the Bistones in Thrace.[1] The strangeness of this is a little mitigated when one recalls the ancient and persistent traditions of Thracians in Boeotia and Phokis. It may be indeed, for all we know, that the Aeolian tribes came from Thrace, while the Achaeans and Dorians came from the north-west. There are many things which suggest that, but we need not discuss them here. We cannot, however, omit to observe what is evidently the memory of an actual shifting of peoples in the fact that Diomedes in Homer is king of Argos, while the realm of Oineus is now held by Thoas the son of Andraimon. Diomedes' tribe has been driven out by the rude warriors of the Aetolian hinterland. These, of course, were of North-Western race. It seems clear that they destroyed a prehistoric civilization in the Aetolian coast-lands,[2] which, to judge by its legends, must have been pre-Achaean. The story of the Kalydonian Boar, for instance, originally concerned in the main three people, Oineus, Meleagros, and Atalante, who all belong to an age earlier than the Achaean. Diomedes is of the dynasty of Oineus, which had been superseded in Aetolia; by lineage therefore he is not Achaean. I believe it would not be wrong to call him an Aeolian. Thoas might perhaps be an Achaean. But if he was, then his people must have been different from Diomedes' people whom they drove out. The true inference to make, however, is surely that Thoas represents the Aetolians of history and Diomedes the older Aeolian population of Kalydon and Pleuron. Diomedes' companion in arms Sthenelos was the son of the pre-Achaean Kapaneus,[3] who fought along with Tydeus against Thebes. The Shield-hero Aias, a creation of the popular imagination without any roots in history at all, must originally have been No-man's son or the son merely of *Telamon*, the shield-strap. Yet Telamon has been made a brother of Peleus and both are called

[1] *Homer u. d. Heldensage*, p. 4 f.

[2] Cf. Bury, *History of Greece*, i, p. 50 f.

[3] B 564.

the sons of a shadowy Aiakos, who is held to have been a son of Zeus. As for the other Aias, the Lokrian, he remains the son of Oileus and never, any more than Diomedes, gets directly affiliated to Zeus. Patroklos is connected with Opous; the name of his father Menoitios is the name of a brother of Prometheus, who also had some connexion with Opous; so he may be very early, although the epos makes him the friend of Achilles but, perhaps significantly, a little older. Teukros must have to do with the Teukrians; yet somehow he has got himself made into a son of Telamon, like the Greater Aias, although by a foreign woman.[1] The Achaean principle that all kings are descended from Zeus is extended even to the enemies of the Achaeans: to Priam, who was derived from Dardanos, whom 'post-Homeric' writers call an Arcadian and the son of Zeus; to Aeneas, who is also, and more legitimately, a descendant of Dardanos, and himself, it seems, originally an Arcadian hero. Sarpedon and Glaukos, the leaders of the Lycians in the Iliad, are, the former the son of Europa and Zeus, that is the Cretan Bull-god, the latter of the blood of the pre-Achaean Sisyphos—who nevertheless, as we saw, was called the son of Aiolos the son of Zeus.

It is somewhat different with the heroines in Homer, who are not nearly so thoroughly Achaeanized as the great chiefs, perhaps because it was still remembered that many Northern adventurers had won kingdoms for themselves in Greece by marriage with the native queens. Still there is a tendency to regard the notable women also as Achaean. Helen, the ancient goddess of Sparta, the daughter of the pre-Achaean Tyndareos and Leda, has become the child of Zeus. For the most part, however, the genealogies of the Homeric women remained untouched. Penelope is merely 'the daughter of Ikarios'. Klytaimnestra is without lineage in Homer; from other sources we find that she was the daughter of Tyndareos or Zeus. And the Trojan women have no Achaean relation-

[1] Cf. Soph. *Ajax* 1289 ὁ δοῦλος, οὐκ τῆς βαρβάρου μητρὸς γεγώς. 1263 τὴν βάρβαρον γὰρ γλῶσσαν οὐκ ἐπαΐω. The mother of Teukros was the daughter of the Trojan king Laomedon (1302); which helps to explain his name.

ships in the epos, as some of the men have. And of all the heroines who appear to Odysseus out of the underworld not one is demonstrably Achaean, although they are the ancestresses of heroes whom Homer calls Achaeans. That takes us back to a time when the princely families traced their descent from some mortal woman, or goddess envisaged as a mortal, and the tribal or local god, in the case of the Minyan heroines in the *Nekyia*, usually the Minyan god Poseidon. Zeus, as we have seen, is hardly ever the direct ancestor.

The Achaeanization of the heroes finds its complement in the Achaeanization of the gods, which is also entirely the work of the epos. It was Homer and Hesiod, says Herodotus, who gave the Greeks a theogony,[1] a systematic account of the interrelations of the gods as members of a single great family under the headship of the Achaean Zeus. The Achaeans, if they did not bring him to Dodona, but found him already in his Oak-grove when they settled in that region, at least adopted him as their chief divinity and carried his worship with them in their progress south, honouring him as Zeus of Dodona in Thessaly, and in Achaia of the Peloponnese as Zeus Ἀμάριος. The Achaean prestige, which was at its height when the Iliad began to take something like its present form, ensured the victory of Zeus over the other gods of Greek religion, who are now associated with him in varying degrees of kinship and subordination; Hera, for instance, as his sister and wife (Dione left behind in far Dodona), Athena and Aphrodite as his daughters, Apollo and Ares and Hermes as his sons.

Of the Homeric gods the most prominent after Zeus are in the Iliad Apollo, Poseidon, and Ares; in the Odyssey Athena and Poseidon and Hermes. Regarding Apollo we cannot speak with any assurance either as to his original character or his earliest home. One view represents him as fundamentally a Sun-god, another makes him an agricultural divinity; Wilamowitz thinks he was a Lycian god, while Dr. Farnell supposes that he came from Northern Greece. In Homer he

[1] ii. 53.

fights for the Trojans, and in earlier days had helped to build the walls of Troy for Laomedon. He is called the guardian of Chryse and Killa and Tenedos, and is addressed by the local cult-name Σμινθεύς.[1] He is in fact for Homer pre-eminently a Trojan god. Thus, whether he came originally from Asia Minor or Delos or Crete or Thrace, we ought not to call him an Achaean. The main reason for doing so used to be the association of his name with those of Zeus and Athena to form the triple oath *αἲ γὰρ Ζεῦ τε πάτερ καὶ Ἀθηναίη καὶ Ἄπολλον*; but this combination is itself evidently artificial and political,[2] while in any case Athena is pre-Achaean, so that, even if this were a characteristically Achaean oath, one would not be entitled to infer that Apollo any more than Athena was a genuinely Achaean god. Poseidon we have already discussed. He was the god of the Minyans and Ionians. Ares was the War-god and Sun-god of Thrace.[3] Hera was the pre-Achaean goddess or Kore of Argos, who retains in Homer the epithet *boôpis*,[4] recalling a time when she was worshipped in cow-form, we may conjecture. Athena was a divinity of the same type as Hera, a type indigenous in Greek lands and in Anatolia; she was the Attic or Athenian, as Hera was the Argive, Kore. In Homer she has become the daughter of Zeus, Hera his wife. Aphrodite is associated with Ares both in the Iliad and the Odyssey,[5] and it is not impossible that originally she was regarded as his wife, as in their joint cult at Thebes. Thebes was a city full of 'Thracian' memories; and if Aphrodite was a War-goddess of Thrace, one can better understand her unsympathetic treatment in Homer, for whom Thracians are enemies. But she is also called the *Cyprian*[6] and the *Cytherean*,[7] and has a sanctuary at Paphos;[8] and it is certain that she came to be identified with or assimilated to the Oriental Love-goddess whom the Greeks called Astarte. In any case

[1] A 37 f. [2] *Themis*, p. 501 f.

[3] N 301, θ 361. Prof. P. Gardner, *Ares as a Sun-God*, in *Num. Chron.*, N. S., vol. xx, p. 12.

[4] A 551. [5] E 359 f., Φ 416, θ 266 f. [6] E 330 f.

[7] θ 288, σ 193. [8] θ 363.

she is not an Achaean. Yet in Homer she is the daughter of Zeus and, very curiously, Dione.[1] Hermes, again, was a god of immemorial antiquity in Greece, remaining in popular religion even in historical times little better than a fetish. The contrast between the ithyphallic idols, which even the Athenians of Thucydides' age reverenced, and the ideal figure in the Odyssey 'like a young man in the most gracious season of youth',[2] brings home to us very vividly the spirit and method of Homer's dealings with the gods. In the Odyssey, Hermes, by a process we can only guess at, has become the messenger of Zeus.

In the same way it would not be difficult to illustrate the Achaeanization of other divinities who are less prominent in Homer: Hephaistos, the Fire-god of Lemnos;[3] Charis, his wife in the Iliad,[4] who may be one of the Charites of Minyan Orchomenos; Dionysos, although he perhaps is admitted to be a Thracian.[5] Helios, on the other hand, is simply the personified Sun, and he, together with Dionysos and Demeter and Persephone and certain minor divinities such as Aiolos, who has charge of the winds, Kirke, Proteus, Leukothea, and the many nymphs, river-gods, and the like, including Okeanos himself, belong to a primitive nature-religion older than Homer's Olympianism and plainly irreconcilable with it. Here and there one seems to detect traces of resistance to the process of Achaeanization on the part even of the gods who are prominent in Homer. Hera, for example, is, in the Iliad at least, violently hostile to the policy of her lord, perhaps because she remembers the grudge of her own people against the Northern worshippers of Zeus. In the *Hymn to Apollo* the god scatters terror among the other Olympians (save Zeus and Leto), which implies that he was in some sense at enmity with them. So Zeus, their conqueror, scatters terror among them.[6] Even in the Iliad, I think, a certain independence or detachment in his relations to the other gods is observable in Apollo. Then Zeus detests Ares. Indeed, Zeus

[1] E 370.
[2] κ 278.
[3] A 593, θ 283–4.
[4] Σ 382.
[5] Z 130 f.
[6] A 533 f.

sometimes speaks as if his rule was unpopular among the gods generally, which would be a natural result, if it represents the prestige of one tribe among many.

When one considers where the Achaeanization of the sagas was likely to take place, one must think first of Boeotia. For the Achaeans and Hellenes dwelt along the Spercheios on the northern frontier of the land, and their power and fame in their conquering days would make themselves felt in Boeotia first and most strongly among the great centres of the Aegean culture. Besides, here was a very ancient school of epic poetry, and perhaps the place of its birth. Here the story of the Argonauts and the story of the Theban War took shape. The Argonauts, because of some vitality in the tradition, remained Minyans to the end, yet they came to be regarded as descended from a son of Zeus. In the same way the combatants in the Theban War are clearly pre-Achaean; there is no touch of the Achaean about Adrastos of Argos or Sikyon, or about Amphiaraos of Oropos, or Polyneikes the Labdakid, or Parthenopaios from 'Pelasgian' Arcadia. Yet the invading army is called, as in the *Seven against Thebes*, an Achaean host; only sometimes, although this is the correct appellation, Argeioi. This transformation of the epic heroes is certainly ancient. Della Seta has shown that the name *Achaioi* occurs so much more frequently both in the Iliad and the Odyssey than *Argeioi* and *Danaoi*, that we seem justified in thinking that it was the first to be used as a common denomination for all the Greeks.[1] This favours the supposition that the name Achaeans in this extended sense was adopted into the epics in Central Greece, where the Peloponnesian names Argeioi and Danaoi would not be so firmly planted as in the south. It is well to remember also that the Boeotian poets were the great preservers of the ancient genealogical poetry; and this makes it the more likely that the Achaeanization of the genealogies was their doing. It is essentially part of the process which made the gods subject to the Achaean Zeus and for the most part allied to him in

[1] *Rendic. della R. Accad. d. Lincei*, ser. v, vol. xvi, pp. 133-210.

blood. That process is most systematically carried out in the Boeotian *Theogony*. And what is done for the gods in the *Theogony* was done for heroes and famous women in many epics now lost of the Boeotian school.

So far we have been considering the Achaean contribution to the actual content of the Homeric Poems, and we have found how it appears to shrink under criticism so far as it concerns the actors, divine and human, in the Iliad and Odyssey. Let us now approach the question from the other side and, by disengaging the certainly pre-Achaean elements, thereby attempt to get a little closer to its solution. Partly this has already been done in discussing the Achaean claim. But we must now extend our investigation to the older religion as a whole, avoiding as far as possible what is still in dispute in a matter so problematical. It seems advisable also to keep specially in mind the conditions of the Boeotian Plain, because it was there that, on our hypothesis, the Odyssey, in which we are chiefly interested, began to take coherent form, and because it was there that Achaean and pre-Achaean first came into touch. It happens besides that we get certain surprisingly definite impressions of the old Boeotian religion. No other part of Greece was so full as Boeotia of the graves of the worshipped dead, caverns in the earth leading to the underworld, and the oracles of buried prophets. This *chthonian* religion, the worship and tendance of the 'Earth-people' (χθόνιοι), we now know to have been of immemorial age in Greece. The worship of the dead is only possible among a people who bury them and do not burn them, as Homer's Achaeans do; for you may feed a corpse with blood and honey and meal and believe that the dead man accepts the offering, but the little grey dust in the urn, which is all that remains of the cremated body, cannot by any liveliness of faith be pictured as retaining the passions and desires and force of the living. The earlier inhabitants of Greece, who had the Cretan culture, almost invariably buried their dead entire, and the worship of ghosts, of dead ancestors perhaps in particular, was prevalent among them.

No very high kind of religion, it may be thought, can have a basis such as that.[1] Yet it would be wrong to fix one's mind wholly on the gloomy and ferocious aspects which the worship of the dead certainly presented, and not think also of its gentler side—the love of the dead for the living and of the living for the dead, the sense of intimacy between worshipped and worshipper, all that is expressed in the beautiful word *pietas* surviving the shock of bereavement. It is fear that makes men cruel, and, although horror of the ghost has often driven them to the commission of dreadful things in the name of religion, they cannot and do not fear all their dead, and may get some real aid for the conduct of life from kindly thoughts about them. Besides the good spirits of the hearth, and the countless and often maleficent spirits outside the family and the tribe, there were many 'heroes' yet strong in death—some nameless, some with famous names, Amphiaraos and Mopsos and Teiresias and Trophonios—dwelling often in caverns and having the gift of prophecy; and, greater yet than they, a god of many names and of none—for his titles are all adjectival—Hades-Plouton with his bride Persephone, whose beauty shines in that dim earth beneath the earth, with its Abhorred and Forgetful Waters and its tormented River of Fire. Yet perhaps in attempting to reconstruct the older beliefs of Greece we should not think too much of Hades and his realm, because in thinking of them it is difficult to avoid too great a definiteness and picturesqueness in our ideas, but should be content with the simple conception of the Earth-people, each sentient and effectual even in the grave. It was a later thought which gave a king and queen to the famous nations of the dead.

It is clear that the worship of the dead was universal in Boeotia 'before the Sons of the Achaeans came'. The ritual survived there throughout the classical age, and the voices of the buried prophets were never quite put to silence by the Delphian Oracle. King Kroisos sent messengers from Lydia

[1] It should not be forgotten, however, that the Minoans had an *ouranian* as well as a sombre *chthonian* religion.

to consult Amphiaraos at Oropos and Trophonios at Lebadeia.[1] Kleanthes stamped with his foot upon the ground that the dead might listen, and cried aloud a line from the *Epigonoi* of Sophocles: 'Hearest thou, Amphiaraos, in thy dwelling under the earth?'—*Audisne haec, Amphiarae, sub terram abdite?* as Cicero gives it in the translation of Accius;[2] words which Shelley took as a motto for the most elemental of English poems. Apart from tombs of heroes and *nekyomanteia* demonstrably pre-Achaean, the mythology of Boeotia is redolent of the rites and beliefs connected with these things. The legend of Oidipous and his race is full of chthonian elements. With him and his house is closely associated, to bless and to curse, Teiresias the blind prophet of Thebes, who alone kept his wisdom among the witless dead. The most famous of the Seven Champions was the old-world prophet Amphiaraos. The Minyan legends, too, have many traces of the cult of the dead. The Sailing of Argo had for its object the laying of the ghost of Phrixos calling for rest from the far-off palace of Aietes;[3] while Trophonios was accounted a son of the king of Orchomenos.

But in all Homer there is only one reference to the worship of a buried hero, namely Erechtheus, whom the Athenians honoured with sacrifice of bulls and rams; and this is in the *Catalogue*, which in the opinion of many scholars is an intrusion in the original Iliad. The practice in Homer is to burn the dead, not to inhume them; and this involves a wholly different theory of the soul's nature and destiny. Instead of the extremely materialistic conception of the ghost natural to minds accustomed to think of the body in its grave, lying there vigorous and watchful yet, a people who practised cremation could only imagine the soul as a helpless and fugitive vapour exhaling from the ashes of the pyre, and thereafter leading a forlorn and unimpassioned life like a dream or a smoke or a shadow (σκιά). The Achaeans must have burned their dead, for on no other assumption does it seem possible to account for the prevalence of cremation in the Homeric Poems; and, since they burned their dead, the

[1] Her. i. 46. [2] *Tuscul.* ii, ch. 25. [3] Pind. *Pyth.* iv. 159–60.

conception of the disembodied spirit surviving death was theirs also. It is an Achaean practice then, and the Achaean doctrine of the ghost, which prevail in Homer. Yet, when we look at the matter closely, this predominance is only superficial. Just as the matter of the Poems is not of Achaean origin, but embodies the legends of the older peoples, who inhumed and worshipped their dead; so we find the older practice and the older conception of the ghost constantly implied in Homer. One thinks at once of the eleventh book of the Odyssey. There, as we have seen, we have a most curious mingling of the older and newer ideas concerning the dead. The drinking by the ghosts of the blood in the *bothros* is part of the older way of belief; and so we may accept that incident as retained from the earliest form of the *Nekyia.* Teiresias himself, the central figure, was, it must be repeated, one of many buried prophets in Boeotia; and that is why a black ram, the appropriate victim, is sacrificed to him by Odysseus. The heroines who appear to Odysseus are pre-Achaean, ancestresses of families which must have buried their dead. Thus, although in the eleventh book all the subjects of Persephone are represented as mere 'shades', and the philosophy of the soul which goes with cremation is expressed there quite clearly by Antikleia,[1] still traces of that other conception of the life after death, of corporeal ghosts to be fed with blood, can be discerned in what must be the oldest parts of the *Nekyia.* There has not been perfectly effective harmonization. And outside the *Nekyia* the same confusion appears in the use of certain expressions appropriate to the practice of inhumation, but employed by Homer in describing the burning of a dead warrior.[2] The explanation must be that in the Iliad and Odyssey cremation has succeeded to the preservation of the body, but has not been able completely to expel from the traditional language of the epos every reminiscence of the earlier practice. Not only that, but Homer is often at variance with the general tradition. According to the description in the last book of the Odyssey,[3] Achilles was

[1] 217 f. [2] Π 456, 674; Ψ 170; ω 67. [3] ω 65 f.

duly burned, and the ashes of his body mingled in one gold urn with the ashes of Patroklos, as he had desired. But the ancient epic called the *Ethiopian Poetry*, which carried on the story of Troy from the point at which our Iliad stops, said that Thetis snatched her son from the burning pyre and conveyed him to the happy island of Leuke.[1] We must not reject the account in the *Aithiopis* as unauthentic simply because it contradicts Homer. It is plainly an attempt to reconcile what Homer says with the current belief that Achilles was not burned, but was carried away bodily to some White Island of the happy dead, where he reawakened to a divine and immortal existence. Originally, Achilles was a god, and he remained a god in popular estimation, among the Aeolians at least, who knew him as Lord of the Pontus,[2] and identified Leuke with an island at the mouth of the Danube; so we cannot be sure that the story of his carrying off is not really the older and authentic one. It certainly belongs to a definite class of myths which must be referred to a dateless antiquity. But if in the oldest form of his legend Achilles was not burned, neither probably was Patroklos, especially if the funeral in the twenty-third book of the Iliad is a replica of the funeral of Achilles described in another epic.[3] In the Iliad Hector is burned at Troy. But his tomb was shown at Thebes, the tomb of a buried hero. Agamemnon was buried at Amyklai, where according to Pindar he died.[4] Menelaos was buried at Therapnai, as the people there believed; but Proteus, in the Odyssey, prophesies that he will not die at all. The *Little Iliad* expressly said that Aias, the son of Telamon, was not burned,[5] and Sophocles, in his *Ajax*, agrees with the *Little Iliad* in this. The other Aias, the son of Oileus, was lost at sea. And the mysterious prophecy of Teiresias concerning the end of Odysseus makes no allusion to the manner of his funeral, perhaps because of the tradition that he was spirited away in

[1] Procl. epitome of *Aithiopis*.
[2] Cf. Alcaeus, *Fr.* 75 (Hiller) Ἀχίλλευ, ὃ τᾶς Σκυθίκας μέδεις.
[3] See Mülder, *Die Ilias u. ihre Quellen*, p. 266 f.
[4] *Pyth.* xi. 32.
[5] Eustath. *Il.*, p. 285.

the hour of death.[1] All these contradictions may be resolved if we assume that the custom of habitual cremation was introduced by an invading people, whom we may identify with the Achaeans, among a people who had hitherto almost invariably practised the other custom of inhumation, and that this has affected the Homeric Poems, where the heroes are spoken of as being burned after death, although when they belong, as so many of them do, to the pre-Achaean saga, they could not have been treated so in it.

It has always been a difficulty, this rule of cremation in Homer. No investigations have discovered a period in the history of Greek lands when cremation alone was practised; we always find inhumation along with it and much more commonly in use. Apparently we must think of the Achaeans as regularly burning their dead when they first penetrated into Central Greece, and stamping this custom upon the language of the epic, as they introduced their name into it. It no more follows that they made cremation universal in Greece than that the Homeric Greeks were all genuine Achaeans, and the absence of evidence for its general use at any time is an argument against the theory of a universal Achaean Conquest. Homer has caught up and, as it were, stereotyped the name and the custom of a particular tribe, which at some spiritual crisis of the race was especially famous and powerful. It was, doubtless, in their early home near the forests of Central Europe that the Achaeans learned to burn their dead. But, since it does not appear that the Achaeans when they come into the full light of Greek history were distinguished from other Greeks by the regular practice of cremation—certainly the Dorians were not, as Professor Ridgeway has remarked—, we must conclude that they speedily conformed to the native custom of inhumation. But it is possible, as has been argued, that the stress of war and wandering had the effect of reviving a custom already falling

[1] Some such legend must lie behind the statements that he was restored to life by Kirke (schol. Lykophr. 805) and buried in Aiaie (Hyg. *fab.* 127). At any rate he was not burned.

into desuetude.[1] 'To be gnawed out of our graves, to have our skulls made into drinking-bowls, and our bones turned into pipes, to delight and sport our enemies, are tragical abominations escaped in burning burials.' The objection that, if the motive for burning the corpse was to prevent its dishonour, a mound would not have been piled above it to advertise its position to an enemy, does not take into account the sentiment involved. The natural man is a great deal more disturbed by the mutilation of a body than by the scattering of a handful of ashes. And besides this, there are two quite different conceptions of death implied, for the buried man, it was thought, could feel, while the charred bones could not. Then, on one occasion at least in Homer, there was a practical reason for burning. When Apollo took vengeance upon the Greek host for the insult to Chryses, there was no other safe or effective way of disposing of so many plague-stricken bodies.[2] Still the historical difficulty remains. It must be supposed that cremation was the normal practice of the Achaeans in peace as well as in war; and in that case we should expect it to be adopted, at least to some extent, by the pre-Achaean peoples of Greece. In effect that is what we do find. At Kakóvatos, near Zacháro, which he identifies with the Homeric Pylos, Doerpfeld found three beehive tombs of the Mycenaean type, contemporary perhaps with the shaft-graves at Mykenai, and in them both burned and unburned bones. It must have been a settlement, Doerpfeld argues, of Northerners who had assimilated the Aegean culture, but retained their tribal custom of cremation. At Olympia and in Leukas he has found a culture similar to that of Kakóvatos, and in Leukas a burial place has been revealed, enclosed in a rectangle of slabs, which was once covered with a mound of earth, making us think of the

[1] *Rise of Greek Epic*, p. 94 f.

[2] Cf. Thuc. ii. 52. 4. Robertson Smith says in *The Religion of the Semites*, p. 353, n. 3: 'In Amos vi. 10 the victims of a plague are burned, which is to be understood by comparing Lev. xx. 14, xxi. 9, Amos ii. 1, and remembering that plague was a special mark of divine wrath (2 Sam. xxiv), so that its victims might well be regarded as intensely *taboo*'.

barrow heaped above the dead in Homer. But I think we must admit this does not carry us very far.[1]

What does emerge from a general view of the evidence is that there has taken place an amalgamation of Northern and native religion, an assimilation of the old to the new, to some extent an actual identification of Achaean with pre-Achaean gods.[2] The earliest inhabitants of Greece probably had two main forms of worship: the cult of the dead, and, secondly, the worship of many goddesses here and there of a fundamentally identical type, whose function was to promote the fertility of the country-side over which they ruled, of its folk and its cattle and its fields. We have had something to say already of these and of the buried heroes. A characteristic of this religion was that it avoided or did not feel the need of distinctive names for those whom it worshipped. Of the local goddesses, as of the heroes, most would be nameless; but now and again some accident, some acquisition of power or reputation by her special community, would bring a particular Kore into prominence, and she would come to be accepted beyond the limits of her native reign, acquiring a name in the process as a necessary condition of her being recognized outside the circle of her first worshippers, though perhaps only a local title, as *Paphia* or *Kypris* or *Athenaia*. The importance of the Argive Kore Hera—*Ἥρη Ἀργείη*—was, no doubt, largely a consequence and proof of the early

[1] See Dr. Leaf's *Troy*, pp. 18–19.

[2] So Zeus-Amphiaraos, Zeus-Trophonios, Zeus-Agamemnon, Zeus *Lykoreios* (?) &c. The last is of special interest to us if it implies the identification of Zeus with the Wolf-god of Parnassos. Steph. Byz. *s. v.* Λυκωρεία κώμη ἐν Δελφοῖς. ἔστι καὶ Λυκωρεῖος Ζεύς. Miss Harrison suggests that there may have been an identification of an incoming Wolf-god with an old Light-god on Mount Lykaios in Arcadia.—It is possible again that Apollo was an Achaean brought to Delphi by his tribesmen, if his name is derived from the North-Western word *apella*. It is obviously easier to understand this possibility if we think of the Achaeans as a North-Western people living along the Spercheios so near to Delphi. But if Apollo is Achaean, he has been identified with the ancient Kouros-god of Delos whom the Ionians worshipped. See Murray, *Four Stages of Gk. Religion*, ch. ii, p. 69 f. But see also supra, p. 152.

importance of Argos. But one can never be sure of the true reason why a particular goddess, a Hera or Artemis, an Athena or Aphrodite, won her way to the position of a national divinity. The causes may actually have been very different in each case, although the promotion of these goddesses illustrates a tendency which is common to all their cases, the tendency for some local Kore to extend her influence at the expense of neighbouring divinities of the same nature, who came to be identified with her. This tendency, which operated among the gods as well as the goddesses, received a powerful impetus from the successive waves of the Hellenic Conquest, which, introducing the characteristic Aryan institutions and a patriarchal form of society into one in which the mother and, as a natural concomitant in the religious sphere, the mother-goddess counted for so much, brought with it the conception of a divine family ruled over by a father-god. Then followed the long process of assimilation, the blending of the invading religion with the native; a process already completed in Homer, for whom certain great deities of diverse origin form a kind of national pantheon, the members of it all related to Zeus, and yielding him at least an enforced allegiance. But although this development involved to a great extent the dethronement of the Korai, they never lost the whole, perhaps they never lost very much, of their power over the minds of their worshippers. A proof of this is the profound and permanent influence exerted on the history of Greek religion by the worship of Demeter and Persephone. Yet of this worship of Mother and Maid there is not a trace in Homer. Artemis, almost the most typical representative of the primitive Kore among all the Olympians, plays a very secondary and somewhat inglorious part in the Poems. And while Hera and Athena are no doubt very prominent, especially Athena in the Odyssey, there is an obvious avoidance of the conceptions which accompany the worship of the Earth-goddesses, from whom after all Hera and Athena were evolved, and an unmistakable reluctance to speak of such divinities at all. This may be due to contempt or hostility, it cannot be due to ignorance. Homer is not ignorant of Demeter and Persephone and Artemis. But they are not Achaean, they belong to the old religion; and so they are excluded from the Iliad and Odyssey, which are in this as in other things carefully Achaeanized. For reasons we can scarcely hope to discover now, Demeter and Persephone were less amenable to the process which turned Hera into the wife of Zeus and Athena into his daughter. So in Homer they are disregarded.

Yet one may see how deeply the old goddess-worship penetrated the stuff from which our Iliad and Odyssey have been woven by reflecting that for the Trojan Poetry the central theme, the bare plot, is the contest for Helen, and that for the Odyssey it is the contest for Penelope. To Homer indeed, Helen and Penelope are Achaean women, but originally they were pre-Achaean goddesses of Sparta or Therapnai and Mantineia. Their legends are necessarily pre-Achaean too, since they have arisen out of the worship paid to them from so remote an antiquity. The Rape of Helen, the Wooing of Penelope, are in origin 'sacred stories' of dateless age, and recur in other contexts besides the Trojan. Then, as if to show how little that is actually Achaean inheres in the substance of the epic traditions, the really operative deities in Homer are apt to be goddesses rather than gods. In the Iliad, certainly, Zeus and Apollo are especially prominent—Zeus in his capacity of king of the gods, and also perhaps as the tribal divinity of Achilles—Apollo as the great deity of the Troad. But if we except these, it is rather Thetis and Hera and Athena who are most deeply engaged in the conflict. The action of Thetis is an integral part of the Tale of Troy; the story of Achilles could not be told without telling also of his goddess-mother, the silver-footed daughter of Nereus, whose immortality was not beyond the touch of mortal sorrow. But the connexion of Athena with Troy is even more vital. She was the guardian goddess of the town, and her sacred image—the Palladion—had to be carried off before the citadel could be taken.[1] The significance of that for the Trojan Poetry as a

[1] Z 297 f., where the Trojan matrons visit Athena's temple and lay the

whole is not readily exhausted. In the Iliad, however, Athena fights against Troy, because she is the protector of certain Greek heroes, Menelaos, Achilles, Diomedes, above all Odysseus. In the epos generally she often appears in this part of 'strong siding champion' to Herakles or Tydeus, to Perseus or Bellerophon. In the same way, Hera aids Jason and Aphrodite Paris. If you analyse the epic legends, you find as a rule that they recount the achievements of a mortal hero with an urgent and protecting goddess at his side; *dux femina facti*. One is tempted to explain this from the constant association in the old religion of a subordinate male divinity, consort or son, with the goddess; but at present we are scarcely entitled to draw this conclusion. One cannot be mistaken, however, in thinking that these legends arose in an age when men instinctively turned for divine aidance not to a god but to a goddess; and that would not be natural among a people like the Achaeans, whose religion reflected so faithfully the patriarchal character of their institutions. There is, indeed, one god who is also a companion and protector of heroes, namely Hermes. He is a 'Pelasgian', that is a pre-Achaean, god in all but the most superficial points; and it is not at all certain how far this special function of his is primary and original.

Why is it that Athena has so great a place in so many adventures of heroes? Perhaps because she is a War-goddess. But in the case of Odysseus, at least, most readers will feel that some less general explanation is called for, his relation to the goddess being obviously exceptional and, as it were, more personal than we find with others. For indeed, in the process of his idealization from a mere type of primitive cunning, Odysseus came to embody the characteristic qualities of the goddess herself, wisdom and self-control and valour and skill in handicrafts. He has been called[1] the ideal Ionian man;

peplos upon the knees of her statue. Since she is regarded as ῥυσίπτολις (305), it matters little whether Homer knew the story of the Palladion. I myself believe the passage in Z to be late and to imply a knowledge of the Palladion.

[1] By Wilamowitz.

at least he is the masculine counterpart of Athena. We must try then to discover how and where and when their alliance was formed. It is certainly ancient, since it is so deeply rooted in the saga, and although we may well believe that Athena came to play an increasingly important part in the later developments of the Odyssey, especially if we regard these as having taken place at Athens, her association with Odysseus is evidently traditional and not an Athenian invention. As it was in Boeotia that the earliest tales of Odysseus grew up, it is natural to look there for the historical conditions of a connexion apparently so ancient. According to Istros[1] Odysseus was born 'in the neighbourhood of the Alalkomeneion', the temple of Athena *Ἀλαλκομενηΐς*. A tradition so precise and so well attested cannot be disregarded. Still, although Odysseus is connected in so many other ways with Boeotia, we could hardly accept the statement of Istros without confirmatory evidence. But we do find this. The chief city of Ithaca or, as some said, Asteris[2] was called Alalkomenai or Alkomenai,[3] and was founded from the Boeotian town. The latter statement, it might be argued, was a conjecture based upon the similarity of names; and then upon this conjecture another was built, namely that Odysseus was born at the Boeotian Alalkomenai, for people would remember that Antikleia was the daughter of Autolykos who lived on Parnassos.[4] But we find that there was a spring near Mantineia called Alalkomeneias, and when we remember that Mantineia was on the line of the Minyan migration from Boeotia to Ithaca and has given so much to the Odysseus saga, we see that the recurrence of the name cannot be accidental; the name must have travelled from the Boeotian town through Mantineia to Ithaca. Indeed, if our analysis of the

[1] In Plutarch, *Qu. Graec.* xliii, p. 301.

[2] Cf. δ 846.

[3] Strabo, p. 327; p. 457; Plut. l. c.

[4] Lykophron actually says (*Alex.*): *ὃν* (Odysseus) *Βομβυλείας κλιτὺς ἡ Τεμμικία | ὕψιστον ἡμῖν πῆμ' ἐτέκνωσέν ποτε* (786–7). The old scholia add: *Βομβυλεία ἡ 'Αθηνᾶ τιμᾶται ἐν Βοιωτίᾳ. Τεμμικία δὲ ὄρος τῆς Βοιωτίας· λέγει οὖν, ὅντινα ἡμῖν ἡ Βοιωτία κακὸν ἀνέθρεψε· λέγει δὲ τὸν 'Οδυσσέα· ἐν γὰρ Βοιωτίᾳ ἡ 'Αντίκλεια τὸν 'Οδυσσέα ἐγέννησεν.*

saga has any truth in it, nothing is more likely than that there should be a tradition of Odysseus' birth in Boeotia. When we have admitted this, we may accept the story in Istros as having a real historical basis. Athena appears twice in the Iliad with the epithet Ἀλαλκομενηΐς[1]; so that we can assume a great antiquity for her worship in the Alalkomeneion and a certain significance for it in the epic tradition. The Boeotian legends also dwell upon its immemorial age. Alalkomeneus was the first man, and his wife, according to one account, Athenais; and tradition reported that Alalkomenai was the actual birthplace of Athena,[2] as it was of Odysseus. Alalkomenia was the daughter of the primaeval Ogygos,[3] her sisters Thelxinoia and Aulis and herself were worshipped at Mount Tilphousion under the title of *Praxidikai*. We have seen that the cult of the Erinys was imported, with the name Tilphousion itself hardly disguised in Thelpousa, from the Boeotian mountain into Arcadia. And at Asea, on the border of Arcadia and Laconia, Odysseus founded a temple of Athena the Saviour and Poseidon,[4] and here lived the 'Ogygian' Ladon, the father of Daphne.[5] These surely are undesigned confirmations of the traditional connexion between Odysseus and the goddess of Alalkomenai. So the intimate relation between Athena and him in the Odyssey goes back to the Boeotian legends, which form the lowest stratum of the poem.[6]

It has already been remarked that the divine actors in the Iliad and Odyssey are apt to be goddesses. This is especially true of the Odyssey. Hermes, however original in the story, plays but a little part in the action of it. Poseidon and Helios, although the wrath of each is an essential element of the plot, operate mainly in the background; while Zeus is almost unnecessary. But Odysseus never loses the counsel and guidance of some goddess, Athena or Kalypso, Kirke or Leukothea; and when we consider that Penelope, too, was a

[1] Δ 8, E 908. [2] Strabo, p. 413.

[3] Paus. ix. 33. 5; *fr.* 3 *Fr. Hist. Gr.* 4. 394. [4] Paus. viii. 44. 4.

[5] Dionys. *Periegesis* 417; Tzetzes on Lykophron 6.

[6] In that stratum the goddess was probably the Ἀλαλκομενηὶς Κόρη, not yet identified with Athena.

goddess to begin with, we must conclude that the story of the Odyssey grew up among a people very observant of goddess-worship, among a people also very reverent of women, as the Odyssey uniformly is. The old religion was the spiritual expression of a society in which women were held in special honour and enjoyed special privileges; and this attitude to women is reflected in the Odyssey with singular beauty and dignity. There is nothing in Greek literature at all like it until we come to the ideal portraits of women in Attic tragedy. But the heroines of Attic tragedy are taken from the epos, and the dramatists are only maintaining and developing the convention, if we call it a convention, of the epic poetry. The honourable treatment of women which we find in Homer is inexplicable except on the assumption that it met the sympathies of those who listened. Later audiences were trained to sympathize, but the first audiences may have sympathized instinctively. The Odyssey, in its treatment of women, recalls a society in which they held a great place. But to find such a society we must pass out of recorded Greek history throughout which they held in Ionia and Athens, the preservers of Homer, a very different position, and awakened a somewhat different sentiment. We must go back to a pre-Achaean age, for, even if we suppose that the Achaeans had Homer's high regard for women, they must have learned it from the older population of Greece, since it goes naturally with matriarchal institutions, of which we find many traces in prehistoric Greece, while the institutions of the Achaeans were nearly all patriarchal. We may argue that the high and delicate respect for women surviving in the Odyssey is a characteristically 'Mycenaean' sentiment, the characteristically Hellenic feeling being expressed in the words with which Telemachos bids Penelope seek her chamber and ply her loom, for Telemachos is of one mind with Perikles and would have his mother conform to the model of the Athenian *hausfrau*.[1] It is true that the seclusion of women was stricter at Athens than in some other parts of Greece.

[1] φ 350 f.; α 356 f. Cf. Thuc. ii. 45. See Additional Note, p. 237.

The Athenians may have learned this of the Ionians, and they from the Oriental peoples of Asia Minor, for the earliest settlers in Ionia married the women of the native races. It was, on the whole, in the less progressive communities that the privileges of women were greater. Sappho was a Lesbian, Korinna a Boeotian. Lesbos and Boeotia, as we have seen, had very close affinities, and, since Lesbos was early colonized, we are entitled to assume that the comparatively high estimation in which women were held there and in the Boeotia of Korinna's day was a relic of the ancient 'Mycenaean' civilization of the Boeotian Plain. That was the land of the Aeolians, who, we cannot doubt, held women in high honour. The roll-call of the Minyan-Aeolian heroines in the eleventh book of the Odyssey proves that; probably the mere fact that the Minyan culture was of the Aegean or Mycenaean type proves it. And the respect for women in the Odyssey suits the conclusion that it is in substance a Minyan poem.

Yet the sentiment in Homer is normally patriarchal. The husband is master of the house and, in the absence of the husband, the son. 'Men bought their wives,' as Aristotle remarks,[1] the Homeric Greeks being in this respect less advanced than their descendants, who, when they gave their daughters in marriage, furnished them with dowries. The divine family upon Olympos probably reflects pretty accurately the economy of the Homeric human family; Zeus is absolute, 'lord of the household', δεσπότης, although, perhaps for metrical reasons, the word itself does not appear in Homer. I do not wish to dwell upon this contradiction which pervades the Iliad and Odyssey, but merely to suggest that it disappears when we recognize that they were composed for a race with patriarchal institutions out of materials derived from an older matrilinear society. In this sense, too, the saga has been Achaeanized.

The difficult questions raised by the critical study of Homeric warfare and armature seem capable of at least partial solution on the same lines. These questions have more importance for

[1] *Pol.* ii. 8. 12.

the Iliad than for the Odyssey, yet they have their bearing upon the Odyssey too; and I think that the theory of its Boeotian origin and early development among a people who cherished the Minyan traditions will help us in this matter as well. . . . In the oldest form of the Odysseus myth the hero was an archer. That will be admitted even by those who hold that he was from the first a spearman also. Most readers of Homer feel that the bow has no longer the honour it possessed in the days of Herakles and Eurytos. 'Thou archer, thou thing of naught!' cries Diomedes to Paris in the Iliad.[1] It was a finer, perhaps because it was thought a more perilous thing, to be a spearman than a bowman; so that when a warrior is praised for valour he is called a good man with the spear (αἰχμητής). The greater heroes, Achilles and Hector, Aias and Diomedes, Idomeneus and Odysseus himself in the Iliad, never use the bow in battle. Yet there are conspicuous fighters who do, Teukros and Paris and Pandaros, and it is remembered that Herakles was an archer. Of these Teukros has an Asiatic name, Paris is a Phrygian, Pandaros a Lycian, Herakles a pre-Achaean Greek associated with Hera of Argos. Apollo, a god and therefore tenacious of what is old, is an archer, and so is his sister Artemis. The objects of art found in Crete and the Mycenaean sites sufficiently indicate the importance of the bow in the warfare of Minoan and Mycenaean times. The Lokrians, of whom the Iliad says that they had no bronze helmets nor shields nor spears, but came to Troy trusting in their bows,[2] remained down to historical times a comparatively primitive people, who would not forget so quickly as more advanced communities the weapons and customs of earlier days.[3] The bow, then, being so ancient a weapon in Greece, must have been pre-Achaean. And Odysseus must have been a bowman from the first. Moreover, the contest in archery is so necessary a part of the Odyssey that it must be original in the story. In

[1] Λ 385.

[2] N 712 f.

[3] For instance, women held a high position among the Lokroi, who were divided into 100 families derived from 100 heroine-ancestresses. Timaeus in Polyb. xii, ch. 5.

the Odyssey again—and this is somewhat curious, since in the Iliad he never appears as an archer, not even in the games of the twenty-third book—Odysseus boasts among the Phaiakians of his skill with the bow at Troy.[1] Then, if one leaves out of consideration for the moment the Iliad, which after all is an episode, and thinks of the Trojan legend as a whole, one must find it significant that Paris, the prime cause of the war, the hero of the *Kypria*, the slayer with Apollo's aid of Achilles, is an archer, and that the conqueror of Paris, Philoktetes, is also an archer, whose bow, according to the tradition, which has the appearance of being older than that which makes the capture of the city the achievement of so obviously secondary a figure as Pyrrhos-Neoptolemos, was necessary for the taking of Troy. One may add the unpleasant anecdote told by the false Mentes in the first book of the Odyssey, how Anchialos gave Odysseus a man-slaying drug with which to anoint his arrows.[2] That piece of savagery must belong surely to quite the earliest stratum of legend about Odysseus and implies that in it he was an archer.

An archer cannot conveniently use a shield, for, in the first place, he needs both hands for the bow, and then, even if we suppose the shield to be hung upon his body, as the Homeric shields are often fastened by the *telamon* to their wearers, he would not have free play for his shooting. Therefore the archers in the Iliad have no shield, at least in their capacity of archers. At best, a bowman may take advantage of a spearman's shield to shoot from behind that, as Teukros sends his arrows from behind the covert of his brother's tower-like defence. For his own part the archer had to content himself with the simple *laiseion*, a leopard skin such as Paris wore[3] or the hide of a wolf, like Dolon.[4] In the great moment when the disguised Odysseus leaps upon the threshold of his house with the bow of Iphitos in his hands, he strips himself of his rags, and so fights like the archers one sees in Mycenaean art, in the siege scene, for instance, depicted upon the well-known fragment of a silver vase from Mykenai. Must we think,

[1] θ 215 f. [2] α 260 f. [3] Γ 17. [4] K 334.

then, of Odysseus as a shieldless bowman in the oldest legends? Not necessarily. In the Mycenaean vase-fragment the archers are fighting side by side with slingers and spearmen, and in the Iliad we find this too, and, what is more to the purpose, archers like Paris and Teukros laying aside their bows, and fighting with shield and spear.[1] Meriones also, although a spearman, can use the bow as well.[2] So, whatever may be said for the theory that in the *Slaying of the Suitors* we have a conflation of two varying accounts, one representing Odysseus as an archer, the other representing him as a spearman, so far as the archaeological evidence goes there was nothing to prevent his being both. Accordingly, for the purpose of this discussion we may assume that he was in fact both.

If then we allow Odysseus even in the oldest tradition a spear and a shield as well as a bow—the Odyssey has no reference to breastplates—, of what fashion was his shield? Was it the great leathern 'Mycenaean' shield or the round metal buckler? As every one knows, this question of the shields in Homer has awakened a great noise of controversy. But no doubt the majority of competent critics recognize the existence of both kinds of shield in Homer, although they would disagree as to which was meant in particular cases. As to the relative antiquity of the two types in Greece, it is certain that the Mycenaean is older, for the other is characteristic of the Greek hoplite of classical times, while there is no proved trace of it among the Mycenaean remains; and we have besides the definite statement of Herodotus.[3] The older type survived into historical times in the form of the Boeotian or Dipylon shield; and it has been argued that the so-called 'Mycenaean' shields in Homer are, strictly speaking, rather 'Boeotian', since they are carried by warriors riding in chariots, as in Dipylon vases and in the Theban saga, whereas the Mycenaean *aspistes* does not use a chariot. It is, in fact, remarkable how clearly the tradition insisted upon the chariotry

[1] Γ 330 f.; Ο 472.

[2] Ν 650; Ψ 860. Meriones came from Crete.

[3] i. 171.

of the Seven who fought against Thebes; in the drama of Aeschylus it is reverted to again and again.[1] That the Homeric manner of fighting was actually followed in Boeotia is proved by the persistence there of the terms παραβάται and ἡνίοχοι, combatants and charioteers, designating members of the Theban Sacred Band. Indeed, some scholars regard the chariot-fighting in the Iliad as modelled upon the example of the *Thebaid*.[2] All this will be suggestive enough to any one who believes that Boeotia contributed a great deal to the early stages of the epos. But we may be content for the present to accept the great shield as pre-Achaean without claiming it as specifically Boeotian. On the other hand, the round metal targe evidently came with the Achaeans. Its introduction into the saga is another sign of the Achaeanization of Homer.

This special problem has, of course, affected the Odyssey less than the Iliad, but it may be worth while spending a few words on the shields in the Odyssey. That which is worn by Odysseus in the *Slaying of the Suitors* was evidently of the pre-Achaean type, for it was 'of four layers of hide', and he 'put it about his shoulders'.[3] The great leathern shield goes with the archery of Odysseus, since, as Andrew Lang observed, it was more or less a survival from a time when archery was all-important.[4] And surely, too, the antique shield of Laertes, which Melanthios took, was Mycenaean, for it is called 'broad', and the strings of leather with which its folds had been sewn together had burst.[5] Then, in a greatly disputed passage, the *megaron* of Odysseus is described as having shields and helmets hanging upon its walls.[6] This may be a genuine part of the tradition, at least the custom it implies is an historical one. A fragment of Alcaeus, writing about the end of the seventh century before Christ, describes the hall of a warrior as agleam with bronze, 'adorned for Ares' with

[1] See Verrall's edition, Introd., p. xxiii.
[2] Mülder, *D. Il. u. ihre Quellen*, p. 72.
[3] χ 122.
[4] *Anthropology and the Classics*, p. 57.
[5] χ 184, 186.
[6] π 281 f. Cf. τ *ad init.*

helmets and greaves and shields and breastplates.[1] Moreover, the presence of the arms within reach of the Suitors is an element of danger in the situation which cannot be removed without weakening the dramatic intensity of the moment when they realize that the defence on which they had counted so securely had disappeared, and left them helpless before the Archer on the threshold. But if we allow the circumstance of the armour upon the walls as belonging to the original tradition, we must admit that the description in the Odyssey will not bear thinking out. Odysseus and Telemachos contrive and ultimately carry into execution a plot to remove the shields and helmets from the *megaron*; when the Suitors miss the armour, Telemachos is to reply in soft words: 'I have taken them down out of the smoke, since they were no longer like the arms which Odysseus left of old when he went to Troy, but have been marred as far as the breath of the fire reached.' Is not that the reflection of a poet who lived after the custom of hanging armour on the walls had fallen into disuse, perhaps for the very reason given here? One thing, at least, is certain—he is thinking of metal shields; for the Mycenaean shield of wood and leather would take no hurt from the smoke and heat. That he is mistaken, and that the shields were really Mycenaean seems to follow from the circumstance that the shields of Odysseus and Eumaios and that old one of Laertes were taken from the storeroom where the armour from the walls had been deposited.[2] That the shield of Eumaios was Mycenaean, like those of Odysseus and Laertes, is at least very probable, for the spear of Ktesippos grazed the shoulder of Eumaios 'above his shield', and we gain a much clearer picture of how this happened if we imagine the bull's hide on its wooden frame standing before the swineherd (as the fighters in the Iliad rest their great shields before them on the ground) than if we think of him as carrying the round metal buckler.[3] What has happened is surely clear enough. A poet who was familiar with

[1] *Fr.* 56. [2] π 825. [3] χ 279, 280.

metal shields only, and therefore concluded that the shields in the *megaron* of Odysseus were of metal, thought it incredible that they should be thus exposed to the smoke and heat, and so composed the speech of Telemachos to meet this self-created difficulty. As a matter of fact, the speech was never made. The Suitors do not miss the weapons until too late. There I think we revert to the genuine tradition.

Odysseus also says, 'Moreover, God has put this better thought too in my heart—that ye do not become drunken with wine, and set up strife among yourselves, and wound one another. For the iron of itself draweth a man to it.'[1] This poet is wrong again.[2] He has forgotten that the Suitors wear swords,[3] as Homeric warriors regularly do, according to a practice universal in early Greece, as Thucydides and Aristotle have recorded. Monro concludes that the poet lived in an age when the custom of carrying weapons had fallen into desuetude. The inference is surely inevitable, and we are reminded of the statement in Thucydides that the Athenians led the way in discarding the ancient practice.[4] If one combines that with what we know of the recitation of Homer in Athens and with the poet's apparent unfamiliarity with another custom described by Alcaeus, it will seem a plausible guess that the lines were composed there. . . . Obviously this poet was not 'Homer'. But what he did, somewhat awkwardly it must be confessed, was certainly done less conspicuously, partly unconsciously, by others. To search out the evidences of this is not a very pleasing task, nor yet perhaps a very profitable one, for the Iliad and Odyssey, full as they are of hidden inconsistencies, have the organic structure of things

[1] τ 7-13. Cf. π 288 f.

[2] Yet I do not think he invented this excuse but found it in some other part of the epos and used it here to get over the difficulty. The excuse in itself is an excellent one and based upon experience. At Emain Macha 'It was the custom with the men of the Red Branch, if one of them heard a word of insult, to get satisfaction for it on the moment. He would get up in the feasting-hall itself, and make his attack; and it was to prevent that, the arms were kept together in one place'. *Cuchulain of Muirthemne,* Lady Gregory, p. 43.

[3] χ 74.

[4] i. 6. 3.

that have grown and draw their life from a deeper soil than other poems. To think of them as deliberately put together like a mosaic or a pattern is deplorably to misunderstand the theory that they are Traditional Poems. They had an inward principle of vitality which assimilated and wrought into unity every extension of their material, and I am not sure that the unity of the Homeric Poems was not profounder, because it was so much richer in content, at the end of their long development than at the beginning.

CHAPTER IX

THE SONS OF HOMER

> 'Ερχόμενον δ' ἀν' ἀγῶνα θεὸν ὣς ἱλάσκονται
> αἰδόι μειλιχίῃ, μετὰ δὲ πρέπει ἀγρομένοισιν·
> τοίη Μουσάων ἱερὴ δόσις ἀνθρώποισιν.
> ἐκ γάρ τοι Μουσέων καὶ ἑκηβόλου Ἀπόλλωνος
> ἄνδρες ἀοιδοὶ ἔασιν ἐπὶ χθόνα καὶ κιθαρισταί,
> ἐκ δὲ Διὸς βασιλῆες.

WE appear to be constantly misinterpreting Greek literature from forgetfulness of certain elementary enough differences between it and modern literature. We may think that, since Greek poetry produces upon us an effect which we cannot assume to be the same as, or even very like, that which it produced upon those who first heard it, its sole value now is the value it has for us. But that value is a variable quantity. Every work of art means to the critic all that it *can* mean. He knows that, unless he puts himself at the point of view of the ancient poet and his audience, he will never comprehend the total meaning of the art they constructed between them; and this is particularly true of poems like the Odyssey, which expected in its audience a deep familiarity with a tradition only partially recoverable now. So he must make it his aim to recover what he can; to recover what the poet himself found in his poem, and even what his hearers found in it. This, like all other ideals worth following, is never quite attainable, and it is so far incomplete that the critic must, of course, add something of his own, and proceed to interpret, and to relate to other things in the history of Art, what he has thus learnt to understand. We need all the knowledge we can get to save us from the sort of personal impression that is not criticism at all. Criticism is the adventures of a soul among the masterpieces, but not of an uninstructed soul. If we read the Odyssey as if it were at all points comparable with *Paradise Lost* or *Sigurd the Volsung*, if we read Euripides with an eye to Ibsen or Shelley, we shall gain something, but there is a risk of our losing much more. The comparative method has this double edge. Where there exists a spiritual resemblance between an ancient and a modern masterpiece, it is sure to strike an ordinarily intelligent reader. But it is more important that the differences should impress him also, because these are more likely to elude him.

Greek epic poetry was composed for an audience, not for a reading public; it is not inventive, because it professes to deliver the tradition; it is conservative in style, because it is conservative in matter; it is attributed—all the heroic epic is attributed—to a single name. Modern poetry, on the other hand, is composed to be read; it seeks new subjects and new forms; it desires to be individual in manner; and it is so eagerly self-assertive, that it has become hard for us to believe again in the possibility of that proud humility in which artists have been content that their names should be hidden from posterity, if only their work survived.

Whether we hold that the Homeric Poems were composed in an Achaean or Ionian court, or for such popular gatherings as the Panathenaic Festival at Athens, or perhaps were court-poetry to begin with, but were afterwards developed and modified by the practice of recitation before the people—we must on any theory allow for the effect of oral delivery upon the form and character of the Iliad and Odyssey. Epic poetry is spoken poetry, *epê*. It is 'natural' in proportion as it is sensitive to the subtle interrelations of word and speaking voice and listening multitude. This is the true distinction between the natural and the artificial or literary epic; for the art of Homer, although it follows a simpler convention, is as conscious and deliberate as the art of Milton. Neither is *Paradise Lost* artificial because it remembers all great poetry that has gone before it, for the Iliad does that, but because it employs a dramatic form of narrative which was invented to hold the attention of an audience and, in the absence of an audience, becomes inappropriate, and in a quite real sense artificial. If we could recapture the mood in which the long-robed Ionians assembled in Delos listened to the minstrels with such rapture that one would have said that old age and death would never come to them, or the emotions with which the Athenians at the festival of the Goddess hung upon the words of the rhapsode[1]; that would be the spirit in which to read the Odyssey, if it is to mean to us what it meant to the Greeks themselves.

Homer was recited at the *Panathenaia*, as the fourth century statesman Lycurgus tells us.[2] The reciters were called *ῥαψῳδοί*, 'stitchers of songs'—'singers of stitched verses', as Pindar explains the word.[3] It is a colloquial expression for *poets*, and must have arisen in an age when the functions of bard and reciter were not yet separated. So Homer and Hesiod are spoken of quite frankly as rhapsodes, the legends telling how Homer wandered from city to city, an old man and blind, winning a livelihood by the recitation of his poetry. The bard of the Delian *Hymn to Apollo* personates Homer. Pindar tells how Homer related all the virtue of Aias 'according to the rod', which the rhapsode bore in his hand when he was reciting[4]; while Hesiod says that Homer and himself chanted once in Delos 'songs stitched in new hymns' in honour of Phoibos Apollo of the Golden Sword.[5] The rhapsode is, in fact, the lineal descendant of the *aoidos*, and the words are often

[1] Plato, *Ion* 535. [2] *In Leocr.*, p. 209. [3] *Nem.* ii. 1-3.

[4] *Isthm.* iii. 56 f. κατὰ ῥάβδον ἔφρασεν. Prof. Murray writes to me, 'Does κατὰ ῥάβδον imply a stick cut into notches and knobs as a record or *memoria technica*? The Spartan σκυτάλη . . . is not quite parallel'. Some kind of tally of the verses must have been kept by some one. From the analogy of the *skeptron* in the Homeric Assembly and the myrtle bough in the singing of *skolia* it seems likely that at an Agon there was only one rhabdos, which the reciter who had just finished passed on to the rhapsode who was to follow him. κατὰ ῥάβδον might thus mean according to this procedure.

[5] *Fr.* 265 Rzach. The authenticity of the passage is not in question here.—Is not the metaphor 'stitcher of lays' a good deal misunderstood? It can only mean one who adds lay to lay, or verse to verse, as a woman sews one piece of cloth to another. So I think ῥάπτειν βουλάς means to devise a plot by sewing counsel to counsel. If this is the right interpretation of the metaphor in ῥαψῳδός it explains a good deal. Homer and Hesiod in the Ἀγὼν Ἡσιόδου καὶ Ὁμήρου are eminently 'song-stitchers'.

used interchangeably. At first the bard recites his own verses. Among a simple people it would seem an unnatural thing if he did not. Xenophanes of Kolophon, who went about Greece reciting his own verses, might be regarded as a rhapsode,[1] and is at any rate a type. Solon declaims his elegies before his fellow-citizens, adding the force of his personality to increase the effect upon his hearers. Before him Archilochos and Hipponax directly addressed the people, and their invective had the effect of a curse to drive their enemies to suicide. But, sooner or later, the separation was made between composer and reciter, and at last we have the professional rhapsode of the sort depicted in Plato's *Ion*; certainly a recent type, for Ion's art is markedly histrionic, and Aristotle says it was long before the histrionic element invaded tragedy and the epic recitations.[2] Perhaps the growth of professional acting, consequent upon the development of the drama, had its effect upon the character and methods of the rhapsodes. Ion is a very different person from Xenophanes or Kynaithos.

The rhapsode is the *aoidos* in a new guise. But there are points of difference between them which, although not vital, are curious and not unimportant. The rhapsode, for example, carried in his hand a staff or long wand, the *rhabdos*, while Phemios and Demodokos in the Odyssey chant their lays to the accompaniment of the *phorminx*. We cannot tell at what time the lyre was laid aside for the rod; but it must have been early, for we read that the Muses gave Hesiod a staff of laurel wood,[3] and Herakleitos of Ephesos, when he said that Homer ought to be whipped, meant, as the word he used implies, with his own *rods*,[4] and Pindar also, as we have seen, speaks of the reciter's wand. But there is even stronger proof than this of the antiquity of the poet's rod, which is, indeed, far older than the lyre; for it is clearly derived from the staff which the speaker in an Homeric assembly must

[1] All that Diogenes says is ἀλλὰ καὶ αὐτὸς ἐρραψῴδει τὰ ἑαυτοῦ, ix. 18.

[2] *Rhet.* iii. 1, 3 (1403 B) καὶ γὰρ εἰς τὴν τραγικὴν καὶ ῥαψῳδίαν ὀψὲ παρῆλθεν (τὰ περὶ τὴν ὑπόκρισιν).

[3] *Theog.* 30 f. See Additional Note, p. 237.

[4] ῥαπίζεσθαι, *Fr.* 42 Diels.

hold in his hand while he addresses his audience. Therefore, in the *Theogony*, the rhabdos is definitely called by its Homeric name *skeptron*. What, then, is the significance of the staff in the hand of the rhapsode? That it has significance is proved by the fact that it was, as Hesiod says, of laurel, Apollo's sacred tree. The rhabdos comes from Apollo then, Apollo *Mousagetes*; and so it is the Muses who present it to Hesiod. Clearly it was charged with some virtue from the god, exactly as the king's sceptre in Homer, which came originally from Zeus, has some divine quality inherent in it. The sceptre of Agamemnon was worshipped at Chaironeia.[1] It was a δόρυ, or wooden staff, and had a priest of its own, and sacrifices made to it. Such a staff was not of ordinary wood, but was an instrument of magic as well as a sceptre, and the man who possesses it is not only a king but a magician as well, like every primitive king. Achilles swears by the staff he holds while speaking in the assembly of the Achaeans, declaring that the need of him will come upon them so surely as this sceptre will never again break forth into leaf or twig.[2] It was the oath of the Pope to Tannhäuser which was made void by the blossoming of the holy staff. These rods are not cut from any stock, but from some special tree, like the hazel rods which play so great a part in Irish mythology. The rhabdos was cut from the bay-tree, reminding us that the Delphian priestess chewed leaves of the bay that she might become possessed of the god, literally eating him, as I understand the practice, in the sacred tree which embodied him.[3] No one who remembers in how actual a sense the ancient poet felt himself to be inspired will be inclined to doubt that the laurel bough had some relation to the process whereby the bard became ἔνθεος, full of the god. Plato, as every one knows, defined poetry as a kind of madness, 'a mania communicated by the Muses.'[4] It is the old doctrine restated with a touch of Platonic irony. Even the rhapsode shares in the divine

[1] Paus. ix. 40. 11 f.

[2] A 234 f.

[3] See Additional Note, p. 237.

[4] ἀπὸ Μουσῶν κατοκωχή τε καὶ μανία, *Phaedr.* 245 A. Cf. *Laws* iv. 719 C.

effluence proceeding from the Muse, though only indirectly, through the poet whose verses he recites.[1] As to the rhabdos, doubtless in later times it came to be regarded as a symbol. But symbolism of this merely picturesque kind is not primitive, and originally the bard by grasping the sacred wand put himself *en rapport* with the god, who was at once the Nurseling and the Leader of the Muses. The rhabdos became in its degree a medium of inspiration. Without it, it was presumed, the poet could not give proper utterance to what was in him. In a word, it had, like the king's sceptre, like the thyrsus of the Maenad, like the wand of the enchanter, like the Golden Bough, what we should call magical powers.[2]

The recitation of Homer in historical times took the form of a contest, an Agon, in which the rhapsodes contended for a prize of victory. The poet in the Delian *Hymn to Apollo* tells how the gathered Ionians celebrate their god with contests of boxing and dancing and chanted verse (ἀοιδῇ), and bids the maidens of Delos declare his songs to be the sweetest who is a blind man and lives in craggy Chios[3]: while elsewhere in the *Hymns* we find formulas like 'Grant that I win victory in this contest, and grace my lay'. Tradition told of a contest between Homer and Hesiod at Chalkis, in which the poet of truth overcame the poet of romance.[4] There is the story in Herodotus how Kleisthenes the tyrant put down the competitions of rhapsodes at Sikyon because Homer was

Poets compose *φύσει τινι καὶ ἐνθουσιάζοντες, ὥσπερ οἱ θεομάντεις καὶ οἱ χρησμῳδοί*, *Apology* 22 C. Cf. Ezekiel iii.

[1] *Ion* 533 D f. The rhapsode here is of course the professional reciter of poetry not his own.

[2] I think these must be regarded as all pretty nearly identical in their essential character. The matter can hardly be gone into in a note, but it is full of interest. The golden rhabdos of Hermes, which is the necromancer's rod, was given to him by Apollo (*Hymn to Hermes*, 528 f.; Apollod. *Bibl.* iii. 10. 2, 7), and this must be the same as the rhabdos with which Hades leads the dead along the Hollow Way (Pind. *Ol.* ix. 33 f.). The Golden Bough has also power over the dead and is sacred to Juno Inferna and must be put in the hands of Proserpina (Verg. *Aen.* vi. 136 f.). Behind everything, no doubt, is the simple idea of the sacred wonder-working tree or *klados*.

[3] Cf. Thuc. iii. 104. 3 f.

[4] *Erga* 654 f.

so full of Argos and the Argives.[1] Accordingly, while it is true that the bards in the Odyssey do not chant their lays in competition, for these are court-poets; we may assume that the public 'singing' of Homer at festivals was from the first competitive, just like the wrestling and the running and the dancing; for, however much we may dislike the spirit of rivalry in art, we cannot deny that the Agon is a characteristically Greek institution, and that it has had a prodigious influence over almost all the masterpieces of Greek poetry. Aeschylus and Pindar, Sophocles and Aristophanes wrote for victory. That is not the less true because it has not injured the quality of their art, and it is worth remembering when one hears the argument that the art of the Homeric Poems could never have evolved itself under the conditions of public recitation. After all, the prize for which the poets were contending was always understood to be something more than the material one; it was the suffrage of a poetically minded nation, such an audience as no poet has ever had since.

If we understood better the rules observed in the contests of the rhapsodes, we might come to feel that the external form at least of the Iliad and Odyssey has been more definitely moulded by these influences than one had thought. But our information is defective and of doubtful import. At the Panathenaic Festival the rhapsodes were required, in the fourth century before Christ, to recite in such a manner that one took up the story at the point where another left off. This was the method ἐξ ὑπολήψεως.[2] Diogenes of Laerte says they were made to recite ἐξ ὑποβολῆς,[3] but probably Diogenes and the author of the *Hipparchos* mean the same thing. Matters are complicated for us by the attribution of this ordinance regulating the procedure of the reciters by one writer to Solon, by another to Peisistratos or his son. Hence we cannot assume that the method observed at the *Panathenaia* was the method before the institution or revival of the festival by Peisistratos. The tradition about the new ordinance does in fact imply the opposite. Before the time of Peisistratos—

[1] iv. 67. [2] *Hipparch.* 228 B. [3] 1. 2. 57.

and even those who reject the claim made for him that he helped to shape the *corpus* of the Homeric Poems do not question this — the rhapsodes could not have recited in sequence, one beginning where another left off. How then did they recite? If only we could attain a clear notion of that, we might come very near to solving the central difficulty of the Homeric Problem.

The Contest between Hesiod and Homer (Ἀγὼν Ἡσιόδου καὶ Ὁμήρου) is the title affixed to the composition of a scholar of Imperial times embodying some verses attributed to the sophist Alkidamas living towards the beginning of the fourth century B.C. The value of this piece for us—it has no literary value—lies in the evidence it affords of the character and method of that famous combat of wits, as a learned man, a contemporary of Plato, imagined it. Alkidamas, moreover, was working upon a tradition. Accordingly, however much he may invent in the actual words put into the mouth of Homer and Hesiod, it is not likely that he invented the external form taken by the Agon, an amoebean contest in which one poet caps the verses of the other. It will be admitted that, if the rhapsodes of the fourth century declaimed consecutive passages of Homer and the contest among them resolved itself into a mere competition in elocution, this Agon is of quite a different nature. That it is modelled upon a genuinely ancient, naïve literary form is, I think, certain.[1] The question is whether Alkidamas (if we accept him as the author of the existing verses) is right in thinking that such a method of recitation as this form corresponds to was really observed in the contests of the ancient rhapsodes, for of course it is a rhapsodic contest in which Homer and Hesiod are engaged. Most of us will be instinctively impatient of the suggestion that the great epic poetry of Greece can ever have been recited, still less that it can ever have been developed, by a method in which one bard strove to outdo his fellow with finer verses on the same subject. But we must consider the evidence without prejudice. For example, is not some sort of amoebean contest implied in the story which we meet

[1] See T. W. Allen in *J. H. S.* xxxii, Part ii (1912), p. 254 f.

with in the second book of the Iliad, telling how the Thracian Thamyris boasted that he could overcome the Muses in minstrelsy (ἀοιδῇ)?[1] For the Muses sing 'answering one another with sweet voice', ἀμειβόμεναι ὀπὶ καλῇ.

The relation of the poet to the Muses helps us to understand. He is the representative of the Muse, the vessel of her inspiration, her προφήτης; he becomes ἔνθεος and she dwells for a moment within him, she or Apollo, the *Kouros* of the Muses, so that the poet for the time being is himself in some sense divine, θεῖός τις, as Plato expresses it. So Apollo entered into the Pythia. The Muses are the source of all knowledge and song for the bard: 'Ye are goddesses and know all things, but we have heard a rumour only, and nothing at all we know.'[2] He can only say what the Muse puts into his mouth. That is why he begins his lay with *Sing, O goddess*, or *Begin now, Daughter of Zeus*. Such a theory of direct, really physical, inspiration, it may be argued, can be held naturally enough by an original poet, but is grotesque when it is held by a rhapsode like Ion. Perhaps Plato thought it grotesque, although the *Ion*, for all its persiflage, does not prove that. There seems no reason to doubt that Plato is considering, whether favourably or not matters nothing here, a claim made on behalf of the rhapsodes to a secondary kind of inspiration; for, as we saw, the rhapsode of earlier days, the descendant of the *aoidos*, would never have consented to be bound by a text, if indeed a text existed; and in fact literal adherence to any received version, of the Iliad for example, would never have been insisted upon by a Greek audience before the age of Peisistràtos: the rhapsode was in his degree inspired. We must remember that the *aoidos*, Homer or Hesiod, does not claim that he himself is the sole author of his poetry. He is only telling over again an old tale of 'true things' taught him by the Muses the daughters of Memory. That is language which a rhapsode like Kynaithos might have employed with entire propriety. It is language exactly suitable on the lips of any one who is helping

[1] B 595 f. [2] B 485 f.

to transmit a Traditional Poem to posterity. The inspiration of the *aoidos* is not different in kind, although it is greater in degree than the inspiration of the rhapsode, as the ring farther from the magnet has a weaker hold than the ring next to it.[1] But in truth we should have found it hard to tell in the case of any ancient bard when *aoidos* became rhapsode, the reciter of verses made before his day, or of any ancient rhapsode when he shared in the primary inspiration of the *aoidos*; and therefore the ancients themselves did not at first think of them as different. Both are performing the same task, the task of remembering and transmitting. Phemios and Demodokos, to be sure, are not rhapsodes. They do not chant in competition with other bards. But then they are figures of the heroic past as much as Aias and Agamemnon; and we cannot assume because the Odyssey is familiar with such court-poets, who seem an invariable element of every feudal society, that it is the product of an art like theirs. The Greeks themselves never thought so. For them Homer was a wandering minstrel, the father of the Homeridai, the first and greatest of rhapsodes. If this be all a romantic invention, we are not left without evidence from the Poems themselves. We hear of 'the race of bards', φῦλον ἀοιδῶν, evidently a division of the people; and Hesiod says: 'Beggar is envious of beggar, and bard of bard'.[2] Hesiod was no court-poet. And, although Phemios and Demodokos are not rhapsodes, they follow the ways of the rhapsodes.[3] Each rhapsode before he proceeded with his *oime*, the portion of song which he selected or which fell to him to recite, uttered a *prooimion*, a brief appeal for the favour of a god, usually Zeus, or it might be no more than a reverential phrase. Thus when Odysseus asks Demodokos to repeat the tale of the Wooden Horse the minstrel 'starts from a god', and then proceeds with his lay, 'taking the matter up at the point when they went aboard their well-decked ships and sailed away'.[4]

[1] *Ion* 533 f.

[2] *Erga* 26.

[3] Yet Plato actually calls Phemios a rhapsode. *Ion* 533 B.

[4] *θ* 499 f.

Even when Phemios says 'I am my own teacher and the god has breathed all manner of lays in my heart',[1] he is merely claiming to be directly inspired. A rhapsode of the earlier days would have said the same. He too was directly inspired, although he would have said with Blake that the real author of the poem he was reciting was in Eternity —the Muse who has charge of the traditions.

The Muses inspire the poet and are themselves poets. Therefore the manner in which they chant their verses will be modelled upon the method of the bards their servants upon earth; since, of course, the bards drew their conception of the Muses' singing from this method. Pindar says: 'The Sons of Homer, the singers of stitched verses, for the most part begin with Zeus in a prelude.'[2] So doubtless did the Muses—

> First hymn they the Father
> Of all things: and then
> The rest of Immortals,
> The action of men.

Hesiod says that they sang *φωνῇ ὁμηρεῦσαι*,[3] which must mean the same as *ἀμειβόμεναι ὀπὶ καλῇ*. And it is epic poetry that is being chanted here, the *Theogony*. The Muses celebrate 'first, the awful race of Divine Beings from the beginning, the children of Earth and the broad Sky, and the gods that were born of these; then Zeus in turn; and last, the race of men and the Giants.' They dance and play upon the lyre as well; this no doubt owing to the association in primitive times of singing and dancing and poetry, an association which the Muses preserve with the conservatism of divinities. But we are concerned here with the manner in which they chant the *Theogony*, which is the manner of the rhapsodes, one Muse taking up the strain from the lips of another, just as they did when they made lament for Achilles.[4] Now since the Muses sang to Hesiod upon Helikon in

[1] χ 347.

[2] *Nem.* ii. 1–3.

[3] *Theog.* 36 ff. Τύνη, Μουσάων ἀρχώμεθα, ταὶ Διὶ πατρὶ | ὑμνεῦσαι τέρπουσι μέγαν νόον ἐντὸς Ὀλύμπου, | εἰρεῦσαι τά τ' ἐόντα τά τ' ἐσσόμενα πρό τ' ἐόντα, | φωνῇ ὁμηρεῦσαι. Cf. Pind. *Nem.* v. 22 ff.

[4] ω 60.

some manner analogous to that observed by the rhapsodes at the *Panathenaia* in their recitation of Homer, we must admit that the method was not a new one, that it was in fact the traditional method. It is simply the ancient, apparently indigenous, 'amoebean' method carried a little further. One remembers the contests of shepherd with shepherd in Theocritus: how many centuries before had the herdsmen of Sicily and Arcadia so contended? Then there was the banquet-song or *skolion*, accompanied usually by the lyre, like the chanting of the Muses and the bards in Homer. One guest took up the strain from another in due sequence and in some manner of rivalry, as the myrtle-bough, corresponding to the laurel-wood staff of the rhapsode, passed from hand to hand. And it is quite relevant here to think of the choral lyric with its elaborate responsions and correspondences, its strophes and antistrophes, and odes and antodes; a sort of friendly Agon between rival semichoruses. In the same way there was some kind of friendly Agon among the Muses. And it will now perhaps seem clear that an Agon of rhapsodes was based upon the same principle. At first it would be an amoebean contest between bards such as tradition represented the Agon of Homer and Hesiod, the prize falling to the poet who should recite the most and the most beautiful verses. Then from something like a battle of wits between rival minstrels reciting, perhaps improvising, their verses, it became a competition in the recitation of 'Homer', that is to say, the great body of epic poetry which these contests of bards preserved and increased. And still it remained in a quite real sense amoebean, one reciter following and striving to outdo his fellow, much as we may suppose the Muses to have done without jealousy and for no prize, in chanting the generation of the gods. Without some element of challenge, indeed, it is hard to imagine how there could be any Agon at all. But now the challenge consisted in leaving your opponent to continue the familiar story at the point where you left off. Here there was still, one may reasonably presume, some opportunity for originality, if not actually in the composition of new lines, yet in the choice of the best version of the passage recited by you: otherwise one must believe that there already existed a fixed text of Homer to which the rhapsode must keep *verbatim*. Certainly in time an official text, of the Iliad and Odyssey at least, came into being, and the rhapsodes addressed an audience familiar with that. But then rhapsody had become simple elocution.[1]

So there is justification for our view. The phrase applied in the *Theogony* to the Muses to describe their manner of chanting epic hexameters, φωνῇ ὁμηρεῦσαι, if it is to have a meaning conformable to Greek usage in the recitation of the epos, and is not to conflict with the regular phrase ἀμειβόμεναι ὀπὶ καλῇ, must mean 'fitting together with the voice' in the sense that one Muse takes up the song at the point where another leaves off. And since this is what the rhapsodes did, they also might be said φωνῇ ὁμηρεῖν and might be called οἱ ὁμηρεῦντες. What if the ὁμηρεῦντες imagined for themselves an ancestor 'Homer' and called themselves Homeridai, sons of Homer, just as the δαιδάλλοντες gave themselves a mythical ancestor in Daidalos and called themselves his sons, Daidalidai? The process at least is familiar to us from many parallel examples.

That Homer is no more than a type, the representative of all the minstrels who preserved the poetry passing under his name, must, I think, be accepted by any one who gives the most obvious interpretation to certain things which we know to be true of the ancient Greek epos. It is almost enough to remember that the ascription of the Iliad and Odyssey alone to Homer was the result of a continuous process of criticism among the Greeks themselves, which began very early and extended beyond the age of Aristotle, who thought that Homer wrote the *Margites*. Our oldest authorities indicate that in the original tradition Homer is the author of the entire Epic Cycle, as it came to be called; that is to say, of the whole body of epic poetry recited by the rhapsodes. These were the Sons of Homer and all that they sang was his. This does not necessarily imply that they did not inherit much

[1] See Additional Note, p. 237.

ancient poetry from an age anterior to their own, an age, if one cares to think so, of court-poets like Demodokos. But this court poetry, if it existed, was not Homer's, if Homer is the typical rhapsode; so it must have been anonymous. And in fact the assigning of the whole Epic Cycle to one name proves that the Cycle was really anonymous, the Iliad and the Odyssey along with the rest. For it is misleading to speak of an extension of Homer's name from these to other ancient epics not at first attributed to him. The evidence indicates the exact contrary, suggesting that Homeric authorship was only gradually restricted to the Iliad and Odyssey. And it was on purely aesthetic grounds that ancient criticism was led to think of these as alone the work of Homer because only they seemed worthy of him. The principle, which has become explicit in so much modern criticism of Homer, that a unique work of art presupposes a single author, was silently, perhaps only half consciously, accepted in the period of Greek literary criticism following the ages of creative activity. The principle may be true or false in itself, or rather it is true when correctly stated and justly applied. But as applied to Homer it has never sought to base itself upon historical considerations, although it is these which furnish us with our only means of knowing in what sense, and to what extent, the maxim is really applicable here.

When we have a literature of the spoken word, it is the audience that chooses the subject. The relation of the bard to his hearers was so much closer, so much more personal and immediate, than that of the modern poet to his readers that he could not for a single instant put his audience from his mind; the mere necessity of addressing them prevented that. Indeed he was even more dependent upon them than they upon him. He had no other public, no appeal from them to another tribunal or to posterity; if he failed to charm them he was left to present and future oblivion. So, if he was to hold the attention of the people, he must speak of the things for which they cared most: else all the beauty of his art, spent upon a subject about which they had not accustomed themselves to feel vividly, might only serve to puzzle or even irritate them. He was the more bound to consult their tastes, if he was to gain the prize in competition with others. Now one thing above all else, one may almost say to the exclusion of everything else, interested an early Greek audience as a subject for poetry, namely their heroic traditions. Therefore the poet's matter was given him. He might handle the legend it fell to him to recite with as much inventiveness as still left intact its essential elements, with as much novelty of art as seemed consistent with the familiar and consecrated manner of the epic poets—that style which in spite of its vividness and its flexibility is after all so formal. He might do this because 'men give the greater glory to that song which is the newest in their ears'. But the subject itself he could not change.

The Greek epic is saga. If the word *saga* suggests a certain formlessness or artlessness in construction, we may describe it as saga raised to a higher artistic power. The gain on the side of art, however, has involved loss in another direction. By giving perfect form to the Tradition it has checked its further development. The epos is the saga crystallized. We, whose thoughts are so much engaged upon the form of Homer, miss the full understanding and appreciation even of that unless we realize of what it is the form. We know that Roman poetry, and almost all modern poetry, is the product of personal culture, and we forget that Greek poetry is the flower of a great traditional culture. Does that seem too strongly expressed? But what is Greek literature but an epic and a dramatic and even a lyrical version of the myths?[1] And what were the myths but a vast popular literature? One must not deny this the name of literature because it was oral; and after all it has got itself partly written in Homer and Pindar and the Dramatists, on the Parthenon and the vases. I cannot help thinking that Greek scholarship in the immediate future will be very largely concerned with the rebuilding of this Tradition; and I think that the most vital contributions to the study of Greek in recent

[1] Cf. Plato, *Phaedo* 61 B.

years, in religion and art and philosophy, have all been in the direction of such a reconstruction. In the meantime let us at least recognize that the Tradition was there, living a vigorous life of its own, as the slightest acquaintance with Greek Art will show; and that while the individual poet, an Aeschylus or Euripides, would mould it to his own purposes, he, too, was in the tradition, giving the people 'slices from the great banquet of Homer'; in a word a popular poet. Now the matter of the Homeric Poems is the Legend of Troy, something which had a history traceable at least in outline; and the form which now expresses it has also had its evolution parallel to that of the legend itself. The Odyssey is the final stage in a development of style as much as of the matter contained in the poem; the one process accompanies and involves the other. The matter of the saga is not the creation of any individual poet; neither is the style, and for the same reason. The tradition grows and grows: *labitur et labetur in omne volubilis aevum.* The secular trunk puts forth ever new branches, new leaves and blossoms; when it ceases to do this you know that it is dead. Then follows decay, a decay visible enough in much of Hesiod, where, beside a great deal that is really more primitive in substance than anything in Homer, there are clear traces of a decline in the authentic saga spirit, its 'old vigour' and adventurous imagination, and a style which one might almost call pedantic. By a unique and happy fortune one spacious growth of the Greek saga was preserved from decay at the very moment of its richest bloom, and endowed by the magic processes of a perfectly accomplished art with a kind of perpetual life in death. It is perhaps this which in the last resort constitutes the special attraction of Homer for modern readers—the union of marmoreal form with a living body of popular belief dating in its oldest parts from an immemorial antiquity. Here, for once, conscious art and unconscious instinct combine to form a poetry at once 'natural' and 'artificial', at once popular and fastidious. This is why some readers find Homer *naïf*, others almost too deliberately occupied with mere expression, the polished epic style. In reality he is both at once, he is the Greek genius.[1]

The style of the Homeric Poems is, like their matter, traditional. It is constantly reminiscent, it is rich in epithets and expressions inherited from so distant a past that the poet appears only dimly to apprehend their meaning, and in general requiring for their existence, and for this habitual, almost unreflecting use of them, a long period of continuous development in which these perpetually recurring phrases would have time to deposit themselves, little indissoluble crystals, in the epic style. No one who understands the meaning of style would argue that this is the invention of any single poet. But it seems a reasonable position to hold that a single poet may have brought the epic style to the perfection it reveals in the Iliad and Odyssey. The difficulty is that an individual poet will have an individual style, and the greater the poet the more markedly personal will it be. By the Dantesque, the Shakespearian, the Miltonic manner we mean a thing of intensest idiosyncrasy. But the manner of Homer is absolutely impersonal. It does not 'bear the stamp of a master', for that implies some quality personal and peculiar enough to make the style of the master distinguishable from that of his pupils and of all other poets; whereas the style in the *Hymn to Aphrodite* is the same as in *The Deceiving of Zeus*. The ancients, Aristarchos himself, could make no use of this criterion to determine what was the work of the poet Homer and what was not. They might define certain characteristic usages of particular words and idioms in the Iliad and Odyssey which were absent in the apocryphal epics. But these things are not style, and in any case they are trifling enough to be

[1] This is not to deny that one seems to feel in certain places the influence of a later hand at work upon the older material. My argument has reference only to what is most characteristic of the Homeric style. And it is interesting to observe that, just where these personal touches begin timidly to obtrude themselves, as evidently in the *Doloneia*, the style immediately becomes less 'Homeric'; and this although the diction of K—its vocabulary—is not markedly different from that of the rest of the Iliad.

negligible. If we insist on them, we shall have to acknowledge that there are certain differences of the same kind between some books of the Iliad and others, and between the Iliad and the Odyssey as a whole; from which one could only conclude that Homer did not write them both, the inference which Aristarchos was most anxious to destroy. The truth is that the Homeric manner is not so much a style as—may we say?—an institution. How different it is from the manner of every individual poet who has ever written epic, Panyassis for example or Apollonios, steeped as they were in Homer and—Apollonios at least—so frankly imitative! It is of all styles the one most nicely adapted to its matter, yet it is also perhaps the most conventional. That is the price, if one may use the word without suggestion of any artistic loss in the bargain, which it had to pay for just that exquisite adjustment to its theme, the heroic tradition. This is not language of philosophical precision. The distinction between form and matter, however convenient and indeed necessary, tends always to bring confusion into the discussion of any question of art, since it is just this distinction that art is continually striving to abolish. But on this higher ground the character of the Homeric style only appears the more clearly. You cannot separate it from the tradition for which it finds a voice. It is itself a tradition, an aspect of the tradition.

Hence comes another paradox of the Homeric style, that it is at once archaic and archaistic; genuinely archaic because it is the traditional saga style, but archaistic also because it is conservative of all archaic elements from a conscious artistic intention. This archaizing tendency, so characteristic of all serious Greek poetry, is comparable to, or rather is a necessary consequence of, the instinct which leads not Homer only but Stesichoros and Pindar and the Attic Tragedians to go back for their subjects to an ideal past. Words dignified by ancient use, glimmering with the magic of old associations, the authentic speech of the gods, are needed to reproduce the colour and sentiment of that ideal, to the Greeks very present, world. For, as Aeschylus says in the *Frogs*, it is natural that the heroes of old should use a larger utterance than we, 'for indeed their garments are much more imposing!'[1] The Homeric style is particularly sensitive to this feeling, and it is so just because it is a traditional style. And it was Homer more than any other single influence who taught all subsequent Greek poetry to charge itself as fully as possible with the colour and sentiment of a heroic past and who teaches epic poetry to do so still.

We can understand what is meant by a traditional style without a definition, for we have many examples of the thing itself. A perfect instance is the style of the Ballads. Those who believe in a single author of the Iliad and Odyssey argue that it may be true that the style of Homer is traditional, but it has a power and splendour which traditional poetry, the Ballads for example, does not elsewhere possess and of which it is, when left to itself, apparently incapable. Therefore we must suppose that this unique power and splendour are a contribution to the traditional epic style from a unique poet. This is pretty much the argument of Matthew Arnold in the essays *On Translating Homer*. Homer, he says, differs from the Ballads by his possession of 'the grand style', and that can belong only to a great individual poet. Now the Homeric Poems exhibit the grand style throughout, and therefore they are from beginning to end the work of one great poet, say rather a supreme poet—Homer. It is this argument which beyond all other seems persuasive to lovers of poetry who have not had the time or the training—I do not say this of Arnold, although he has clearly not thought out the historical problems connected with Homer—to understand the conditions under which the arts evolved themselves in ancient Greece; and it appeals to the instinct of hero-worship. But in fact it is surely a mere begging of the question.[2] How do we know that a traditional style cannot rise above a certain elevation? We may deny (although the denial is quite arbitrary) the possibility of 'the grand style' in ballad poetry: but that does not at all destroy the force of the analogy. If in the

[1] 1060 f.

[2] Cf. Jebb's *Introduction* to Homer, p. 156.

Iliad the traditional epic style has been raised to a higher power, so has the ballad style in *Clerk Saunders*. But *Clerk Saunders*, we say, owes its present perfection of form to constant rehandling and, at the last, a little selective editing; we do not assign it to a single unknown poet. Well, if a ballad can gather beauty in this way, so could the epos. What right have we to say: 'Thus much beauty can the Iliad have gathered in this way and no more'? Neither ought we to forget among what people the Iliad came to birth. Obviously the only critical method of deciding the question at issue is to study them and the methods of their poets.

Thus the argument for a single author which is based upon the style of the Homeric Poems becomes in the end a simple appeal to the feeling we have that the finest qualities of art, at any rate art of so elaborate and costly a kind as that of the Iliad, can never belong to popular poetry. The feeling is probably a just one. But traditional poetry is not necessarily popular poetry, and certainly the Homeric Poems cannot be described simply as popular. The epos belongs to a genus of its own which dispenses with the necessity of feeling about it in any such way at all; it is not too strong to say, makes any such feeling appear unintelligent. We should be merely deceiving our imaginations if we talked of the Homeric style as if it were somehow created by the poetical instinct of the people. It is really the product of the interaction through long ages of development of two complementary forces, the poet and his audience. The poet contributed his personal gift, his exceptional instinct for form; the audience determined his choice of a subject and the general character of its treatment. We should remember that the audience of the minstrel or rhapsode was not, as in our theatres, a more or less haphazard collection of people with nothing in common but an interest in the performance, but the people itself, the Polis, burningly conscious of its solidarity, still capable of imaginative emotions, and therefore supplying a profound stimulus to the artist addressing it. It was an audience of this kind which made the Attic and the Elizabethan drama possible, and it was just as necessary for the development of Homer and the Homeric style. It was even more necessary because, while the Attic tragedians dealt with the saga, Homer was the saga itself, the spiritual inheritance of the people. It was only so long as the saga was alive in the popular heart that the Greek epos could grow, as, in spite of a certain formality or conventionality of expression characteristic of traditional poetry everywhere, it has grown in Homer, naturally as a flower.

It is, however, possible to argue that, while the style of Homer is traditional and therefore no criterion, there is proof of a single poet's dominating influence in the structure and conduct of the plot in the Iliad and Odyssey, what Arnold would have called the architectonics of such complex masterpieces. Style, it may be said, is within the reach of any competent craftsman trained in a good tradition, but construction cannot be taught, construction is invention. But must it be the invention of a single mind? Every one knows it need not be so. Plots are constantly produced by collaboration. In the case of Homer we can put the matter even more definitely. The effectiveness of the Odyssey in respect of its plot is that of a perfectly told story. It was a very ancient story and it had been told by many minstrels before any credible 'author of our Iliad and Odyssey' could have been attracted to it. Is the inference not clear? With each successive telling the story must have tended to adapt itself more and more nicely to the tastes of those who listened, to become more dramatic, to become more effective simply as a story, to improve the plot. To this end, here as in the formation of the Homeric style, the poet and his audience worked together. The latter gave as its contribution the general imaginative exaltation of a people still in the mythopoeic age, fusing the scattered elements of tradition, unconsciously moulding and remoulding their unforgotten tales of gods and heroes. The poet gave his art. These two influences co-operating through many generations—deliberate skill working experimentally upon the native story-telling faculty—were certain in the end, among Greeks at any rate, to produce a model of narrative art. They did so in the Odyssey. There the two influences are clearly discernible: the popular imagination combining the diverse elements of the story, Boeotian, Arcadian, Ithacan, into an organic whole; and then, on the other hand, the skill of the professional story-teller cunningly heightening the interest, making it all as dramatic and exciting and lucid as possible.

But it is necessary to find some answer for another and really penetrating question, which may be thus expressed: 'Granted that the Odyssey has attained to its present excellence through a progressive concentration of the diffused imaginative ardour of a poetically minded people and the perfecting of the plot by constant rehandling, we have still to explain how the Iliad and Odyssey came to be regarded as exceptional among the poems of the Heroic Cycle and alone worthy of "Homer". Was it not because they were wrought into their present form by Homer indeed, by one poet greater than the rest by the measure in which the Iliad and the Odyssey excelled the *Kypria* and the *Thebais*?'—The answer is that at a certain point in the development of the whole Epic Cycle (to use the convenient later term) the attention of the minstrels was centred upon these two poems to the exclusion or comparative neglect of the rest, with the result that the latter remained in a relatively rude and artless state, while the former were carried ever nearer perfection. Then the question takes a new form: 'What was it in the Iliad and Odyssey that engaged the interest and labour of the bards in this special degree? Was it not some peculiar excellence which these poems had, and the others had not, already? And does not this imply that an exceptional poet had been at work upon them?' The answer to this has been anticipated. Where we have a traditional recited poetry it is not the bard but the audience that chooses the subject. Accordingly, to say that the poets concentrated on the two Homeric epics for their quality as literature is a manifest *hysteron proteron*. What then was it that attracted the interest of the people to the Iliad and the Odyssey? That is the right form in which to put the question. But, after all, we are not bound to find an answer. For some reason, now perhaps past finding out, the tale of the Wrath of Achilles, the tale of the Wanderings and Vengeance of Odysseus, more than other stories captured the imaginations of the Greeks. There is nothing singular in this, it is what has always happened. We cannot tell why the death of Hrodland of the Breton March awoke such echoes in mediaeval Europe, nor why King Arthur became so great a subject of song and story, or Siegfried, or Cuchullain, or Beowulf. Suppose that in each case it was some poet who sowed the seed from which sprang so great a tree, such a poet would not answer at all to the ordinary conception of Homer as the author of the finished Iliad and Odyssey. And suppose that the analysis of the Odyssey attempted in this book is even partially right, how are we to think of Homer? As an Athenian or an Ionian, as Achaean or pre-Achaean? These questions are insoluble; and so is the question what it was that recommended the two great epics to the early Greeks. Even if very plausible reasons were suggested, it is extremely probable that none of them would be the true one; it might be something more apparently capricious. To account for the attraction of the Odyssey, with which we have been more specially concerned, several suggestions have been made. One is that the opening up of the Western Seas gave new life and meaning to the old saga of the mariner who sailed into the Sunset, just as the exploration of the Black Sea appears to have given a fresh lease of life to the epic of the Golden Fleece. Another, more perilous, suggestion is that Peisistratos had a personal interest in a hero with whom he claimed to be, though indirectly, connected by descent, and whom in many points he really resembled and perhaps in some degree imitated.[1] But for us the best explanation will be found in the history of the saga

[1] In the story of Phye he appears as the favourite of Athena like Odysseus. Her. i. 60. Solon said to Peisistratos when the latter mutilated himself that he was imitating Odysseus. Plut. *Solon* xxx.—For the genealogy of Peisistratos see Seeck, *Quellen der Odyssee*, p. 327 f., p. 342 f. But see also Toepffer, *Attische Genealogie*, p. 85, n. 3.

itself. Long before Peisistratos, the Ionians loved to hear it. So many of them, so many of their princes at least, claimed to be Sons of Neleus, children of the race which so long ago occupied Ithaca. Thus the Odyssey was in a peculiar degree their 'national Epic'.

CHAPTER X

HOMEROS

τὸ ὑπ' ἐνίων λεγόμενον ὡς Ἀπόλλων αὐτὰ ποιήσας τὸν Ὅμηρον ἐπέγραψε τῇ ποιήσει. Philostratos, *Heroicus*, 317.

The Muses had their earthly analogues in many maiden-choirs worshipping their god with dance and song in his temple or at his Festival. But there is one chorus whose analogy with the Muses is so complete, that it excites a special interest. This is the chorus of Kourai or Maidens addressed by the poet in the Delian part of the Homeric *Hymn to Apollo*. They are 'servants of the Far-Darter. First they hymn Apollo, then Leto next and Artemis the Archer; then celebrate in song the men and women of old, enchanting the tribes of folk assembled; and they can imitate the speech and the castanet-music of every man, that he would say it was his own voice he heard. So fairly is their song fitted together.'[1] Well, the Muses sing the same things and in the same order, and are pre-eminently 'servants of Apollo'. But this is not all. Apollo himself, that is the *Delian* Apollo, has grown out of the ritual-dance of his Kourai, which goes back to the very beginning of his worship in Delos. There he is *Letoides*, the son of Leto, a women's god, of whom his father

[1] 157 ff.
κοῦραι Δηλιάδες Ἑκατηβελέταο θεράπναι·
αἵ τ' ἐπεὶ ἂρ πρῶτον μὲν Ἀπόλλων' ὑμνήσωσιν,
αὖτις δ' αὖ Λητώ τε καὶ Ἄρτεμιν ἰοχέαιραν,
μνησάμεναι ἀνδρῶν τε παλαιῶν ἠδὲ γυναικῶν
ὕμνον ἀείδουσιν, θέλγουσι δὲ φῦλ' ἀνθρώπων.
πάντων δ' ἀνθρώπων φωνὰς καὶ κρεμβαλιαστὺν
μιμεῖσθ' ἴσασιν· φαίη δέ κεν αὐτὸς ἕκαστος
φθέγγεσθ'· οὕτω σφιν καλὴ συνάρηρεν ἀοιδή.
My translation of the last three lines is tentative. Hesychios says *s. v.* κρεμβαλιάζειν· κογχύλια καὶ ὀστᾶ ἅμα συγκροτοῦντας ἐρισμόν τινα ἦχον ἀποτελεῖν ὀρχουμένοις.

'took no heed'.[1] Just as Dionysos cannot be understood apart from his thiasos of dancing Maenads, so Apollo of Delos is only understood from his relation to his singing Maidens.[2] Yet we know so little of these Maidens, that the inference I have drawn no doubt requires further confirmation.

The existing *Hymn to Apollo* is simply the latest, the most complete and finished, form of the ancient ritual chant, which related the Birth of Apollo in Delos, just as the Dithyramb was concerned with the Birth of Dionysos.[3] It had been the business of the Kourai, from a time we do not know how remote, to chant this hymn. In other words it was a Traditional Poem. Such a poem will have a traditional author; the author of the Delian hymn was Homer. 'And I bid you hail, Maidens every one! And do ye make mention of me hereafter also, whenever any other of the toilsome race of mortal men shall come hither and ask you, *Maidens, of the minstrels who frequent this isle which is the sweetest in your thoughts, and in whom do ye most delight?* Answer fairly with one accord, *A blind man, and he lives in rocky Chios.*'[4] The blind man of Chios is Homer. But of course no one now believes that our *Hymn* was composed by the man of Chios; it is only attributed to him. The real author is personating Homer.[5] The impersonation, let us observe, must have been

[1] *Hymn to Hermes* 557 πατὴρ δ' ἐμὸς οὐκ ἀλέγιζεν.

[2] For Apollo as Kouros see *Themis*, pp. 439–44.

[3] Plato, *Laws* 700 B ἄλλο, Διονύσου γένεσις οἶμαι, διθύραμβος λεγόμενος.

[4] 166 ff.
χαίρετε δ' ὑμεῖς πᾶσαι· ἐμεῖο δὲ καὶ μετόπισθε
μνήσασθ', ὁππότε κέν τις ἐπιχθονίων ἀνθρώπων
ἐνθάδ' ἀνείρηται ξεῖνος ταλαπείριος ἐλθών·
ὦ κοῦραι, τίς δ' ὔμμιν ἀνὴρ ἥδιστος ἀοιδῶν
ἐνθάδε πωλεῖται, καὶ τέῳ τέρπεσθε μάλιστα;
ὑμεῖς δ' εὖ μάλα πᾶσαι ὑποκρίνασθ' ἀμφ' ἡμέων·
τυφλὸς ἀνήρ, οἰκεῖ δὲ Χίῳ ἔνι παιπαλοέσσῃ,
τοῦ πᾶσαι μετόπισθεν ἀριστεύουσιν ἀοιδαί.

For the reading of line 171 see T. W. Allen, *Hom. Op.* v. (Oxford text) ad loc. Cf. Thuc. iii. 104 τὸν γὰρ Δηλιακὸν χορὸν τῶν γυναικῶν ὑμνήσας [Ὅμηρος] ἐτελεύτα τοῦ ἐπαίνου ἐς τάδε τὰ ἔπη, ἐν οἷς καὶ ἑαυτοῦ ἐπεμνήσθη· ἀλλ' ἄγεθ' κτλ. (165 ff.).

[5] Thus Chrysothemis personated Apollo. Proclus (Phot. *Bibl.* p. 320) Χρυσόθεμις ὁ Κρὴς πρῶτος στολῇ χρησάμενος ἐκπρεπεῖ καὶ κιθάραν ἀναλαβὼν εἰς μίμησιν τοῦ Ἀπόλλωνος μόνος ᾖσε νόμον. Cf. the story of Arion, Her. i. 24.

like the hymn itself traditional. As an innovation it would have been meaningless and intolerable, above all on a solemn occasion like the Delian Festival and in chanting the ancient hymn of the god. It clearly goes along with the tradition that Homer was the author. Whatever the new minstrel might add of his own was added in the name and in the character of Homer. To chant the hymn as his own composition would have seemed a lie and an impiety.

The relation of the minstrel to the choir is explained by several passages in the Iliad and Odyssey, as well as elsewhere. When Demodokos was about to chant his Lay of Ares and Aphrodite, he stepped into the midst of the Phaiakian youths and so with harp and voice led their dancing.[1] On the shield of Achilles was depicted a dance of young people, and in the middle of the dancers a divine minstrel sang to the lyre.[2] On another part of the shield Hephaistos had wrought a different company of dancing youths and maidens, whose minstrel was not any professional *aoidos*, but one of themselves: 'In the midst of them a boy made pleasant music on a clear-toned phorminx, and sang thereto the sweet *linos* with delicate voice,' while they followed dancing and crying aloud.[3] The minstrel therefore acted as ἐξάρχων or χορηγός of the choir. Hence Apollo is sometimes called *Mousagetes*, Leader of the Muses: they dance and sing, Apollo in the midst with his lyre. According to the Pythian *Hymn*, when Apollo appears the Muses and the gods join in the dance, while he makes music among them[4]; and the Hesiodic *Shield of Herakles* speaks in the same way: 'There, too, was a sacred dance of Immortals; and in the midst accordingly (ἄρα) the Son of Zeus and Leto played sweetly on a golden lyre,' while 'the goddesses, Muses of Pieria, struck up the song'.[5] On the Chest of Kypselos were represented the Muses singing, and Apollo leading the song.[6] Dionysos, one of whose titles

Assuming the στολή was a way of assimilating oneself to Apollo Kitharoedos.

[1] θ 262 ff. [2] Σ 590 ff. [3] Ibid. 567 ff. [4] 186 ff. [5] 201 ff.

[6] Paus. v. 18. 3 πεποίηνται δὲ καὶ ᾄδουσαι Μοῦσαι καὶ Ἀπόλλων ἐξάρχων τῆς ᾠδῆς.

was *Melpomenos*, in like manner leads the dance of his votaries[1]; nay, the very Moon and Stars dance in his train.[2] Thus, whatever modifications may have been introduced in later days by the development of rhapsody, the original custom at Delos must have been for the minstrel to act as Exarchon of the Maiden-choir.

The learned author of the *Certamen* tells us that Homer visited the Panegyris at Delos. 'And standing upon the Altar of the Horns he recited the hymn to Apollo which begins: *I will remember and will not forget Apollo the Far-Darter.* When they had heard the hymn, the Ionians made him a citizen of their League (πολίτην κοινόν), while the Delians engraved the verses on a tablet and dedicated it in the temple of Artemis.'[3] We are put in touch with a genuine tradition. The white tablet or λεύκωμα undoubtedly existed, and its existence explains the second part of the legend. But what is the explanation of the first part? There the evidence fails us. This, however, is clear; the chanting of the hymn somehow centred about the Horned Altar. It does not seem an unwarrantable inference to suppose that by immemorial custom the Delian Maidens in chanting their hymn danced about the *Keratôn.* Round it, we know, was performed the Delian Crane-dance.[4] The actual scene of the Maiden-dance, however, does not immediately concern us. But, with regard to Homer, observe that, whether we think of him as founding the contest of minstrels at the Delia or as taking part in the contest already existing, he remains the type of the victor. This is clearly implied in our *Hymn*, as Thucydides has remarked. The poet, personating Homer, being indeed, in the opinion of Thucydides, Homer himself, prays Apollo and Artemis and the Kourai to grant him the victory.[5] An apocryphal fragment of Hesiod evidently refers to some

[1] Eur. *Bacchae* 140 ὁ δ' ἔξαρχος Βρόμιος. Cf. 115.

[2] Soph. *Antig.* 1146 ff. χοράγ' ἄστρων. Cf. Eur. *Ion* 1074 ff.

[3] 316 ff.

[4] Plut. *Life of Theseus* xxxi ἐχόρευσε δὲ περὶ τὸν Κερατῶνα.

[5] iii. 104.

tradition of an Agon between Homer and Hesiod at the Delian Festival. 'Then for the first time Homer and I chanted our minstrelsy in Delos, stitching song in new hymns, chanting in honour of golden-sworded Apollo, whom Leto bare.'[1] Thucydides at least is quite definite. The Ionians used to assemble with their wives and children at Delos, and 'there was an athletic competition and a competition of minstrels, and the various states sent choruses to the god'.[2] The Athenians in 426 B.C. merely revived the competitions, which had fallen into desuetude.[3]

We have got two results. Homer, as Aoidos of the Kourai, must have been thought of originally as their Exarchon. Secondly, Homer was victor in the contest of minstrelsy. The tradition must reflect the historical practice at the Delia. The practice may have been changed or discontinued quite early. But at first the contest was to decide who should be the Leader of the Maiden-choir when they chanted their ancient hymn to the god; who, in fact, was to personate Homer. We shall find an exact parallel to this at Olympia. The Games decided who was to be Exarchon of the kômos chanting the traditional hymn of Archilochos; and on the part of the Olympian Victor also we find just such an impersonation. And here we may note, as an additional confirmation, that the Delian choir not merely chants the hymn to Apollo, but goes on to chant of 'the men and women of old', the reference unmistakably being to the heroic epos, to 'Homer'. We see that the Muses are a replica of the Delian Maidens; and that Homer, as their Aoidos and Exarchon, stands to the Kourai precisely in the relation in which Apollo Mousagetes or Mousarchos stands to the Muses.

[1] *Fr.* 265 (Rzach) ἐν Δήλῳ τότε πρῶτον ἐγὼ καὶ Ὅμηρος ἀοιδοὶ μέλπομεν, ἐν νεαροῖς ὕμνοις ῥάψαντες ἀοιδήν, Φοῖβον Ἀπόλλωνα χρυσάορον, ὃν τέκε Λητώ.

[2] l. c. καὶ ἀγὼν ἐποιεῖτο αὐτόθι καὶ γυμνικὸς καὶ μουσικός, χορούς τε ἀνῆγον αἱ πόλεις.

[3] Ibid. τὰ δὲ περὶ τοὺς ἀγῶνας καὶ τὰ πλεῖστα κατελύθη ὑπὸ ξυμφορῶν, ὡς εἰκός, πρὶν δὴ οἱ Ἀθηναῖοι τότε τὸν ἀγῶνα ἐποίησαν καὶ ἱπποδρομίας, ὃ πρότερον οὐκ ἦν.

The reader will recall the expression used to describe the chanting of the Muses: *φωνῇ ὁμηρεῦσαι.*[1] The same expression is entirely applicable to the chanting of the Kourai; indeed, the phrase actually used in the *Hymn*, *οὕτω σφιν καλὴ συνάρηρεν ἀοιδή*, is but a variant of it. But if the choir is composed of *ὁμηρεῦσαι* and its minstrel is called *Ὅμηρος*, we have here the basis of a philological explanation of the name Homer. To explain *Ὅμηρος* without relation to the *ὁμηρεῦσαι* would be as futile as to explain *Δαίδαλος* apart from the *δαιδάλλοντες*. We all understand Daidalos. He is the imaginary founder of their craft evolved by the *δαιδάλλοντες*. In the same way Homer is the legendary first Aoidos imagined for themselves by the *ὁμηρεῦσαι.*[2] Analogous is the process by which so many peoples and communities, so many tribes and families in ancient Greece invented for themselves a divine founder or ancestor. The invention was sometimes, but not very often, deliberate. Few things are more remarkable in so rational a people than the *naïveté* with which the Greeks would accept the historical existence of figures like Doros or Ion, like Dardanos or Dolops or Eumolpos, or even 'Tekton Harmonides' (*E* 59).[3] The explanation is a psychological one. The Greeks believed in these people because they did *not* consciously invent them.

But we may go farther. The verb *ὁμηρέειν* (*ὁμηρεῖν*) can only mean 'to be *ὅμηρος*'; as *φιλεῖν* means to be *φίλος*, *ἀδικεῖν* to be *ἄδικος*, *εὐορκεῖν* to be *εὔορκος*.[4] Now we can tell what it is to be *ὅμηρος*; it is to dance and sing like the

[1] Hes. *Theog.* 39.

[2] Cf. Fick, *Personennamen*, 2nd ed., 1894, p. 423; also p. 367. To Fick's list we may add Τέκτων Ἁρμονίδης E 59, Εὐάγγελος, ancestor of the Εὐάγγελοι or Εὐαγγελίδαι, functionaries at the oracle of Apollo at Branchidai. Konon, 44. Euangelos was *ἄγγελος τῶν μαντευμάτων.*

[3] Many instances in Fick, op. cit., esp. pp. 356 ff.

[4] Hesych. *s. v.* *ὁμηρεῦσαι· ὁμοφωνοῦσαι, ὁμοῦ λέγουσαι.* *Et. Mag. s. v.* Ὅμηρος . . . Ἡσίοδος '*φωνῇ ὁμηρεῦσαι*' *τουτέστιν ὁμοῦ εἴρουσαι.* This etymology was probably suggested by the previous line (38) of the *Theogony*, *εἰρεῦσαι τά τ' ἐόντα τά τ' ἐσσόμενα πρό τ' ἐόντα.* P. D. Ch. Hennings, *Homer's Odyssee*, 1903, p. 3, says, 'Abgeleitet von *ὅμηρος* ist jedenfalls das Verb *ὁμηρεῖν*.'

Delian Kourai (including, we may suppose, their Exarchon), like the Muses, like any similar chorus of men or women. *Ὅμηρος*, then, the imagined Head of the *ὅμηροι*, has come into existence by exactly the same process as that whereby Amphiktyon was 'projected' from the Amphiktyones, or Bakchos from the Bakchoi and Bakchai. However we may conceive the process, the direction of it is here quite clear and certain; it is from the *ὁμηρεῦντες* or *ὁμηρεῦσαι*, the *ὅμηροι*, to *Ὅμηρος*. Their existence was a preliminary condition of his. And it is quite natural and according to analogy that the leader of the Kourai should personate, or even be identified with, Homeros himself. 'A number of difficult passages', says Professor Murray, 'in Euripides' Bacchae and other Dionysiac literature find their explanations when we realize how the god is in part merely identified with the inspired chief dancer, in part he is the intangible projected incarnation of the emotion of the dance.'[1] The meaning of this will be developed as the argument proceeds.

In the meanwhile we may stop to consider certain initial advantages in the result we have obtained. It does give us an intelligible account of the name Homeros; and that is much. Again, it explains, and in a manner justifies, the confused stories about Homer current in antiquity. If 'Homer' was really a functionary in the Delia, we can understand why so many states might claim to be the birth-city of the poet, and why he was so generally regarded as an Ionian. Apollo was the Theos Patrôos of the Ionian race.[2] The minstrel of the Delian hymn must have been, at least usually, an Ionian.[3] Now this

[1] *Four Stages of Greek Religion*, p. 43.

[2] Plato, *Euthyd.* 302 C *οὐκ ἔστιν, ἦν δ' ἐγώ, αὕτη ἡ ἐπωνυμία* [Ζεὺς ὁ Πατρῷος] Ἰώνων οὐδενί . . . ἀλλ' Ἀπόλλων πατρῷος διὰ τὴν τοῦ Ἴωνος γένεσιν. At Delos he had the title Γενέτωρ. Diog. Laert. viii. 1. 13. Seeing that the Delia was a Pan-Ionic assembly, this evidence, taken with the statement of Plato, is surely decisive. If it were not, the story of Ion would make it so. Ion would not have Apollo for his father, unless the god had been Patrôos of the Ionians before the legend arose.—The evidence for Athens is abundant, and accepted by every one.

[3] And if not, the Kourai could speak his dialect. This appears to be the meaning of the obscure words *πάντων δ' ἀνθρώπων φωνὰς καὶ κρεμβα-*

state and now that must have had the distinction of producing the Homeros for the current Festival; and so would arise all those conflicting claims to the possession of the authentic Homer, claims which would naturally be most loudly asserted where some famous Homeros had succeeded in founding a school. Such, apparently, was the Homer of Chios; and we know of historical Homeridai there.[1] The author of the existing *Hymn* was perhaps a Homerid of Chios. In the same way, Melesigenes and Maionides may have been real people—Homeroi at the Delia. Melesigenes, it is true, belonged to 'Aeolian' Smyrna; and so, it seems, did Maionides, if he is rightly distinguished from Melesigenes. But, even if we reject the statement of Strabo that it was originally colonized from Ephesus,[2] we can be sure that there was always an influential Ionian element in Smyrna, and we know that after 688 B.C. the town became definitely Ionian.[3] The Smyrnaean Homer had a shrine (*Ὁμήρειον*), because in his lifetime he had assumed a sacred function. There was a Homer born in Ios, and evidently buried there and honoured as a Hero. Another Homer, perhaps, was Kreophylos of Samos or Chios or Ios—the variation is instructive—but probably really of Samos, since he appears to have left descendants there.[4] A certain Thestorides of Phokaia may have played the part of Homer. Kolophon also has a claim. The traditions are not all of equal value, and some of them are manifestly built upon conjecture. We know what to think of a story which assigns Homer to Athens or Argos or Ithaca,

λιαστὺν μιμεῖσθ' ἴσασιν (160 f.). See Sikes and Allen, ad loc. It looks as if the strange passage δ 277 f. concerning Helen and the Wooden Horse had some bearing on the point. See esp. 279 *πάντων Ἀργείων φωνὴν ἴσκουσ' ἀλόχοισιν*. Yet I admit the connexion eludes me.

[1] Suidas *s. v.* *Ὁμηρίδαι· οἱ δὲ γένος ἐν Χίῳ ἀπὸ τοῦ ποιητοῦ ὠνομασμένον*. Cf. Harpokrat. *s. v.* *Ὁμηρίδαι*; Schol. Pind. *Nem.* ii. 1–3. The chief sources for the Homer stories are of course the *Lives* and the long article *Ὅμηρος* in Suidas. They are most conveniently found in the Oxford text, vol. v. A careful discussion in Monro's *Appendix* to the Odyssey, pp. 385 ff.

[2] xiv. 634.

[3] Mimn. 9; Herod. i. 16; 150. Paus. vii. 5. 1; ix. 21. 2.

[4] Heraklid. *Pol.* 2—the Lykourgos story.

not to mention Egypt or Rome. But it is different with the legends which have gathered about an actual tomb or temple, and our explanation supplies them at any rate with a *vera causa*. If they seem to us now purely fabulous, that may only be because the spirit of romance has been at work upon a little core of fact in each, until the whole has been transformed. For the popular imagination loves

> Blind Thamyris, and blind Maeonides,
> And Tiresias, and Phineus, prophets old.

I have put these stories at their highest historical value, because, wherever an historical explanation is possible, it should be considered first. But another, and I incline to think a more probable, theory of the origin of at least some of them may be advanced. The *Homereion* at Smyrna may have been built, not to some bard who personated Homer, but to Homer himself. The grave which probably existed in Ios may have contained no human bones, any more than the graves of Adrastos or Penelope. The Homeridai of Chios, we can hardly doubt, claimed descent from the original Homer. The very existence of such a γένος implied, for Greeks, the existence of a hypothetical ancestor or hero-founder. And so with the Homeridai in the wider, more conventional sense, in which the name was given to the rhapsodes. Monro argued that these were Sons of Homer in a spiritual, not in a physical sense.[1] We can at least see how naturally the claim might come to be made. There are limits to impersonation, even on the part of the artist. The growth of self-consciousness, perhaps also the instinct of self-assertion, would make it increasingly difficult for the bard to say, quite simply, 'I am Homer.' Yet his relation to Homer had to be expressed somehow. Quite naturally, and quite in accordance with Greek feeling in such a matter, he would express it by saying now, 'I am a "son" or descendant of Homer,' Ὁμηρίδης or Ὁμήρου παῖς. Soon we hear of bards with names which look like authentic personal names, such as Arktinos of Miletos,

[1] *Appendix*, pp. 398 ff.

Eumelos of Corinth, Kinaithon of Sparta.[1] Finally we have the epic poet, not even writing now in the name of Homer; historical figures like Panyassis of Halikarnassos or Antimachos of Kolophon.

But in this vast interval of time what a distance we have travelled from 'Homeros'! Apart from this, nothing could be much more unlike the conception of Homer as the typical epic poet than that strange and remote figure, the Exarchon of the choral song. The name itself has survived; its content has changed utterly; as oak succeeded beech, but kept the old name of φηγός. Accordingly, we have got to face the problem of this evolution. How did Homer, from being something like a personification of the tribal dance, come to be regarded as the author of the Iliad and Odyssey?

The Muses and Apollo their leader are the reflections against an imaginary, supernatural background of exactly such a company as that of the Delian Maidens and Homeros. That is, the human group came first. Consequently we have to envisage an earlier state of things, in which the goddesses were not yet separated from the singing women, nor the god from Homeros. The women, then, possessed some more than human quality, which made them the prototypes of the Muses; their leader was, potentially, Apollo Mousagetes himself. We reach the same conclusion by studying the phenomenon of inspiration, as the Greeks understood it. The notion of a god or goddess entering into or 'possessing' the human bard is not in reality a very primitive one. Behind the *vates*, half poet and half prophet, we discern the still less specialized figure of the Medicine-man or Magic-King, with his rhabdos and his murmured *carmina*, drawing his inspiration altogether from within, because himself endowed with superhuman powers. Thus Hesiod was prophet as well as poet. He says of the Muses, 'they breathed in me the inspiration of song, that

[1] Other names, Ἀγίας, Ἡγησίας (cf. Alkman's Ἀγιδώ, Ἀγησιχόρα), Στασῖνος (cf. Στησίχορος), may mean 'Choir-Leader'. This would be interesting in the light of Ὅμηρος.

I might publish things past and things to come.'[1] More primitive still is the type embodied in the mythical Amphion, whose singing built the walls of Thebes.[2] The leader of the Delian Maidens must have been at first one of these semi-divine beings. Then, I suggest, with the progress of religious thought, he shook off his supernatural qualities, which now crystallized about the imagined personality of a god, Apollo. His merely human self, so to speak, remained the Exarchon of the choir. Still in that capacity some lingering *aura* of sanctity rested upon him; he was the *θεῖος ἀοιδός*, the *vates sacer*, the divine Homeros. The personation of Homer by the later minstrels had a religious significance, for it was part of a ritual. Being religious, it must, according to all analogy, have had for its motive some more or less consciously realized theory of reincarnation. And even 'Son of Homer' was scarcely a mere figure of speech. During the moment of inspiration, Homer, it was dimly felt, had come to life again in the poet, as he told of Troy and Ithaca.

The evolution of the poet from the leader of the magico-religious dance seems reasonably clear. Such a dance, we should remark to begin with, is originally communal or tribal. So much the evidence makes abundantly clear. All over the world in primitive communities we find the dance in vogue, and it might without exaggeration be called a characteristic feature of the ancient Greek life. Doubtless in historical Greece the magical and communal aspects of the dance were apt to be obscured. Yet, in however atrophied a form, they were there. We hear of armed dances engaged in by the warriors of the tribe, like the *pyrrhiche*; of mystery-dances, like the Kouretes'; of commemorative dances, like the Crane-dance at Delos. To Lucian is attributed a whole treatise

[1] *Theog.* 31 ff. *ἐνέπνευσαν δέ μ' ἀοιδὴν*
θέσπιν, ἵνα κλείοιμι τά τ' ἐσσόμενα πρό τ' ἐόντα.
Cf. A 70 *ὃς ᾔδει τά τ' ἐόντα τά τ' ἐσσόμενα πρό τ' ἐόντα*, of Kalchas. The Muses themselves are prophetic, *Theog.* 38. For the characteristics of the Medicine-man see F. B. Jevons, *Graeco-Italian Magic* in *Anthropology and the Classics*, pp. 94 ff.

[2] Apollod. *Bibl.* iii. 5. 5. 10.

Concerning Dancing. But such distinctions as I have indicated are not ultimately tenable. The dance of the Kouretes, for instance, was an armed dance, a mystery-dance, and commemorative, all in one.[1] We can probably reduce every traditional Greek dance, however singular in its details, to one original type, the communal, magic-making χορός. Such a dance is not engaged in for the mere pleasure of it, nor even, at first, 'in honour of' any definite god. It is to stimulate the fertility of the tribe and its possessions, especially to increase the food-supply.[2] We are perhaps only now beginning to realize how important is the tribal dance in barbaric societies, although we know that the social importance of the savage is fixed by the number of his dances. The tribal dance—the dance, that is to say, of people representing the tribe, for every member is not able or qualified to dance—has, perhaps always, a magical intent, and is accompanied by some kind of chant or music-making. The Cretan Hymn of the Kouretes is typical. The Greatest Kouros is summoned to the dance at the head of his Daimones, and bidden to 'leap' for the fruits of the field and for young citizens and for Themis, while the Kouretes make music upon harps and flutes.[3] The dancers naturally have a leader, an ἐξάρχων or ἔξαρχος. Thus Bromios is the ἔξαρχος of his thiasos.[4] Sometimes we find a more specialized name, ἀρχίβακχος or πρωτοκούρης.[5] As the tribal dance is perhaps the most elementary demonstration of the solidarity of the tribe, the leader of the dance is in the evolutionary sense much older than any functionary holding an independent and personal authority. For, while the latter has to some extent asserted himself at the expense of the society which produced him, the former is—may we say?—a mere epiphenomenon of the social consciousness. It is im-

[1] *Themis, passim.*
[2] Cf. ibid., pp. 42 ff., p. 139.
[3] Ibid., p. 7 f. *Hymn of the Kouretes*. B. S. A. xv, p. 357.
[4] Eur. *Bacchae* 140.
[5] πρωτοκούρης at Ephesos, where there was a college of Kouretes, Dittenb. *Syll.* i². 1861, 1. ἀρχίβακχος at Athens, J. E. Harrison, *Prolegomena*, pp. 475, 656.

portant therefore to seize the characteristics of the Dance-leader. These are simply the characteristics of the *choros* concentrated in an individual. The tribal dance is magical, the dancers for the nonce magicians, making rain, say, or somehow bringing increase to the tribe. It follows that the Chief Dancer is at the same time Chief Magician. Thus Melampous, a typical witch-doctor,[1] having undertaken to cure the mad daughters of Proitos, 'took the young men who were most fit, and with hallooing and some kind of inspired dance (μετ' ἀλαλαγμοῦ καί τινος ἐνθέου χορείας) chased the women from the hills into Sikyon.'[2] The impression of a special sanctity attaching to the leader of the dance tends to outlive the occasion which generates it. He is then on his way to becoming the Medicine-King, the permanent chief-magician, a figure somewhat like Numa, who made thunder on behalf of the state.[3] It must be remembered that 'public' magic, performed by the king as head of the community, is older than 'private' or professional magic, practised by the wizard for his own ends.[4] The professional witch or wizard is an antisocial being, and no member of a very primitive society is habitually antisocial. When the Medicine-King disappears, his functions are distributed and specialized. His magic-making duties pass to the Medicine-man, still in his way a public institution. His strictly regal duties are taken over by the Basileus or secular King. Naturally, the division is rarely quite clean. The king usually retains a sacrosanct or priestly character, which is only gradually deputed to subordinate officials. This is so well known, that I need merely refer to the evidence from the case of the Spartan kings, and from the survival at Athens and Rome of functionaries like the *Βασιλεύς* and the *rex sacrorum*.

But the Chief Dancer has another aspect besides the magical. He is the Chief Singer and Music-maker. It is in this capacity

[1] μάντις ὢν καὶ τὴν διὰ φαρμάκων καὶ καθαρμῶν θεραπείαν πρῶτος εὑρηκώς. Apollod. *Bibl.* ii. 2. 2. 4.

[2] Ibid. ii. 2. 2. 4 f.

[3] Plut. *Life of Numa*, xv.

[4] *Themis*, pp. 76 ff.

that he develops into the Aoidos, who, as we have seen, acted as Exarchon of the *choros*. The Aoidos, in fact, is just the Exarchon become, as it were, professional, and gradually detaching himself altogether from the dancers; while the Exarchon is a clear development of the Chief Dancer. The Aoidos sings to the lyre, *cithara* or *phorminx*, as is apparent from the examples of Phemios and Demodokos. He is thus at once poet and harp-player. But, as the arts of poetry and music progress, this double function of the Aoidos gives rise to two more specialized types: the Kitharoedos or professional harp-player, and the Rhapsode or professional reciter of verses.[1]

Let us see how this scheme fits the evidence.

The Muses and Apollo are the divine antitypes of the Delian Maidens and Homer. Now Apollo, as Mr. Halliday remarks,[2] 'has all the attributes of the Medicine-man,' or perhaps rather the Medicine-King. He is *vates*—prophet and poet; he inflicts and cures diseases; and he is Basileus. The last characteristic alone requires emphasizing. Yet it is as certain as the others. He is constantly called ἄναξ in the epos.[3] The papyrus-fragment dealing with the Rape of Proserpine calls him the Basileus of the Muses.[4] 'King of the Muses'—that title gives us the clue to Apollo's origin. He is, primarily, Leader of the magical dance. Then he becomes Paian, the Healer—for primitive medicine is magic—

[1] The following diagram may elucidate this paragraph:

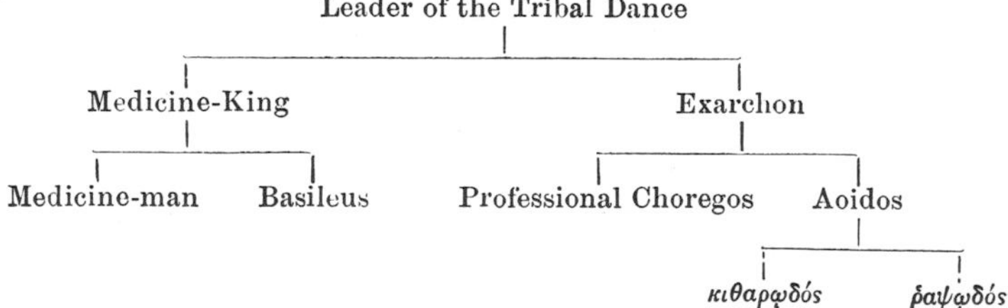

[2] *Greek Divination*, p. 59.

[3] Cf. *Hymn to Apollo* 15 Ἀπόλλωνά τ' ἄνακτα καὶ Ἄρτεμιν ἰοχέαιραν: 179 ὦ ἄνα.

[4] *Berl. Klassikertexte*, vol. v, *Epische Fr.* 2, p. 8 τῶν δὲ Μουσ]ῶν βασιλεὺς Ἀπόλλων.

Basileus, Prophet, Aoidos, Kitharoedos; summing up in his undying existence the development of ages. And as Apollo is Basileus among the Muses, so Zeus as king of the gods leads the sacred dance or procession of the gods and daimones in Heaven.[1] This conception reappears in a quaint line preserved by Athenaeus and attributed by him to 'Eumelos the Corinthian or Arktinos': 'And in the midst of them danced the Father of gods and men'.[2] That takes us back, I believe, to the very beginnings of Zeus's sovereignty. He is king of the gods because he leads them in the dance.

The human parallel to Zeus is the Olympian victor. Zeus himself, it should be remembered, overcame Kronos at Olympia and so became *'Ολυμπιονίκης*.[3] The Victor was treated as a divine person and a king.[4] The immense honours heaped upon him in his own state were but extensions of the honour he received at Olympia, where, according to immemorial custom, he led the kômos. The kômos was essentially a *χορός*; indeed, in its Attic form, it reappears in the Chorus of Athenian Comedy. The friends of the Victor accompanied him to the altars of the gods, singing the triumph-song or 'hymn of Archilochos'. The Victor himself was Exarchon. In the hymn Herakles was saluted as Lord or King (*ἄναξ*). Herakles was reputed to have been the first Olympic victor.[5] Whether we agree or not that the purpose of the foot-race—the original Agon at Olympia[6]—was to decide who was to be Basileus for the year, it is clear that in some sense the Victor was regarded as a Basileus and representative of Zeus.[7] Thus the Victor was at once Daimon, Basileus, and Exarchos of the

[1] Plato, *Phaedr.* 246 E.

[2] 22 C *μέσσοισιν δ' ὠρχεῖτο πατὴρ ἀνδρῶν τε θεῶν τε.*

[3] Paus. v. 7. 10. See A. B. Cook, *Folk-Lore*, vol. xv, p. 399 f. Aesch. *Ag.* 168 ff. evidently refers to this story, and *Ζῆνα δέ τις προφρόνως ἐπινίκια κλάζων* must allude to the kômos.

[4] A. B. Cook, l. c.

[5] Lykophron, *Alexandra* 40 ff. with Tzetzes, ad loc.; Pind. *Ol.* ix. 1 and schol.

[6] Paus. v. 8. 6; Plut. *Sympos. Qu.* v. 2. 675 C.

[7] F. M. Cornford in *Themis*, ch. vii.

hymn; and all this because in the first instance he was Leader of the kômos. The parallel to the Zeus of the *Phaedrus* is complete. In the Platonic myth Zeus, as Basileus, appears as Exarchos of what is, exactly, a kômos of gods and daimones. And the Hymn of the Kouretes speaks in the same sense, calling upon him as Megistos Kouros to come to Dikte at the head of his kômos of daimones.[1]

The Roman Salii had two officials, a *praesul* and a *vates*. It is reasonable to suppose that the functions of Chief Dancer and Bard had originally been united in the person of one man, the Leader of the Salii. Their god, identified with Mars, is clearly begotten of the ritual; he is their imagined divine Leader. Again, we find King Numa in intimate association with the Salii; so that the regal office somehow fitted into their hierarchy.[2] Here also we seem to discern the complex of Chief Dancer, Bard, God, and King all derived from the original head of the Dancing Brethren.[3]

If our general theory is correct, then, wherever we find a company of dancing and singing people, we shall expect to find attached to it, as normal developments of its leader, three typical personages: a God, a Basileus, and an Aoidos or Vates. Yet, partly because the evidence is very scanty, partly because the development has often been arrested, we cannot always make out the complete triad; a failure which does nothing to invalidate the scheme, into which the knowledge we do possess fits perfectly well. Professor Murray has shown how the ordinary civil king is the descendant of the antique Medicine-King, the chief public magician of the

[1] l. 5 *δαιμόνων ἁγώμενος*. Terpandros says, *Ζεῦ πάντων ἀρχά, πάντων ἁγήτωρ*. Cf. Eur. *Fr.* 593 (Nauck[2]):

> *σὲ τὸν αὐτοφυᾶ, τὸν ἐν αἰθερίῳ*
> *ῥύμβῳ πάντων φύσιν ἐμπλέξανθ',*
> *ὃν πέρι μὲν φῶς, πέρι δ' ὀρφναία*
> *νὺξ αἰολόχρως, ἄκριτός τ' ἄστρων*
> *ὄχλος ἐνδελεχῶς ἀμφιχορεύει.*

[2] Ovid, *Fasti* iii. 371 ff.; Livy i. 20.

[3] For the Salii the chief authorities are Dion. Halicarn., *Ant. Rom.*, pp. 70, 71; Ovid, *Fasti* iii. 259 ff. We have also their Carmen.

tribe or community.[1] It would be possible to explain in great detail how 'public magic' normally takes the form of a communal or tribal dance; how the Old Men or Gerontes who form the Council of the King are those who 'know the dances', the rites and customs of the tribe.[1] On the other side, one might compile from Greek sources alone a considerable list of bards, who, when they are mythical like Olen or Mousaios, are obviously projections of a ritual chorus, and, when they are historical like Alkman or Stesichoros, are the 'teachers' of such choirs. But the evidence for all this cannot be satisfactorily presented here. And in fact our task is a more special and testing one; to put a complex scheme to proof.

Taking first the Muses as a typical *choros*. We find them called by various titles, Pierides, Olympiades, Helikoniades, and the like. It is not a sufficient explanation to say that the Muses 'had seats' on Olympos and Helikon and Parnassos. It is not impossible that a single cult spread from its original home (whatever that was) to the other mountains. But it is far more probable that each hill had its independent group of divine Dancers, They of Helikon, or They of Parnassos, as the case may be. But all these groups belonged to a uniform type, and naturally enough came to be regarded as the same group manifesting themselves here and there. Their generic name was Muses. Each group, we may be sure, was the centre of a local cult, because each group must have been developed by a cult. If we knew the facts of the local worships, we could gather much regarding the characteristics of each group. As it is, we must deal with the groups separately. That is the only scientific method.

The Helikoniades, as we may see from the proem to the *Theogony*, have associated with them a God, Apollo, and

[1] *Four Stages of Greek Religion*, p. 40 f.; *Anthropology and the Classics*, pp. 78 ff.

[2] See esp. J. G. Frazer, *Early History of the Kingship*; *Golden Bough*[3], vol. i for magic-making dances; *Themis*, pp. 42 ff. The importance of the initiation-dance in savage societies is also to be recognized.

a Bard, Hesiod. Who is their King? Evidently Apollo again, as 'Basileus of the Muses'. But it is worth remarking that the cult of the Helikonian Muses at Askra was founded by the twin-brethren, Otos and Ephialtes,[1] whom the saga regards as human 'sons of Aloeus', and who may therefore be considered as representing the normal King. Their connexion with the Helikoniades is doubtless older than Apollo's; hence this apparent conflict of claims to the position of Basileus. There was a festival called the Mouseia held every four years at Thespiai near Askra, at which there was a competition in minstrelsy.[2] Askra was a mere village, and may have been robbed of this festival by its more important neighbour. Unfortunately our information is so defective, that we cannot tell if there was a choir of maidens corresponding to the Kourai at Delos to celebrate the Muses. Yet the essential part of every religious festival was a *choros*; and some kind of *choros* there must have been at Thespiai. Presumably, almost necessarily, it would be composed of Thespian maidens. But that scarcely matters. The existence of a chorus of some sort being granted as a necessary and original part of the Mouseia, what was the relation of Hesiod to this choir? Was it the same as that of Homer to the Deliades? The name *Hesiod* is obscure. It is perhaps the name of a famous minstrel; it is perhaps a traditional name like Homer.[3] The latter supposition appears to me the more probable, because it explains the Hesiodic *corpus* on the same principle as the Homeric.

The Muses of Kastalia or Parnassos had for their God and Basileus, Apollo; for their Bard, Philammon. Philammon

[1] Paus. ix. 29. 1.

[2] Paus. ix. 31. 3.

[3] The *Etymologicum Magnum* says (452. 37) Αἰολεῖς τὸ Ἡσίοδος καὶ ἡμίονος Αἰσίοδος καὶ αἰμίονος λέγουσιν. Accepting the tradition that Hesiod was a native of Kyme in Aeolis (*Erga* 636), Hoffmann, *Griech. Dial.* ii. 420 f. Cf. 324 f., and Fick-Bechtel, *Personennamen*, p. 4, regard Αἰσίοδος as the genuine form. The Boeotians called the immigrant Ἠσίοδος, which afterwards became Ἡσίοδος under the influence of ἵημι or ἥδομαι. This involves a good deal of hypothesis. Yet if Ἡσίοδος is original, it is not easy to explain. One may perhaps compare ἠσιεπής.

was represented as the son of the god,[1] and was closely associated with Delphi.[2] He was the father of Thamyris or Thamyras, who strove with the Muses on Mount Dorion[3]; and the brother of Autolykos.[4] The last detail is interesting. Autolykos represents the ancient Wolf-god of Parnassos, identified with Apollo. Now, if the Parnassiades were indigenous and not a mere importation of 'Thracian' Muses, they would, according to our scheme, naturally produce a God and a King before they received Apollo; and these would naturally be the God and the King of the mountain, the Wolf and Autolykos. Similarly at Helikon, we may suspect, Apollo supplanted an indigenous God, probably Helikon himself.[5] But we may be content with Apollo and Philammon.

The Pierides or Olympiades or Leibethrides or Pimpleides have associations rather more difficult to elucidate. They are more definitely 'Thracian' than the southern groups, and we hear of them on Mount Pangaion and by the Hebros and Strymon. But perhaps this only means that there was another, strictly Thracian, group with whom the Pierides were confused. Their God was apparently not Apollo, at least originally, but the Thracian Helios-Ares; their poet, Orpheus; their Basileus, perhaps Rhesos.[6]

Another dancing company is the thiasos of Dionysos; and here again we ought to take the local groups separately.

[1] Hes. *Fr.* 111 (Rzach); Ovid, *Metam.* xi. 316 f.

[2] Paus. x. 7. 2.

[3] B 594 f.; Apollod. *Bibl.* i. 3. 3.

[4] Hes. l. c. (Philonis) *ἣ τέκεν Αὐτόλυκόν τε Φιλάμμονά τε κλυτὸν αὐδήν.*

[5] For Helikon as Daimon see Wilamowitz, *Berl. Klassikertexte*, vol. v, *Epische Fr.*, p. 26 f.; Korinna's *Helikon and Kithairon*; Fick, *Personennamen*, p. 441. Or, since the Muses dance about the *ἵππου κρήνη* (*Theog.* 6), was their god a Horse, Poseidon Helikonios?

[6] For Orpheus, Eratosthenes, *Catast.* 24, p. 140, referring to the *Bassarai* of Aeschylus, *τὸν μὲν Διόνυσον οὐκ ἐτίμα, τὸν δὲ Ἥλιον μέγιστον τῶν θεῶν ἐνόμιζεν εἶναι, ὃν καὶ Ἀπόλλωνα προσηγόρευσεν.* The identification of Helios with Apollo is here attributed to Orpheus. The bard was torn in pieces by the Bassarids on Pangaion and buried by the Muses at Leibethra. For Rhesos, see esp. the speech of the Muse his mother at the end of the play, 919 ff., also 970 f.

As we might expect, it is harder to make out the Minstrel of each group than in the case of the Muses. On the other hand the Basileus is generally obvious enough. Beginning with the Thracian Maenads, whom we may call the Bassarides, we note that their God is, of course, Dionysos, and that they are associated with the Edonian king, Lykourgos. The story is in Homer.[1] Admittedly it reflects a ritual. The Bassarides did not develop a Bard, or, if they did, he has been merged in the typical Thracian minstrel, Orpheus, whom they rent in pieces.

The Bakchai of Kithairon have, besides their God, a King, Pentheus of Thebes. We call Pentheus a 'form' of the god, and in a sense he is. But it would be more accurate to call him a form of the Archibakchos or leader of the thiasos, who enacts the central part in the mimetic *σπαραγμός* or ritual tearing in pieces, and thereby shapes the conception of Dionysos on the one hand, and of Pentheus on the other. We hear of no Bard definitely connected with the rites on Kithairon. If we regard the triumph-song of Agave in the *Bacchae* of Euripides as modelled upon an actual chant of the worshippers upon the Boeotian mountain, we can only say that this chant had apparently no traditional author. Some kind of traditional chant, however, must have belonged to the ritual. It would be interesting to know if it was wrought upon in any of the Dithyrambi composed by the Theban Pindar. But we do not know.

The Bakchai of Parnassos seem to break our rule, for apparently they produced neither Bard nor King. The arresting influence no doubt was Delphi, which had to reconcile many conflicting claims to recognition in the systematized Pan-hellenic religion which it promulgated. Orestes, who has affinities with Dionysos at Delphi,[2] has no certain associations with the Bakchai, although, like Pentheus, Orestes is pursued by Avenging Women. Philammon, Chryso-

[1] Z 130 ff. The story of Lykourgos was treated by Aeschylus in a lost trilogy composed of the *Bassarai*, the *Edonoi*, the *Neaniskoi*.

[2] H. Usener, *Arch. f. Religionswissenschaft*, vol. vii, pp. 332 ff.

themis, Thamyris, and Sakadas, who are all connected with Delphi, belong to the service of Apollo.

But Dionysos does not lack for poets. The Attic Drama originated in choruses engaged in his worship, and the dramatists were in a quite real sense elaborating the traditional Dithyramb into Tragedy, and the traditional phallic song into Comedy. As every one knows, the early history of the Drama is vexatiously obscure. Our ignorance is a little less in the case of Tragedy than of Comedy. According to tradition, it was especially the deme Ikaria that was concerned with the first development of Tragedy. 'Ikarios' spread the worship of Dionysos in the land, and was murdered for his pains.[1] 'Thespis' (*θέσπις ἀοιδός*), who composed the first tragedies, was from Ikaria.[2] This gives us a chorus of Ikarians, Dionysos the God, Ikarios the local hero or Basileus, and Thespis the Bard.

The reader may feel doubtful of the validity of this reasoning. What have all these mythical personages to do with actual, human kings and poets? But to this doubt there is a quite simple and conclusive answer. The myths are moulded upon human institutions. As we have seen, every genuine myth goes along with a ritual; one might say that the myth and the ritual together form a single institution. The myths we have been discussing tell us about the rituals to which they corresponded. And they tell us that God and King and Bard develop out of the ritual. Take the case of the Mysteries at Eleusis. These at least were a concrete fact, and they gave rise to a complex mythology, in which we discern Demeter and Kore with Iakchos for Gods; Mousaios[3] and Pamphos[4] for Bards; and quite an array of Kings—Triptolemos, Dioklos, Polyxeinos, Eumolpos, Dolichos, Keleos, Demophon.[5] Mousaios and Pamphos are legendary figures; so are Keleos and the rest. But the hymns attributed to

[1] See Roscher's *Lexikon*, *s.v.* Thespis.

[2] Plato, *Min.* 321 A; Horace, *Ars Poet.* 275.

[3] Paus. i. 25. 7; Eur. *Rhes.* 945 f.

[4] Paus. viii. 37. 9.

[5] *Hymn to Demeter*, 474 f.

Mousaios were real enough; and Eleusinian families claimed descent from the legendary princes. My argument is that, if you search for the germ of the ritual, you will be driven to find it in a religious dance or Drômenon, the chief actor in which was at least the spiritual ancestor of the Eleusinian princes, of the Eleusinian bards or singers, of the divine Child Iakchos himself. The Leader of the Drômenon (not in essence distinguishable from a sacred dance) survived in the Hierophant of historical times. The Hierophant had to be a member of the Eleusinian family called the Eumolpidai or Sons of Eumolpos. Eumolpos was a 'Thracian' Basileus, who founded the Mysteries.[1] He was the father of Mousaios, and his name signifies the Good Dancer and Singer. The Hierophant was the original figure, from whom were developed Eumolpos, the Basileus, representing the princely family of the Eumolpidai, and Mousaios, the Bard, representing the Hierophant's function as 'Chief Dancer'.[2] Finally, he played the leading part in the ritual which shaped the conception of the God.

Plutarch in his *Life of Theseus* tells us the origin of the Crane-dance at Delos. Theseus landed in the island on his voyage back from Crete with the young people he had saved from the Minotaur, and there led them in a dance which imitated the turnings and windings of one threading the Labyrinth. 'They say that the Delians still perform the dance.' That is, the whole story has arisen in connexion with this ritual at Delos. Here then we have King Theseus as Chief Dancer. Who is the divinity concerned? Not, as we might expect, a god but a goddess, Ariadne-Aphrodite. For Plutarch says that Theseus set up at Delos, before the dance began, the image of Aphrodite he had received from Ariadne, and Kallimachos in his Delian Hymn says the dance took place round the altar of Aphrodite.[3] The explanation is that Ariadne, a Cretan goddess identified with Aphrodite,

[1] Apollod. *Bibl.* ii. 5. 12; iii. 15. 4.

[2] For the Mystery-dance cf. Lucian, *Pisc.* 33 *ἥν τινα καὶ τῶν μεμυημένων ἰδὼν ἐξαγορεύοντα τοῖν θεοῖν τὰ ἀπόρρητα καὶ ἐξορχούμενον* (= 'disclosing') *ἀγανακτήσω.*

[3] *H.* iv. 312 f.

was the divine consort of Theseus, and thus may fairly represent the normal God answering to the Basileus.[1] And the Bard? He was Olen of Lycia.[2]

If, to take another dance, we ask ourselves who is the God of the Cretan Kouretes, we can answer at once, Zeus. True, he is not called Zeus in the Hymn; only the 'Greatest Kouros'. But that rather helps my point, for it shows the Leader of the Kouretes half-way, as it were, to becoming Zeus. The King is, I think, Minos. Minos is admittedly the human representative of the Cretan Bull-god identified with Zeus, and is himself the son of Zeus. Now the ritual of the Kouretes included a communal feast upon the living flesh of a bull; and the Bull-god is the god of this feast.[3] In the *Cretans* of Euripides the Koures calls himself an 'initiate of Zeus' (*μύστης Διός*). When the Minotaur was born, Minos sent for the Idaean Daktyls or Kouretes to give him counsel.[4] When he lost his son Glaukos, he sent for them to find the child.[5] These indications, put together, seem to justify us in assuming a real association between King Minos and the *mystai* of his father, Zeus. Their Bard is the historical Epimenides, although he is more *μάντις* than *ἀοιδός*. Epimenides was called 'the new Koures', and had many mystical experiences in Crete. The Cretans were said to have sacrificed to him as a god. Also he composed a *Birth of the Kouretes*, no doubt in hexameter verse.[6]

[1] *Life of Theseus*, xxi ἐκ δὲ τῆς Κρήτης ἀποπλέων εἰς Δῆλον κατέσχε καὶ τῷ θεῷ θύσας καὶ ἀναθεὶς τὸ Ἀφροδίσιον ὃ παρὰ τῆς Ἀριάδνης ἔλαβεν, ἐχόρευσε μετὰ τῶν ἠιθέων χορείαν, ἣν ἔτι νῦν ἐπιτελεῖν Δηλίους λέγουσι, μίμημα τῶν ἐν τῷ Λαβυρίνθῳ περιόδων καὶ διεξόδων, ἔν τινι ῥυθμῷ περιελίξεις καὶ ἀνελίξεις ἔχοντι γιγνομένην. Plutarch's authority is Dikaiarchos.

[2] Kallim. *H.* iv. 304 f. This accords with the statement of Herodotus iv. 35 that Olen was the author of the oldest Delian hymns, οὗτος δὲ ὁ Ὠλὴν καὶ τοὺς ἄλλους παλαιοὺς ὕμνους ἐποίησε ἐκ Λυκίης ἐλθὼν τοὺς ἀειδομένους ἐν Δήλῳ. Olen was regarded as the inventor of the hexameter. Paus. x. 5. 7.

[3] *Themis*, ch. v.

[4] *Fr.* 472 (Nauck). *Berl. Klassikertexte*, vol. ii, *Gr. Dichterfragm.* (2), 1907, p. 73, for new papyrus-fragment.

[5] Apollod. *Bibl.* iii. 2. 2.

[6] Diels, *Fragm. d. Vorsokratiker*, ii, pp. 489 ff.

At Olympia we find, evolved from the kômos through its leader, the Olympic victor, a similar triad of God, Poet, and Basileus; namely, Zeus, superseding the earlier Kronos; Archilochos, composing afresh the ancient anonymous hymn of victory; and at least three Kings—Salmoneus, Pelops, Oinomaos.

I confess it seems to me that our scheme has fairly stood the test of these, almost the first examples that came to hand. It appears that God, Poet, and King are derived from one primitive figure, the leader of the tribal magic-making dance. We were right in supposing that the Delian Apollo and Homer were in origin identical.[1]

We have reached the true ground of that traditional connexion of the epic poet with the Basileus on the one hand, and the inspiring god or Muse on the other. To speak of the epos as 'court-poetry' is to use unworthy language. If the poet ever really became the appendage of a court—and, although this is often assumed, there is no evidence for it at all—he fell beneath his vocation, which was of equal age and dignity with the king's, although it was developed in a different direction. For, parallel to the evolution of the Aoidos, which has been described, there was a concurrent evolution from dance-song to epos. There may be a trace of this in the Homeric term for a lay or portion of epic song, *οἴμη*.[2] But the only conclusive method is to begin with the most rudimentary form of the choral hymn and trace its gradual elaboration.

The chant accompanying the magical tribal dance is at first almost what one might call an ejaculation, a mere *ἰυγμός*.

[1] A coin of Smyrna shows a laurelled head of Apollo, and on the reverse Homer reading a scroll. *B. M. Cat.* '*Ionia*', Pl. 25. 7. At Delos the question of the Basileus does not arise. We have to do there with a theocracy. In other words, Apollo himself is Basileus.

[2] Cf. *οἶμος, οἶμα, οἰμάω*. The movement of dancers is described by the word *ἐρρώσαντο*. The Phaiakian youths evidently dance the *οἴμη* of *Ares and Aphrodite*. A *προοίμιον* would then be a preliminary dance, such as the Delian Kourai perform in honour of Apollo. The Watchman in Aesch. *Ag.* says (31) *φροίμιον χορεύσομαι*.

This slowly gathers definiteness and articulation, as the dancers come to realize more distinctly the intention of their dancing, which is, to begin with, purely instinctive. The dance acquires an Aition, which they now sing, explaining what it is they are dancing. If it is a Bear-dance, an ἀρκτεία; 'I begin to grow restless in the spring', or 'I take my robe, My robe is sacred, I wander in the summer'.[1] The Aition gradually becomes more complete and detailed. At a certain point in this development the leader of the dance ceases to lead the singing as well, the latter duty falling to a new character, the Aoidos. Thus in the Odyssey it is Demodokos who sings the Aition of the Phaiakian dance, *The Loves of Ares and Aphrodite.* In illustration of this we can follow the long blossoming of the kômos-hymn into the full-blown Olympian ode in Pindar. In the earliest times the Victor sang the simple traditional words. But at a definite moment he sought the aid of an Aoidos—the tradition said, Archilochos—who refashioned the hymn in the form which became so popular. But the Victor and his fellow-citizens could hardly be content with the meagre ritual at Olympia. So, on his return home, the kômos was held over again on a much more elaborate scale. The hymn of Archilochos naturally shared in this elaboration. It became an art-form of ever-growing complexity, requiring an ever greater degree of skill and training on the part of the poet who composed and the choir who sang it. But in essence it was still the Olympic kômos-song, as Pindar himself implies.[2]

Again, Stesichoros composes a kind of lyric markedly epic in character and of almost epic dimensions. His odes were sung at the festivals of various local Heroes in the Western Colonies.[3] Stesichoros in fact did for the festival hymn what Arion did for the Dithyramb, gave it a more imposing and splendid form. He did not invent it. The festival was there in each case before Stesichoros, and must always have had its

[1] *Themis*, p. 112 f., quoting W. McClintock.
[2] e.g. *Ol.* iv. 9 f.; ix *ad init.*
[3] See Christ, *Gesch. d. Gr. Lit.* in Iwan Müller's *Handbuch* 7⁴, p. 162 f.

hymn. Trace any Greek festival to its origin, and you will find there in some form—Thrênos or Paian or Dithyrambos—a χορός. It was exactly the business of Teisias to be a marshal of such choruses, Στησίχορος. Accordingly in his lyrics we have another elaborate art-form wrought, certainly with the aid of earlier poets, out of the ritual νόμος or hymn 'in honour of' god or Hero. And we may say much the same of the odes of Alkman and Ibykos, of Simonides and Bacchylides. Moreover, Stesichoros helps us to understand how the epos could be developed from a choral form. He came very near to being confessedly an epic poet. His *Sack of Ilion*, for instance, is referred to in the same terms as the epic of a 'Cyclic' poet.[1] He had but to change his metre a little, and the transition from lyric to epic was made. The chorus interposed no difficulty. The Muses sing the *Theogony*, the Delian Kourai sing not merely the *Hymn*, but the deeds of men and women in times past, the heroic epos. It would be the purest pedantry to find a difficulty in theory where the ancients found none in practice. And since it is certain that the recitation of Homer by rhapsodes is a later thing than the chanting of a choir so ancient as the Delian, the development of the former out of the latter may be regarded as a matter of history.

The tribal dance is mimetic and magic-working. It commonly takes the form of a mummery simulating the processes that bring fertility. Very often the Chief Dancer, acting the central part in the mime, pretends to die and come to life again. Scholars have recently discovered that this primitive rite is still performed in Thrace and Thessaly and Macedonia.[2] The next stage comes when the Chief Dancer (hitherto himself the god or rather the god in embryo) merely personates the god, who has now become as it were externalized from

[1] Thus Theodoros preferred the version of Stesichoros to that of Arktinos or Lesches in composing the epitome of the Trojan Story followed by the *Tabula Iliaca* (first cent. B.C.).

[2] R. M. Dawkins, *The Modern Carnival in Thrace and the Cult of Dionysos*, *J. H. S.* xxvi, p. 191.

the *choros*. The hymn consequently now tells us the Life-story, more particularly the Birth-story, of the god or Daimon. Such was the Dithyramb, whose proper and original subject was the Birth of Dionysos.[1] Such, beneath the accomplished style, are the Delian *Hymn* and the *Hymn to Hermes*. But, after all, Apollo and Hermes and Dionysos are complex figures, who have drawn to themselves the functions and characteristics of many minor local divinities superseded by them. We get a clearer and juster conception of the primitive hymn, if we put from our minds the great national deities, and think of it as recounting the Life-story of the local or tribal god or Hero or Heroine at the local festival. Even the Homeric Hymns, although in their present form most of them are of no great antiquity, and although they are practically all addressed to the greater gods, sometimes indicate this. The *Hymn to Demeter* is concerned with the child Demophon, an Eleusinian Hero. The *Hymn to Aphrodite* is the Birth-story of Aeneas, the Hero-ancestor of an aristocratic *gens* in the Troad. But the evidence from the choral poets is overwhelming. It is with local festivals and the celebration of the local Daimon that they are concerned. Very often of course some great Olympian has won a connexion with the festival and robbed the old festival-hero of his solitary pre-eminence. But for all that the Hero is the real subject of the poet's celebration. To take the first instance that comes. Pindar writes his Olympian odes in praise of Olympic victors. The Victor himself received divine honours, yet it is not of *this* Daimon that Pindar prefers to sing, but of the established local Daimon revealing himself in the Victor. The hymn is the Life-story of the tribal or communal divinity.[2]

That divinity is normally the imagined ancestor of the *gens* or tribe which worships him. 'Men and gods', says Pindar, 'are born of one mother'.[3] Zeus is 'the Father of

[1] See p. 202, note 3.
[2] Cf. F. M. Cornford in *Themis*, p. 257.
[3] *Nem.* vi *ad init.* ἓν ἀνδρῶν, ἓν θεῶν γένος κτλ. with Bury's note *ad loc.* Cf. Hes. *Erga* 108 ὡς ὁμόθεν γεγάασι θεοὶ θνητοί τ' ἄνθρωποι.

gods and men'. This is not the teaching of a speculative mysticism, but one of the oldest beliefs of man. The tribal god is, simply and literally, a member of the tribe, although a member with supernormal powers and privileges. All this was brilliantly explained by Robertson Smith in *The Religion of the Semites*. I have taken the tribe as the unit; but it is perhaps more exact to say that the god belongs to the circle of his sacrificers, whatever the extent of that may be. He might begin with being the ancestor of a mere *gens* or family, like Iamos the father of the Iamidai, or Aiakos the father of the Aiakidai, or a hundred others. But, if his own little clan grows in power and numbers, he may become the progenitor of a whole race or ἔθνος, as Apollo of the Ionians, or Mars of the Romans. Finally, he may become, like Zeus, the Father of gods and men. This development is reflected in the hymn or Life-story of the god as it increases in extent and complexity. For his Life-story reflects the history of his worshippers, who unconsciously think of their god as doing and suffering what they themselves have suffered and done. We have, however, constantly to remind ourselves that the word *god* does not suggest to a primitive people the clear-cut conception it presents to us.[1] The old Medicine-King was himself a god, 'though in the germ'; and, when this idea perished, his descendant the merely human Basileus retained a certain nimbus of divinity, often, especially on religious occasions, representing or even personating the god.[2] One method of impersonation was to wear a mask, as Minos wore the mask of the Bull-god. Hence a certain confusion or ambiguity in the thoughts of men at this stage of culture. Was the Basileus not the god himself reincarnate in human flesh? The confusion generated a tendency, which operated in two ways. The achievements of the human kings were apt to be credited to the tribal god; while, on the other hand, the fabulous actions of the god were often assigned to the Basileus.

[1] *Four Stages of Greek Religion*, pp. 23 ff.

[2] On this subject see *Early History of the Kingship*, *passim*; A. B. Cook, *J. H. S.* xiv, *Animal Worship in the Mycenaean Age*.

The first movement was much the stronger, because it had more to give, and what it gave was less remote and cloudy. 'It is not we who have done this', said Themistokles after Salamis, 'not we, but Gods and Heroes'.[1] This was like the letting in of waters. The river of saga began to run within the narrow channel of the hymn and quickly overflowed its banks. But we are not yet quite ready to consider the consequences of that.

First came the 'Olympian Conquest'. The worship of some few gods and goddesses flourished, in ways already illustrated, at the expense of other divinities; the process being at least aided by the Great Migrations. The effect of this upon the hymns was exactly what might have been anticipated. As the Olympian passed triumphant from one shrine to another, usurping the honours of the local Daimones and hero-ancestors, the various local hymns and 'sacred stories' were all swept up into one great hymn in his praise, and he became the centre of an almost endless mythology. The present *Hymn to Apollo*, for example, consists of at least two distinct hymns, one to the Kouros of Delos, the other to the god of Delphi. The Delian *Hymn* itself was but the prelude to a great outpouring of song concerning the epic men and women. The hymn has given birth to the heroic epos. For these 'men and women' are the old local Daimones—Achilles, Helen, and the rest. Their legends have combined to form one great legend recited at the Delian Festival in honour of Apollo the Father-god of all the Ionians. Once grasp the fact that the hymn of the Kouros is the germ of the Delian recitations, and the rest follows of necessity. The hymn gradually added to itself more and more of the inherited or borrowed legends of the Ionian race, until it grew to the proportions of all 'Homer'. And as Homer was the traditional author of the original hymn, so he remained the traditional author of all the rest.

No doubt the epos was long in forming. It must have

[1] Her. viii. 109.

been at first an artless, incoherent thing. But it grew by virtue of a natural attractive force within it. The history of the Homeric poetry is the history of this force:—how it became conscious of itself; how it made the vast body it informed more and more an organism, shedding irrelevant members, intensifying the vitality of the rest. This is not a fanciful metaphor; for the saga *was* alive. And, as it became increasingly aware of the nature and direction of the forces impelling it from within, it became more vivid. Vividness, intensity of life, is perhaps what mainly constitutes beauty; it is certainly what mainly constitutes the beauty of Homer. How then does he attain it? The answer is given by Aristotle.[1] The Odyssey differs from the *Herakleis* or *Theseis* in this respect; that instead of recording the whole Life of its hero, it concentrates on a single part of it. The gain in dramatic value is inestimable, and it is achieved in this way. Now what does that imply? It implies that a *Herakleid* or a *Theseid* belongs to an earlier kind of epic than our Odyssey. In other words, our Odyssey has been fashioned out of a great mass of poetry covering the whole Life of Odysseus. And, in fact, this poetry is constantly quoted and referred to in the Odyssey. Our poem knows of the boar-hunt on Parnassos, of the voyage to Ephyra for poison, of Odysseus's adventure as a spy in Troy. The prophecy of Teiresias alludes to a whole lost epic.

We have seen how such a Life-story grows. The original γενεαλογία of the hero, at first quite brief like one of the Birth-stories in the *Nekyia*-catalogue, expands into a Life, which may extend indefinitely as it comes to reflect in its mythical way more and more of the actual history of the tribe. A good illustration of this is the *Herakleia* or versified Life of Herakles. It is a Traditional Poem, which can be traced back to a very considerable antiquity, and the various stages of its expansion exhibited. There was a Rhodian 'kernel' treating of the Twelve Labours. Peisandros and, apparently, a certain Peisinoos, both of Rhodes, worked at the Rhodian

[1] *Poet.* ch. 8.

poem. Finally it was expanded into the *Herakleia* of Panyassis of Halikarnassos.[1] This consisted of fourteen books; the *Herakleia* of Peisandros consisted of two. Now the Odyssey also is a Traditional Poem. Consequently it must have passed through these stages of expansion just like the *Herakleia*. A simple genealogy expanded into a great Life; certain moving incidents selected from the Life and elaborated with great art: that, I suggest, is the history of the Odyssey.

If my analysis of the poem is in the main right, I may probably claim to have proved this already. The Odyssey is part of the Life-story of Odysseus, a tribal hero, which can be traced back stage by stage to its Boeotian original. From Homer himself, but especially from Hesiod and the compilers of *γενεαλογίαι* who succeeded the epic poets and drew upon them, we can see that the unwrought stuff of the epos consisted largely of genealogies. Hesiod weaves together the Birth-stories of gods in his *Theogony*, the Birth-stories of half-divine men in his *Catalogues of Women*. The connexion is of the slightest. A simple 'Or such as' will do to link one woman's history to another's. It is scarcely art at all. Art in the constructive sense begins when one of the Birth-stories extends itself into something like a history of its hero. I am thinking of the *Shield of Herakles*, a little epic which has grown out of one of the 'Or such as' genealogies.[2] There is a good deal of simple genealogizing in Homer, and it is interesting to observe how naturally it leads to the full-blown epos. Every one remembers the meeting of Glaukos and Diomedes in the sixth book of the Iliad. Each declares his lineage to the other. Glaukos begins: 'Sisyphos was the father of Glaukos, and Glaukos of Bellerophon. Bellerophon begat Hippolochos, and Hippolochos begat me.'[3] But when he comes to the great saga-hero Bellerophon, the poet breaks away from the simple enumeration of ancestors. 'Bellerophon, to whom the gods gave the grace of beauty. But Proitos . . .,'[4]

[1] P. Friedländer, *Philol. Unters.*, vol. xix.

[2] It begins *ἢ οἵη προλιποῦσα δόμους κτλ.*

[3] Z 152 ff.

[4] Ibid. 156 ff.

and then comes a quotation from some old epos, the *Korinthiaka* apparently.[1] Diomedes replies with an account of his ancestry: 'Oineus was my grandfather, Tydeus my father. . . . But Tydeus I do not remember, for he left me while yet a little child, when the Achaean army perished before Thebes.'[2] The poet stops in time, but he might have gone on to the whole *Thebais*. Or take the genealogy of Theoklymenos in Odyssey XV.[3] 'He was of the race of Melampous, who . . .,' and then a portion of the *Melampodeia*. And even the genealogies in λ are but fractions and beginnings of whole Life-stories: 'each woman told me the whole story of her race (γόνον).'[4]

All this comes to reinforce the conclusion that the Homeric poetry as a whole was an expansion of the Birth-song of Apollo. The Odyssey must have acquired, not, I think, its final shape—that came from the Panathenaic recitations—but the broad outlines of its present form at the Delian Festival. It shows signs of that. The culminating scenes leading to the death of the Suitors took place during a festival of Apollo.[5] Surely that is very significant. Odysseus himself has at least some of the characteristics of Apollo. He is a Daimon of the Sun-Year. He sojourns for a time among Dark Men (φαίακες) and with the Concealer (Καλυψώ).[6] The Delians believed that their god disappeared for half the year, but always returned with the Summer:

[1] See *Rise of the Greek Epic*, p. 198 f. [2] Z 216 ff.
[3] 225 ff. [4] 234.
[5] φ 258 νῦν μὲν γὰρ κατὰ δῆμον ἑορτὴ τοῖο θεοῖο
ἁγνή· τίς δέ κε τόξα τιταίνοιτ';
υ 276 κήρυκες δ' ἀνὰ ἄστυ θεῶν ἱερὴν ἑκατόμβην
ἦγον· τοὶ δ' ἀγέροντο κάρη κομόωντες 'Αχαιοὶ
ἄλσος ὑπὸ σκιερὸν ἑκατηβόλου 'Απόλλωνος.

[6] Seeck, *Quellen d. Odyssee*, pp. 267 ff., gives twenty reasons for regarding Odysseus as a Sun-hero. The axes in the Trial of the Bow are twelve in number (φ 76). Odysseus has the characteristic weapon of Apollo, and a son named Τηλέμαχος, watched over by the god (τ 86 ἀλλ' ἤδη παῖς τοῖος 'Απόλλωνός γε ἕκητι). He is reunited to Penelope the Moon-goddess at the time of the new moon (τ 307). He returns at the winter-solstice. He disappears underground in the west. He takes vengeance for the slaughter of his herds, &c.

> Qualis ubi hibernam Lyciam Xanthique fluenta
> deserit ac Delum maternam inuisit Apollo . . .
> tela sonant umeris.[1]

So, in a kind of epiphany, Odysseus suddenly appears in his own house, his great bow in his hands.[2] Then there is Penelope. The first settlers in Ionia must surely have felt her kinship with Artemis. How striking that in the holy isle of Leto's Children we should have a poem recited, in which the hero is in some sense a form of Apollo, and the heroine a form of Artemis! Again, every reader remembers the speech in which Odysseus compares Nausikaa to Artemis and the sacred palm of Delos.[3] That would sound finely at the Festival. Again, when Eumaios tells of his birth in the paradisal island of Syrie (*νῆσός τις Συρίη*), watched over by Apollo and Artemis, and describes it as lying 'above Ortygia'[4] —a hieratic name for Delos—what hearer but would glance towards the island of Syra a few miles away? It must be admitted that these things are at least appropriate to the Delia.

Then came Peisistratos the Athenian and 'purified' the island.[5] Thereafter Homer is recited at the Panathenaia, and the Odyssey becomes a specially Athenian possession.

We need not pursue its fortunes farther. But it seems well, before closing, to sum up, as clearly as the case permits, the results of this investigation.

The Odyssey is a Traditional Poem. The Story of Odysseus, which it embodies, is of the greatest antiquity. That story originated somewhere in the Boeotian region of Central Greece, where, according to the legend, Odysseus was born. Here it was remembered and repeated by a people which later sought a new home in Southern Greece, passing by way of the Corinthian Isthmus through Arcadia to Triphylia and the Ionian Islands, including Ithaca. On the way the legend or saga gathered fresh accretions. In particular, at Mantineia in

[1] Verg. *Aen.* iv. 143 ff. with the comment of Servius.

[2] χ *ad init.* The epiphany was characteristic of Apollo. Her. i. 51 mentions the Θεοφάνια at Delphi.

[3] ζ 155 ff. [4] ο 403 ff. [5] Thuc. iii. 104.

Arcadia, where the people of Odysseus found an ancient goddess called Penelope, the saga added to itself the myth of Penelope and her Wooers, she being represented as the wife of Odysseus. Ultimately, when his people had occupied Ithaca, he came to be represented as a former king of the island, and she as his queen. But the wanderings of the race were not yet over. Many joined in the movement which historians call the Ionian Colonization, and must now be accounted definitely Ionian. They took their saga with them. Every four years the Ionians held a great religious festival or Panegyris at Delos, where a traditional hymn, preserved to us in an elaborate and stylized form as the Delian *Hymn* in the Homeric collection, was chanted to Apollo. The traditional author of this hymn was Homer. But, besides the hymn, much other poetry came to be recited at the Festival, and amongst it the Poetry about Odysseus. Gradually, through constant recitation, it acquired the qualities of an artistic epic poem; first at the Delia, afterwards at the Panathenaic Festival at Athens, now regarded as the metropolis of the Ionian cities. Like all traditional literature, the Odyssey and Iliad were at first anonymous; but, owing to their long recitation at Delos, they were attributed to the author of the Delian *Hymn*. Yet Homeros itself is only a ritual name, proceeding from the chorus of Delian Maidens who sang the hymn *φωνῇ ὁμηρεῦσαι*.

I feel drawn to end upon a note which has often recurred to me in writing this chapter. The Homeric Poems are thrilled through and through with the Apolline spirit, the spirit, we must believe, of the Delian Festival. No words must be used but such as are fair and holy, no rhythm but the stately hexameter metre. Above all, no taint or shadow of corruption, no mention of the hostile powers of death and darkness must mar the ritual of the god whose very name, Phoibos, proclaims his purity. The noble morality of Homer echoes the *εὐφημία* of the Apolline Festival. He will not speak, if he can help it, of the worship of the dead, of Hades and Kore and her grieving Mother, of magic and witchcraft. Nothing extravagant, nothing obscene, nothing 'too much': that is the pervading tone of Homer, 'whose poem Phoebus challenged for his own.' It is not a surrender but a discipline, a slaying of the dragon. The spirit of Athena, ruling the Panathenaia, would reinforce rather than qualitatively alter that of Apollo; so closely in the higher aspects of their natures are these two gods akin. Contrast the spirit of the Dionysia as embodied in the Athenian Drama. Yet the origins of Homer and of the Drama are almost identical. Homer begins with the Birth-song of Apollo; Tragedy, if not Comedy, with the Birth-song of Dionysos. There must have been from the first some germ of vital difference, to work out in results so different. It lay in the character of the rituals. For in contrast to that of Apollo the ritual of Dionysos was one of mourning. Dionysios of Halikarnassos observes that the Romans have no mourning feasts like those of Dionysos and Persephone.[1] So Homer will not speak of Dionysos any more than of the goddess. The difference between the epos and Tragedy is the whole difference between Apollo and the Son of Semele; one moving always in the noonday, ardent and pure and deaf to the crying of the mourner;[2] the other nearer to his mother the Earth and her heart of dreams, dying like us, to be born again and dance with the stars upon the heights.

[1] *Ant. Rom.* ii. 19, p. 274 *ἑορτή τε οὐδεμία παρ' αὐτοῖς μελανείμων ἢ πένθιμος ἄγεται τυπετοὺς ἔχουσα καὶ θρήνους γυναικῶν ἐπὶ θεοῖς ἀφανιζομένοις, ὡς παρ' Ἕλλησιν ἐπιτελεῖται περί τε Φερσεφόνης ἁρπαγὴν καὶ τὰ Διονύσου πάθη καὶ ὅσα ἄλλα τοιαῦτα.*

[2] Aesch. *Ag.* 1075 *οὐ γὰρ τοιοῦτος ὥστε θρηνητοῦ τυχεῖν.* Cf. 1079.

ADDITIONAL NOTES

Additional Note to Page 36.

If the name 'Minyans' is equivalent to 'Minoans', and the people themselves came from Crete, a wide field of speculation has been opened up. But, in the present state of our knowledge, one lacks a clue.

Additional Note to Page 38.

The *Etymologicum Magnum* adds: '*Hippios*, epithet of Poseidon. Because it is believed that he created the first horse, Sisyphos, in Thessaly by striking the rock with his trident. Hence a shrine has been built in Thessaly to Poseidon of the Rock.'[1]

[1] 473 *s.v.* Ἵππιος ὁ Ποσειδῶν· ὅτι δοκεῖ πρῶτον ἵππον γεγεννηκέναι Σίσυφον ἐν Θεσσαλίᾳ, τῇ τριαίνῃ πέτραν παίσας· ὅθεν ἱερὸν Ποσειδῶνος Πετραίου καθίδρυται ἐν Θεσσαλίᾳ. Chariot-racing at the *Petraia*, Bacchyl. xiv (Kenyon).

Additional Note to Page 43.

Painted coffer with Ποτνια in Berlin Museum (Furtwängler's Catalogue, No. 306). See *Jahrb. d. Arch. Inst.* 1888, p. 357; H. B. Walters' *Ancient Pottery*, i, fig. 86; *J. H. S.* xxix, p. 289. Cf. the Centaur-Medousa on Boeotian pottery (stamped), J. E. Harrison, *Prolegomena*, p. 179.

Additional Notes to Page 65.

It is said (see Mr. Macan, ad loc.) that Herodotus means the Ionians of Attica, Euboea, and the pre-Achaean Aigialos. But Herodotus does not regard Euboea as Ionian, and in any case Attica and it are excluded by τοῦτον τὸν χρόνον. How the people of Aigialos could be called περίοικοι of the Kadmeians, I do not understand. Surely Herodotus is thinking of an invading race teaching its culture to the native Boeotian population, who 'dwell round' like the Laconian Perioeci.

Aristeides in his Panathenaic oration says of the early Athenian immigrants from Thessaly and Boeotia that they were all Ionians.[1]

[1] i. 177 Dind. οὗτοι δ' ἦσαν Ἴωνες (schol. for Ἰωνία) πάντες.

Additional Note to Page 69.

Et. Magn. s.v. Ὠκεανός· ὁ οὐρανὸς νενόμισται. Berger, *Mythische Kosmographie d. Griechen*, 1904, p. 1 f.; *Themis*, p. 456 f. Okeanos is θεῶν γένεσις, Ξ 302, so = Ouranos. All rivers flow *from* Okeanos, Φ 196, and rivers are διιπετεῖς.

Additional Note to Page 81.

Or did he know a version which placed them in the west, where they were passed by the Argo returning by way of the Istros and Eridanos? But that also would be a version of the *Argonautica*.

Additional Note to Page 122.

See Beloch, *Griech. Gesch.*[2] p. 89 f., also, especially, H. M. Chadwick, *The Heroic Age* (Cambridge, 1912), pp. 280 ff.

Additional Note to Page 168.

Yet perhaps this argument involves a pathetic fallacy. In an early society women may have authority without exciting any very chivalrous emotion. So the chivalry may be Hellenic too.

Additional Note to Page 180.

καί μοι σκῆπτρον ἔδον δάφνης ἐριθηλέος ὄζον
δρέψασαι θηητόν· ἐνέπνευσαν δέ μ' ἀοιδὴν
θέσπιν, ἵνα κλείοιμι τά τ' ἐσσόμενα πρό τ' ἐόντα.

Additional Note to Page 181.

According to some, Hesiod tasted of the laurel. Cf. Tzetz. *Vit. Hes.* 8 *φασὶ δ' ὡς ἐννέα τινὲς ἐλθοῦσαι γυναῖκες καὶ δρεψάμεναι κλῶνας ἐκ δάφνης Ἑλικωνίτιδος αὐτὸν ἐπεσίτισαν κτλ.* See Rzach's commentary, *Theog.* loc. cit.

Additional Note to Page 189.

For the rhapsodes and their methods see P. D. Hennings, *Homers Odyssee*, 1903, pp. 11 ff.; also some remarks by Jevons in *J. H. S.* 1886, vol. vii, *The Rhapsodising of the Iliad.*

INDEX I

GENERAL

INDEX II

AUTHORS

INDEX III

PASSAGES QUOTED FROM THE ILIAD AND ODYSSEY